Live Oaking

Live Oaking

Southern Timber for Tall Ships

Virginia Steele Wood

With drawings by Walter E. Channing
and other illustrations

Naval Institute Press
Annapolis, Maryland

Originally published in 1981 by
Northeastern University Press.
Naval Institute Press edition 1995.

Library of Congress Cataloging-in-Publication
Data

Wood, Virginia S.
  Live oaking : southern timber for tall ships /
Virginia Steele Wood ; with drawings by Walter
E. Channing and other illustrations.
      p.   cm.
  Originally published: Boston : Northeastern
University Press, 1981.
  Includes bibliographical references (p.
and index.
  ISBN 1-55750-933-6 (alk. paper)
  1. Shipbuilding—United States—History.
2. Ships, Wooden—United States—History.
3. Live oak—Southern States—History.
4. Logging—Southern States—History.
5. Timber—Southern States—History.
I. Title.
VM23.W63   1995
623.8' 207—dc20   94-45595
                                        CIP

Printed in the United States of
America on acid-free paper ∞

9 8 7 6 5 4 3 2

First printing

For My Son Jerry

Contents

Preface

A century and a half ago when a shipwright said he was going live oaking, friends and neighbors all knew he was headed south for a winter of cutting trees and hewing out ships' timber. For over a century thousands of skilled craftsmen worked in the live-oak hummocks, and the results of their labor—naval vessels, whaleships, packets, and clipper ships—could be found in seaports around the world. Generally ignored in the chronicles of maritime affairs, live oakers are now virtually forgotten; the aim of this book is to save them from continued neglect, so undeserved.

The idea for writing an account of live oaking was suggested to me several years ago by Marion L. Channing, whose ancestor was one of the live-oaking shipwrights from Massachusetts, and the subject meshed with my own burrowings into the post-Revolutionary history of coastal Georgia and its ties with New England. But my first soundings into these waters were discouraging. Except for acknowledging that certain timbers for the first United States men of war were obtained along the Georgia coast, histories tend to overlook both the live oak and the laborers involved in its procurement.

It has been interesting to discover sources of study. Around New Bedford, Massachusetts, people still mention great-great-grandfathers who went south "to the live-oak fields." And occasionally, some early newspaper item or letter recalling an aspect of the live-oak trade is displayed in one of the local libraries or historical societies. On the other hand, residents of coastal South Carolina and Georgia, who have been living for generations in live-oak country, had much the same reaction to my inquiries as the genial scholar at a southern university: "Lie-voking? Oh, live oaking. Never heard of it. You had better come back down here and tell us more."

This was a natural response. The workers were transients, encampments were isolated, contact with local inhabitants was limited, and records of their work were forwarded either to northern employers or to the federal government. In parts of Florida, however, the term *live oaking* still brings a glimmer of recognition. Some live-oak camps in that state were very large and resumed activity after the Civil War; additionally, a number of New Englanders who went down to work took along families and settled there for good.

In pursuit of information about live oakers, I traveled from Maine and Massachusetts to Philadelphia, Washington, coastal South Carolina, the sea islands of Georgia (St. Simons, Sapelo, Blackbeard, Jekyl) and the Gulf coast of Florida. As a result, many more questions were raised than answered. I have included in this book letters written by men who went live oaking; they represent only a few tantalizing samples of what may still exist, and what one day may emerge from attic trunks before the ink fades to illegibility.

In focusing on the New Englanders who went south and the earliest struggles to obtain live oak for the commercial and naval needs of a young country, I found that other aspects had to be omitted and quantities of source material neglected, including an enormous amount available in the National Archives alone. Volumes can be written on topics related to live oaking, and it is happily anticipated that others will delve into the records and reveal more on this chapter in the annals of American labor.

My object has been neither to enlighten naval architects nor to set down a complete history of live oaking, public lands, and policies of naval construction, but simply to show, for those who chance to wonder, how our most valuable trees were transformed into ships that helped the United States attain international respect as a great maritime nation.

Virginia Steele Wood

Washington, D.C.

Live Oaking

Introduction
Hail the Live Oak

Old age and a generous girth are requisites for admission to the unique Live Oak Society, a Louisiana-based organization of about three hundred members. Only trees are admitted, only trees hold office. Qualifications are a minimum age of a hundred years, and a minimum girth of 17 feet, measured 4½ feet above ground level. In accordance with the constitution's by-laws, each member has a human "attorney" who maintains it, reports accurate measurements, and collects the annual dues of twenty-five acorns for distribution where most needed. First to serve as president was the Locke Breaux Oak at Hahnville, Louisiana. After its demise in 1966, the presidency passed to the Seven Sisters Oak at Lewisburg near Lake Pontchartrain, a tree with matronly measurements: circumference, 36 feet, 7 inches; height, 55 feet; crown span, 132 feet.

A member of the beech family, the live oak (*Quercus virginiana*) dominates our maritime story. The term *live oak* refers to several types of semi-evergreens including *Q. maritime*, often found behind sand dunes; *Q. geminata*, a shrub-like plant; *Q. agrifolia* of California; and *Q. chrysolepis* of the southwestern states. These should not be confused with *Q. virginiana*.

Found only along the coast from southeastern Virginia to the Texas border and the west coast of Cuba, the live oak is usually 40 to 70 feet tall but the crowns of single trees can span 150 feet or more to shade more than half an acre. Trunks are often 20-odd

3

QUERCUS virens

*Leonard Plukenet, the English bota-
nist, is credited with being the first to
classify* Quercus virginiana *in 1696.
The trees were cultivated by Philip
Miller in the Physic Garden near London during 1739, but they required a
warmer climate to mature fully.*

feet in circumference. They divide 5 to 18 feet from the ground to form several immense, horizontal limbs. From colonial times, shipwrights were attracted to these naturally curved branches that demonstrated great tensile strength and resistance to rot; such qualities provided the ultimate combination for shipbuilding.

Because large numbers of these trees were never found in pre-dictably long, straight pieces, the wood had limited use outside the shipyard. However, the firm of C. Drew & Company, estab-lished in 1837 in Kingston, Massachusetts, claimed for many years to make the world's finest live-oak caulking mallets and hawsing beetles. And in the South, live oak had some utility for hubs, axles, and felloes of heavy cart wheels; for screws and cogs of mill wheels; and for submerged piles, locks, and waterwheels. Close-grained and taking a smooth polish, the wood boasted a warm, light brown color that made attractive beams for interior staircases and small decorative pieces in parquet flooring. How-ever, such use was unusual because the wood was simply too hard for the cabinetmaker to work. Today live oak has little commer-cial value, although some is occasionally used in the construction of small craft (e.g., shrimp boats).

From a distance, the trees appear graceful, supple, and even delicate. But the stiff little twigs and leathery olive-green leaves are indicative of its tremendous strength. The simple, narrow leaves are two to five inches long; because they shed only once a year after new growth appears, the trees are known as semi-ever-greens. Most wild animals and birds consume the small, oblong acorns that mature in early autumn, fall by December, and germi-nate rapidly in warm, moist soil. They average about 400 to the pound. In some places the trees harbor mistletoe, but usually they are draped with Spanish moss (*Tillandsia usneoides*). Living on air and water, this nonparasitic plant is harmful to the live oak only when it shrouds the lower branches, blocking sunlight needed for photosynthesis.

Depending on the time of year, green live oak weighs nearly 75 pounds a cubic foot, making it the heaviest of all oak. The weight of a single branch stretching a full 70 feet is calculated in tons; for a trunk to support several limbs measuring 40 to 60 feet

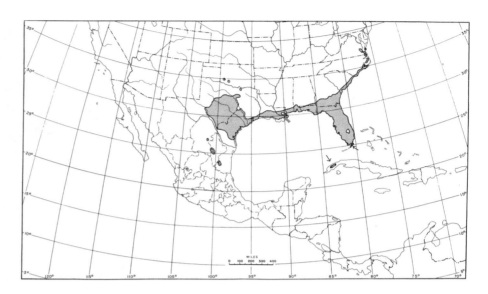

Natural range for live oak, Quercus virginiana

is evidence of toughness and durability. Its unusual density is partially caused by its relative lack of air passages. As the heartwood forms, the vascular system fills with a waxy gum, blocking these passages.

Resistant to disease, the live oak's greatest natural enemy is fire; heat generated by burning grass can kill its thin, rough bark, exposing the trunk to insects and fungi.

Live oak's tolerance to salt spray, a characteristic referred to as "salt spray climax" by ecologists, is an important feature that permits the tree to dominate other hardwoods along river bluffs, and the edges of salt marshes, creeks, and swamps; with good drainage, the roots withstand immersion in water at high tide. The trees can also tolerate annual rainfall of 25 to 65 inches and temperatures ranging from 110° F (43° C) to freezing; they cannot tolerate temperatures dropping to 0° F (−18° C). Live oak thrives in a wide range of soil conditions—from rich, moist hummocks to dry sandhills—and flourishing live-oak forests have even been discovered in coastal sand dunes.

Most of the great live-oak forests of the past have been decimated by construction of coastal recreational facilities and

sprawling residential suburbs. Today's visitor to the South sees the trees most often in gardens or parks and along walkways in quiet old towns and plantations, their ample branches offering relief from the blistering sun. Many agree with the great naturalist John Muir who considered the live oak "the most magnificent planted tree I have ever seen."[1]

Chapter 1

"What a Field Is Open Here!"

The live oak (so called from being an evergreen) is tougher, and of a better grain than the English oak, and is highly esteemed for shipbuilding.

John Bartram, Botanist to
His Majesty for the Floridas, 1766

The voyage was coming to an end. For several days the men had sailed past sea islands with wide stretches of white sandy beaches reflecting the warm sunshine of late October. Scanning the shoreline they saw a flat, subtropical world that was said to be free of rocks and stones inland for some eighty miles or more. It was nothing like the rock-ribbed coast of their native New England.

As they approached the channel the course was altered, putting their backs to the ocean, and soon a pilot came aboard to conduct the schooner past shoals and sand bars, then through a labyrinth of small islands grown head tall with marsh grass. As the vessel moved slowly up the narrow tidal river, the passengers crowded against the rails for a better view. Occasionally they passed the mouth of a creek, where they caught sight of fishing egrets; otherwise they saw only a dense and exotic jungle. Although their fathers, grandfathers, and neighbors had often spoken of this country, no description had prepared the newcomers for reality.

Disturbed by their approach, a full-grown alligator crawled from shore, drifted a few moments in the brackish water, then dropped out of sight. Startled boys gaped and pointed with alarm, but the old timers just laughed, promising that bigger ones lay ahead.

7

Within a quarter of an hour the captain sighted what he judged to be a fair landing place, and the mate gave orders to drop anchor. As the invaders began to disembark, unload supplies, and set up camp in the primeval wilderness, they were observed by no witnesses and encountered no resistance. The operation was well planned. Most of the group were armed, and they had brought vehicles to move heavy objects; but their weapons were axes to wage a bloodless war and their vehicles were to haul timber, not cannon. These men were neither loggers nor lumberjacks; instead, they were shipwrights who journeyed south for a few months each winter to fell and shape live-oak timbers needed to supply the shipyards back home. They called themselves "live oakers."

During the mid-1500s, Spanish explorers in Florida recognized the southern live oak as distinctly different from other oaks; they referred to it as the "green" or "live" oak. As he was establishing St. Augustine, Pedro Menéndez de Avilés wrote to King Philip II of Spain during the winter of 1565 describing the new country's wealth in terms of resources, claiming there is "much hemp, pitch, all kinds of wood that you do not have in your kingdoms; many ships could be built. . . ."[1] An Englishman's description of the Virginia colony, published in 1610, stated "the country yeeldeth abundance of wood, as Oake . . . Ashe Sarsafrase, liue Oak, greene all the yeare, Cedar and Firre. . . ."[2]

Precisely when live oak was first used in constructing sailing vessels along the American coast is unknown, but eventually it became so important for the building of tall ships that expeditions sailed southward for the sole purpose of cutting and carrying off the timber to northern shipyards. Its natural curves especially suited shipwrights; it fulfilled their requirements for a variety of shapes, and permitted them to avoid the weakening effect of crossgrain cuts. With its great tensile strength and resistance to rot, even when exposed to constant wetting and drying, it was ideally durable for wooden ships.

Because water rather than roads linked early American settlers with each other and the Old World, shipbuilding became a vital industry. Their first villages were built in sheltered places safe from the capricious and turbulent ocean, but convenient to bays and harbors, inlets, coves, and rivers because of their dependence on sailing craft for food, trade, and social contact. The stands of virgin timber growing close to shore provided an abundance of choice material for shelter, fuel, fencing, boats, and ships.

Among the earliest vessels constructed were the 30-ton *Virginia*, launched by the English settlers in 1607 on the Kennebec River in Maine; *Onrust*, built by the Dutch of New Amsterdam in 1616; and the 30-ton *Blessing of the Bay*, constructed in 1631 on the Mystic River in the Massachusetts Bay Colony. Within a decade, trade with the West Indies stimulated the building of "top sail" ships of up to 400 tons burthen, and probably a good hundred feet long and twenty-six feet wide. The colonists also produced sloops, pinks, shallops, and ketches for fishermen and coastal traders.[3]

Information about early shipbuilding in the southernmost colonies is meager, but the industry was certainly well established by 1700. Between the settlement of Carolina's Charles Town in 1670 and Georgia's Savannah in 1732, it is clear that live oak's properties were regarded as both unusual and valuable for shipbuilding. At the end of a two-year journey through the region, Thomas Ash published an account of his travels in 1682 including a brief statement about the South's timber resources: "*Trees* for the Service of building Houses and Shipping, besides those and many more which we have not nam'd; they have all such as we in *England* esteem Good, Lasting, and Servicable, as the Oak of three sorts, the *White*, *Black* and *Live Oak*, which for Toughness, and the Goodness of its Grain is much esteemed."[4]

A number of eighteenth-century English travelers to the southern colonies were impressed by the strength of live oak. One gentleman recommended its importation especially for the use of refiners and others requiring very strong fires. Ship carpenters, though, remained the principal craftsmen who found its strength and durability irresistible. In December 1747 Thomas Middleton of Goose Creek offered for sale a new schooner with a keel of 46

Here the lofty Oak,
with all his kindred tribe clad
in Robes of antique Moss,
seems by its venerable Appearance,
to be the real Monarch
of the Woods. . . .

Edward Kimber on the
Georgia coast, 1745

9

Live-Oak chiefly grows on dry, sandy Knolls. This is an Ever-green and the most durable Oak all America affords. The Short-ness of this Wood's Bowl, or Trunk, makes it unfit for Plank to build Ships withal. There are some few Trees, that would allow a Stock of twelve Foot, but the Firmness and great Weight thereof, frightens our Sawyers from the Fatigue that attends the cutting of this Timber. A Nail once driven therein, 'tis next to an Impos-sibility to draw it out. The Limbs thereof are so cur'd, that they serve for excellent Timbers, Knees, &c. for Vessels of any sort. The Acorns thereof are as sweet as Chestnuts, and the Indians draw an Oil from them, as sweet as that from the Olive, tho' of an Amber-Colour. With these Nuts, or Acorns, some have count-erfeited the Cocoa, whereof they have made Chocolate, not to be distinguish'd by a good Palate. Window-Frames, Mallets, and Pins for Blocks, are made thereof, to an excellent Purpose. I knew two Trees of this Wood among the Indians, which were planted from the Acorn, and grew in the Freshes, and never saw any thing more beautiful of that kind. They are of an indifferent quick Growth; of which there are two sorts. The Acorns make very fine Pork.

John Lawson, Surveyor-General of North Carolina, in A New Voyage to Carolina, *1709*

feet, timber "all of Alive Oak and Plank of yellow Pine." In July 1748 the ship *Mary-Anne* (200 tons and 12 guns), built by Ben-jamin Darling from New England, was launched from Winyaw in Georgetown, South Carolina. "The Frame is all of Live Oak, and she is allowed, by good judges, to be the compleatest vessel ever built in America, and inferior to none in Great Britain."[5] Vessels were even named in honor of the timber. The ship *Live Oak*, with a frame of live oak and a bottom of yellow and pitch pine, was completed at approximately the same time as *Mary-Anne*, and in 1772 she was reported still in excellent condition. The surviving eighteenth-century ship registers of South Carolina also list two

Raising remains of the 50-foot Brown's Ferry vessel (built ca. 1700–20) from waters of the Black River, Georgetown County, South Carolina, where it sank with a load of bricks about 1740. Bow stem is of live oak, planking of bald cypress and yellow pine. Discovered in 1976, it has been considered by maritime archaeologists to be "the most important single nautical discovery in the United States," providing much information about construction of local Southern merchant sailing vessels.

schooners christened *Live Oak*, each of 20 tons; one was built in 1761 at Dorchester and the other in 1766 at Port Royal. In Georgia, the Savannah merchant Thomas Rasberry made an entry in his daybook that a ship *Live Oak* came from London in 1758, and during the next few years local newspapers of that active little port reported arrivals and departures of several vessels with the same name, classed as sloop, schooner, and ship.[6]

During this period, property owners advertising land for sale in Georgia and South Carolina newspapers called attention to its fitness for cultivating corn, rice, indigo, and cotton; however, they were just as careful to mention the availability of live oak and pine for shipbuilding. By 1771, orders from England for constructing large ships were "proof that the Goodness of Vessels built here, and the superior Quality of our Live Oak Timber to any wood in America for Ship-Building is at length acknowledged."[7] The *South-Carolina and American General Gazette* of Charleston proudly announced the launching of two brigantines for the West Indies trade and construction of five other vessels, two for the London trade and one for the Bristol trade.

A report sent to England from Florida a few years later reveals details of the British search for timber along the Georgia border.

> In the year 1769 or 1770 a frigate was sent to St. Mary's River with Ship Carpenters to Survey the Live Oaks, & search for the Proper Pieces for 74—64 Gun Ships & frigates. They were found at the Plantation of Jermyn Wright Esquire on St. Mary in a few hours Time without Running half a mile. Live Oak on the Salt water Creek, or Islands is far superior to those on fresh Water with less Sap & a finer grain of Wood—a Difficulty attends the working of that Timber—it must be done while green no Tools can be found to Hew it when once seasoned by the Air & time. . . . The timber is seasoned in Bassin [sic] filled up with water & each piece is taken out as it can be immediately worked up—[8]

Figures of the principal pieces of timber used for shipbuilding in standing trees. This is one of many illustrations from Lescallier's book for French naval architects, published in 1777, and it served to guide shipwrights in choosing which trees to fell. Similar illustrations were published in America during the early nineteenth century.

It was suggested that straight timbers, sawed into boards and scantlings while green, would make durable gun carriages and mortar beds capable of withstanding inclement weather.

Two years later, in 1772, John Montagu, fourth Earl of Sandwich and First Lord of the Admiralty, ordered Charles Inglis to make inquiries about the live-oak timber; he visited nine sea islands from Florida to South Carolina, talking with traders, planters, ship carpenters, builders, and shipmasters. Advantages of the wood for shipbuilding were obvious, but he found it "so hard that Tools seldom can be had fit to work upon it," and getting it to waterways through swamps and over sand hills was viewed unfavorably by property owners.[9] The Georgia planters were realizing such good profits from planting indigo that they were uninterested in cutting timber, even during winter when indigo works were idle, and apparently none of them would even consider becoming involved in hewing it without a competent person to direct the slaves.[10]

Two factions were at odds over the matter of buying American ships and live-oak timber. Although the British Admiralty had traditionally favored promoting the shipbuilding industry of North America, the British Navy Board was opposed to contracting for warships constructed "in any part of America" because of their experiences with rot developing in ships built in New England and purchased during 1694 and 1739.[11] The memory lin-

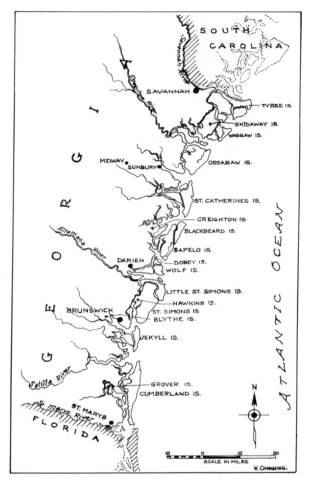

Coastal Georgia

Coastal South Carolina

gered. This factor—and the meager quantity of easily available live oak and difficulty in working it, as well as the established commercial practices, conservatism, and inertia—probably accounted for the Board's lack of vigor in seriously pursuing the matter.

While southern colonists traded mostly with the West Indies, and naval stores were among several commodities available for exchange, New Englanders concentrated on sending their timber and fish across the Atlantic. For this reason, according to Albion,

13

they forced their native white oak on British customers.[12] Although nearly equal to English oak, its reputation suffered in transit. Frequently cut and floated downriver to landings, it was thoroughly wet by the time it was loaded onto vessels, and during the long summer's transatlantic voyage conditions were ideal for dry rot spores to flourish in the warm, dark hold. On arrival at royal dockyards entire cargoes were sometimes declared ruined, thus confirming the already formed prejudice against North American oak among naval officials.

Still, the British needed timber; their shortages were often acute. An eighteenth-century 74-gun ship of the line required 3,000 loads of 50 cubic feet each, which could deforest sixty acres of oak trees. In addition to shipbuilding, the wood was indispensable for house construction and for fuel in blast furnaces. To solve their timber shortage, the British scurried to the forests of Ireland, the Baltic, and Spain as well as the American colonies, but just how frequently they sought out southern timber has not been determined. In any case, any serious commitment by the British Admiralty to set about procuring live oak in large quantities would have been thwarted by events precipitated in 1775.

John Morel of Bewlie Plantation on Ossabaw Island was probably one of few people in the Georgia colony engaged in the business of building ships and selling ships' timber. Early in 1774 his master shipwright Daniel Giroud advertised for one or two good ship carpenters with assurances that "they will meet with good treatment and good wages, and will be paid off very punctually every month in cash."[13] Within the year Morel launched the 200-ton *Bewlie* and offered live-oak frames for ships of any dimensions cut to mould. By October 1775, Morel could supply on short notice "a Quantity of sterns, stern posts, transoms, bow timbers, lower, upper and middle futtocks, aprons, knees, &c."[14]

During the mid-1770s, live-oak activity also flourished in West Florida, an area that eventually became southern Alabama, Mississippi, and eastern Louisiana. As Bernard Romans was studying and mapping the Pearl River region, he discovered "there is a Scandalous illicit Trade Carried on between the inhabitants . . . & the Spanjards at Orleans the former (of which many have taken the

Cross-cut or thwart saw. This type of saw was mentioned in New England records as early as 1633.

Oath of allegiance to & hold Estates under both Governments)
Supplying the latter with Pitch, Tarr, Charcoal, Live Oak & Cattle, by way of St. Johns Creek."[15] On the topic of territorial exchange between Britain and France at the Treaty of Paris in 1763,
he became quite heated over the results of permitting France to
retain New Orleans.

> . . . the grand manufacture to be made of timber here, is SHIP-
> PING, for this purpose no country affords more or better wood; live
> oak, cedar, cypress, yellow pine, are adapted by nature to this. O!
> how just is every *Englishman's* reason for cursing the late peace-
> makers, when he reflects upon the fatal mistake of leaving the isle
> of *New-Orleans* in the hands of the *French* and consequently of the
> *Spaniards!* and when he sees them building such fine frigates as
> they did last year on that island; to add to the misfortune they
> leave their own timber and cut it off of the *English* land, about the
> lakes, for present use; might not *England* herself infinitely rather
> build ships of war, and sell them to her enemies, and so make prof-
> its of them, than to be obliged to behold this with supineness? . . .
> what a field is open here! . . . no empire had ever half so many
> advantages combining in its behalf: methinks I see already the
> *American* fleets inhabiting the ocean, like cities in vicinity![16]

From the point of view of some French citizens, it was deplorable that their country had yielded the port of Mobile to Britain in
the treaty negotiations of 1763. Otherwise, as one observer specu-
lated, "France could have obtained the greater part of her Navy"
from the quantity of live oak, cedar, and other timber in that
area.[17] Because live oak excelled in strength and durability, it is
not surprising that its reputation among shipbuilders steadily
grew and its potential became a matter for comment. On the eve
of the Revolutionary War, authors of *American Husbandry*, published in London, confirmed "the best ships built in America are
those which have their timbers of ever-green oak, and their plank
of cedar," noting also that some was being sent from Georgia to
the West Indies.[18]

Shipbuilders in Philadelphia, among them John Wharton,
Francis Grice, and Joshua Humphreys, were using live oak prior to
the Revolution. Wharton and Humphreys built the frigate *Ran-
dolph* for the Continental Congress, and in 1776 their account

ledger listed receipt of over four hundred pieces of live oak delivered to the shipyard.[19]

Fairly early in the war, Americans took advantage of native southern oak to make frames for two 74-gun ships; the trees were cut at Kilkenny, on the Savannah River, and further south at Sunbury. By the summer of 1778 the Continental Marine Committee in Philadelphia ordered their agent in Savannah, John Wereat, to obtain timbers for repairing two frigates partly burned by the enemy. He was reminded that "considerable quantity of Timber belonging to the Public in your State and under your care . . . will be wanted . . . for the use of our Navy" and he was requested to ship over 1,600 middle and upper "Foothooks," top timbers, half timbers, and other pieces.[20]

Outstanding live-oak vessels of the early Revolutionary War period included the remarkably fast privateer *Hancock*, a 115-ton brigantine owned by John Bayard, James Deane & Company, and others of Philadelphia. Armed with four 6-pounders, eight 4-pounders, and eighty men, she made a record capture of nine British vessels between August and October of 1776.[21] Advertised for sale the following year, the five-year-old, 200-ton British prize ship *Lydia* was described as Philadelphia-built of live oak and cedar, remarkably fast, and "a handsome ship, well found in every Particular."[22] Jesse Hollingsworth, who purchased the vessel for Maryland's Council of Safety, stated: "[she is] as fine a ship as ever I saw, . . . [and] at £4400, I think shee is a bargain."[23] By the war's end, live oak was an acknowledged asset for an emerging maritime nation, though the cessation of funds for wartime expenditures delayed its use in naval vessels for over a decade.

Meanwhile, there was no hesitation about resuming its export. Devastation inflicted along the southern coast during the war left its destitute inhabitants dependent on their land for sustenance, and survival meant reestablishing commerce as quickly as possible. The obvious place to begin was the West Indies, where naval stores, hides, and pork were traditionally the items Southerners traded for Caribbean rum, sugar, and slaves. Immediately following the peace in 1783, British, American, and West

Indian coasting schooners headed for the Caribbean loaded with cargoes of turpentine and lumber variously classed as planking, ranging timber, ships' timber, scantlings, staves, and shingles. In *Three Years Adventures of a Minor*, William Butterworth leaves no doubt that along Georgia's Altamaha River timber was cut in quantity during this period.

> Where our ship lay, the water was salt,—an inconvenience which we obviated by collecting fresh out of numerous sawpits, found in a pine-barren; the road to which lay through a thicket of live oak . . . at the distance of half a mile from the creek. . . . Numerous as the pits have been for a number of years, they continue to increase; for, wherever there are a few trees standing together, that are deemed worth felling and sawing into planks, there a pit is immediately dug, and the trees, mostly of an immense size, cut up, rendering them easy to remove.[24]

The quest for new sources of vital naval timbers became a major concern of Europe's great maritime nations during the late eighteenth century. For southern planters, supplying them was a potentially lucrative means of recouping the losses suffered during the post-war economic depression. Among the planters was the Revolutionary War hero of the southern campaign, General Nathanael Greene of Rhode Island. Given Mulberry Grove plantation near Savannah by Georgia's grateful citizens, he moved south and made a valiant attempt to restore its ruins to a productive state.

In 1783, with expectations of regaining financial solvency by selling valuable stands of live oak and pine, Greene acquired large tracts on Cumberland Island, Little Cumberland, and the adjacent south Georgia mainland. For Greene as well as others, the most likely customer was the French navy. Given the exhausted state of their forests, and sporadic British blockades of the English Channel that hampered importing timber from the Baltic area, it was incumbent on the French to continue investigating American resources. They were well aware of the vast forests and valuable ships' timber on this side of the Atlantic, for there was a strong tradition, dating from the seventeenth century, among botanists and other travelers from France to report on flora of the New World. Seeds and plant material were shipped abroad for propagation, and an active botanical exchange developed among the English, French, and Americans that existed outside the realm of political and national enmity until the Revolutionary War. Even then, Benjamin Franklin, our envoy in Paris, managed to initiate a plan permitting this communication to continue.[25]

General Greene anticipated that the Marquis de Lafayette (his former comrade-in-arms) and the Marquis de Marbois would be excellent contacts in Paris, but French naval officials were nearly as conservative as the British, and Greene's struggles to convince them at least to try a sample of live oak were endless. He had other problems as well. In September 1784, he was greatly perturbed to learn that two or three hundred Loyalist refugees from Florida were illegally cutting and shipping Cumberland Island timber to the West Indies on British transports.[26] Greene's plea for protection from the state of Georgia prompted Governor John Houstoun to comment that he was "really at a loss how to proceed against these lawless People," but their conduct "would justify any steps whatever, . . . their Insolence so great as would render it unsafe for any but a pretty strong force to go against them."[27] Vincente Manuel Zéspedes y Valasco, the Spanish governor of St. Augustine and the province of East Florida, was contacted by the Executive Council of Georgia, but stated that he could exercise no control over British subjects until the territory was evacuated and under the Spanish flag.

Efforts to curtail the thievery must have been successful, for the following spring William Maxwell apprised Zéspedes that Amelia and Cumberland islands both abounded with "Live Oak and Hickory of the largest growth I ever measured," and several people were cutting ships' timber on Cumberland destined for Philadelphia.[28] This was well and good for Greene, but no private shipyard building commercial vessels could use the quantity of timber he counted on selling.

On behalf of several other planters, John McQueen, owner of Sapelo and Blackbeard islands, was also attempting to market live oak. He wrote Greene of his plan to visit Holland to further the project, and he had already successfully contacted "the fountain-head of the Minister of Marine of France," though precisely what he accomplished is uncertain.[29]

Finally deciding to try the highly regarded live oak, French officials dispatched a ship in the fall of 1785 to fetch a cargo of it; however, the ship's captain discovered on arrival that Greene "had not cut one tree."[30] John McQueen offered him several sample pieces, but he rejected them; this is not surprising, because they had lain two years on Sapelo beach and were unfit for use. In any case, the captain's orders had been to accept only the timber from Cumberland Island. This was a tremendous setback for Greene, who was in the North and knew nothing of the vessel until it had set sail for France with an empty hold.[31]

Among many of London's shipbuilders, caution continued to be the watchword when it came to purchasing live oak. Lord Sheffield's book on American commerce, first published in 1783, was indicative of—and helped perpetuate—the prejudiced attitude about American timber and ships. In a footnote he mentioned that live oak was an excellent wood, but had to be seasoned under water many months before being used for shipbuilding; it was too hard and short for planking; and only a small quantity was available. Despite these disadvantages, he acknowledged that live-oak and yellow pine timbers of a ship built in South Carolina were still good at the end of thirteen years.[32]

Perhaps because durability was of paramount concern, the tenaciously held British bias against live oak began wavering. During the winter of 1785–86, General Greene received some reassuring news from both England and France. Lafayette wrote that his government requested him to apply for an assortment of live-oak knees as well as some cedar from Cumberland to be shipped directly to Brest, and he advised submitting an invoice low enough to appear to be a bargain.[33] James Penman sent word from London that he found "no person here willing to Contract for receiving it upon the spot."[34] He was, however, encouraged by the interest of Mr. Barnard, a shipbuilder on the Thames in Deptford

19

who built men of war for the British government as well as ships for the East India Company. Penman promised to enclose the dimensions for a 74-gun ship "having discovered by fatal experience That it will never answer where you Pay superfluous Freight, which you must do if shipped in a Rough State." He also advised that it would be "impossible for you to convert your Timber to the most Advantage without the Aid of a sensible Ship Carpenter and such I suppose you will find no difficulty in Procuring from the Northward upon Tolerable easy Terms."[35] These communications briefly renewed Greene's spirits, but his sudden and premature death on 16 June 1786 at the age of forty-five terminated any hope for significant financial gain from the enterprise. Nearly fifteen years later Phineas Miller, who married Greene's widow, would try again.

Although the French Ministry of Marine seemed to negotiate its purchase of sample timber at a dilatory pace, it should be credited for its persistence in attempting to obtain more information. Unfortunately, the best qualified naval constructors refused to visit the United States for this purpose, but after much searching Sieur Rolland, a former mast inspector from Brest, agreed in 1785 to cover the territory from New England to the South.

Traveling alone, unable to speak English, and knowing little of living trees, he was handicapped from the start, and his 27-month inspection of our vast forest lands from Maine to Georgia was probably as superficial as his critics claimed. His report concerning American white oak was favorable, and he found live oak to be of excellent quality, although limited in quantity among the coastal islands of South Carolina and Georgia. But these observations were obscured by his rambling, poorly written, often incoherent reporting and his adverse comments on other varieties of American timber.[36]

Concurrently, the French royalty realized the necessity of sending a well-trained botanist to study American forests and judge the feasibility of transplanting and acclimatizing certain foreign species to France. The choice fell on André Michaux, who sailed in September 1785, with his young son François-André, a gardener, and a servant. Early the following year he established a nursery near Hackensack, New Jersey, and two years later moved to Charleston, South Carolina, where he purchased a plantation and continued searching for plant material. During the years 1785–1793, he shipped to France some 60,000 specimen plants and ninety boxes of seeds to be distributed among the royal gardens.[37]

Writing of *chêne vert* in his *Historie des chênes de l'Amerique*, Michaux commented on its abundant growth among the southern islands and along the beaches, observing that even when exposed to stormy ocean winds the trees could withstand much abuse, because their roots extended over a considerable area in sandy soil covered by a thick layer of clay. In all America, he reported, live oak was recognized as the finest wood for construction of ships, and it merited the attention of both French and Spanish governments. He suggested that it could be grown successfully in Europe, since soil conditions of the Bordeaux area were so similar to those of South Carolina and Georgia.

However, any plans for carrying out such an experiment were thrust aside by revolution—this time in France. When the royal government fell, Michaux's financial support ended and he returned home in 1795 to discover neglect and destruction among the plantations where the American trees had been growing. In 1801 his son, François-André Michaux, was sent by the French government to make another study of American trees, but there seemed to be little interest in semitropical species; they were impractical for culture in France.[38]

The quantity of live oak used abroad during the eighteenth century is unknown, but Luis Fatio, while commenting on Florida commerce in 1790, claimed it was highly esteemed in French shipyards.[39] Clearly, in some quarters the idea persisted that live oak would also benefit the French navy if a substantial amount could be secured. During 1794–95, a Frenchman residing in Philadelphia, believed to be Antoine Charbonnet Duplaine, devised and drafted a bold scheme for his government to effect a secret purchase of Cumberland Island for its timber. His American contact and advisor was a South Carolina senator, probably Pierce

Butler who was known to be sympathetic with the French Republic, and who indicated a willingness to handle the transaction without compensation. He suggested a purchase price of £20,000 sterling, although the island's timber made it three times as valuable.

In September 1794, Duplaine sent a letter from Philadelphia to an unidentified contact in Paris, describing the excellent timber resources of Cumberland Island and outlining a plan for its purchase. Secrecy, he felt, was vital. Otherwise, the American owners might inflate the price and "if British agents got wind of it, they would spare no effort to abort the enterprise."[40] His proposal was forwarded to the French Commission de la Marine et des Colonies for consideration, and in February 1795 it was sent on to the Committee of Public Safety.

French naval officials expressed doubts about the success of maintaining secrecy. For one thing, the sale of American land to a foreign nation would have to be ratified by the government. If it were purchased through a confidential agent, his heirs could claim ownership of the island and any course of action following these circumstances would upset Congress. In fact, officials felt that full possession of the island would be feasible only through treaty negotiations; therefore, it would be impossible to keep such a transaction secret. The naval officials also warned that Cumberland was uncomfortably close to Spanish-held Florida, and there was no desire to excite the wrath of Spain. There was also a practical concern, left unstated: the cutting, hauling, and shipping of timber from Cumberland Island by a group of Frenchmen would certainly generate curiosity and publicity.[41]

Probably the Commission's skepticism discouraged the Committee of Public Safety, for there is no evidence that any attempt was made to negotiate the island's purchase. It was a novel idea that never materialized. Two years later the United States and France were at war on the high seas.

Chapter 2

Live Oak for a New Navy

The live Oak of Georgia, is thought to be almost indispensable, in the Construction of our largest Ships, to be used in those portions most subject to decay. . . .

Benjamin Stoddert, Secretary of the Navy, 1798

Soon after the Revolutionary War, live oak and ships for a new American navy became vital concerns to the nation. When the war ended the new country was left with a military force consisting of a few local militia companies; in 1785, to avoid paying for costly repairs, it sold the last ship, *Alliance*, into merchant service.

The country was impoverished and exhausted by war. A great many people harbored fear and suspicion of a strong military force, and the Articles of Confederation gave Congress no power to raise funds to establish one. Without a navy to thwart predators, the country soon became vulnerable to foreign aggression; such vulnerability quickly became apparent when American ships began plying the Atlantic and Mediterranean to trade in Europe. No longer protected by the British flag, the merchant fleet was repeatedly attacked by corsairs from Algiers, Tripoli, Tunis, and Morocco. Following the pattern of Britain, France, and other major European nations, the United States government began meeting the high ransoms demanded for release of the suffering captives as well as paying tribute to the Barbary powers to purchase immunity from their attacks. It was believed to be less expensive than fighting a war, but was humiliating, and achieved only temporary relief from harassment.[1]

23

In October and November 1793, eleven vessels were over-taken by Algerine cruisers, adding 110 more American masters and crewmen to the list of captives "in a distressed and naked" state. Among them was Samuel Calder of Colchester, Connecti-cut, master of the schooner *Jay*, who was captured en route from Malaga to Boston. In dire need of food and clothing, he requested a loan of one hundred dollars from Dominick Terry & Company in the Spanish port of Cadiz until aid or ransom arrived from the United States. To describe the deplorable conditions of his im-prisonment, he wrote: ". . . we was all stript of all our Cloaths some Came on Shore without even a shirt, and was immediately put into Chains and put to hard labour, with only the allowance of three small loaves of black bread pr. day & water . . . its not possible to Live long in this situation. . . ."[2]

Such grievous news concerning so many American prisoners in North Africa convinced the outraged American public that continued inadequate protection of its commercial vessels would only guarantee additional capture and losses of men and ships. A congressional act passed on 27 March 1794 authorized President George Washington to form a navy under the War Department with a nucleus of six frigates; funds were appropriated in early June.[3] Construction was to go on simultaneously in six different places: Philadelphia (then still the nation's capital); Baltimore; New York; Boston; Portsmouth, (New Hampshire); and Gosport (now Portsmouth, Virginia). Plans for the ships were drawn up in Philadelphia, mainly by chief constructor Joshua Humphreys, Josiah Fox, and William Doughty.

Barring shipwrecks and other disasters, the life expectancy of wooden warships was only about ten years, mainly because of their constant exposure to the wetting and drying effects of sea water. This being the case, many were firmly convinced that us-ing the superior live oak timber for constructing the frames of the new vessels would be advantageous because its durability was es-timated "at five times that of common white oak."[4] John Barry, Thomas Truxtun, and Richard Dale, all sea captains with consid-erable experience, wholeheartedly supported this view and wrote that use "of the most durable wood in the world (live oak of Georgia) would be a great saving to the United States, as we are well satisfied (accidents excepted) that their frames will be perfectly sound a half century hence, and it is very possible they may continue for a much longer period."[5]

In addition to live oak and red cedar from Georgia, a combination of the best timber—white oak, yellow pine, pitch pine, and locust—was to be used. Humphreys specified live oak for futtocks, knight heads, hawsepieces, bow timbers, stanchions, knees, transoms, and breasthooks. It was essential that "great timbers," those pieces used in the hulls, be large as well as strong; "compass pieces," the curved members used in frames, could be hewn from trees of irregular shape, and live oak met this requirement.

For those directing the operation, it was easy enough to sit comfortably in Philadelphia and demand the finest live oak; however, it was quite another matter to drag it from the malarial swamps of Georgia. In early June of 1794, John T. Morgan, shipwright of Boston and "master builder of considerable abilities," who had been provisionally appointed constructor at the Gosport yard, was detailed to Charleston and Savannah by Tench Coxe, Commissioner of Revenues. Since all the land was privately held, Morgan was to seek out property owners, search along the coastal islands to determine what live oak and cedar was available, estimate the cost of standing and cut timber, and report on its proximity to landings convenient for loading onto scows or coastal vessels. He was not to make any agreements; others would attend to the contracts. He was, however, to take copious notes and perform his duties with dispatch "as the public anxiety is much excited by the circumstances [which] have occasioned this naval armament."[6] After all arrangements were made, Morgan was to superintend the cutting and hewing of timber and to see that it was shipped to the six ports where construction on the frigates was to begin. In addition to expenses, his annual compensation was $2,000, the same as Humphreys'.

Since local labor along the coast was primarily agricultural, skilled shipwrights had to be brought in from the North because the War Department decided that unless moulds or patterns were transported to the site, expensive mistakes would be made. The saving on shipping space and freight charges would also be advantageous.

In mid-June, Jedediah Huntington, Collector of the Customs at New London, Connecticut, was ordered to employ sixty axemen to fell trees and thirty ship carpenters to "form by pattern moulds" the live oak timber.[7] Coxe thought they could best be found at ports on the Connecticut and Rhode Island rivers and in such Massachusetts towns as Dighton and New Bedford. They were to be "able bodied [and] sober:"[8] Later, another twenty carpenters were hired on the Delaware River. For food they would depend mostly on beef, pork, bread, rice, and vegetables that would be sent with them or obtained on the spot. Huntington was to procure a six-month supply of distilled spirits, butter, cheese, and molasses sufficient for one hundred men. Coxe recommended an allowance of half a gill of distilled spirits per day, although it was two gills in naval service, but Morgan's opinion was that three gills per day "would not be too much." In the end, Coxe left the decision up to Huntington based on the men's habits and the climate, but noted that the "cheapest kind of Rum, with which [they] will be satisfied . . . should be preferred."[9]

All provisions, timber carts, tools, and grain were to be sent from New York, New London, and Philadelphia. The contractors in Charleston acting on behalf of the government were Isaac Holmes, Collector of Customs, and Daniel Stevens, Supervisor of the Revenue; in Savannah they were John Habersham, Collector of Customs, and Joseph Clay, merchant. Coxe alerted them of Morgan's arrival with assurances that he was "well acquainted with the state of Georgia and used to the climate."[10]

Some weeks after traveling in the South, Morgan sent word to Joshua Humphreys that he had found no timber in South Carolina "as good as in Georgia nor so cheap by 50 Pr Cent."[11] Therefore, St. Simons and Hawkins islands in Georgia were among the first sites designated for the live oaking. But things got off to a slow start, as Morgan was confronted by unexpected problems. He received the moulds and oxen in August, but no hands to do the work. Furthermore, as he wrote to Humphreys, "I have not

WANTED *immediately a number of sober, industrious Axe-men and Ship-carpenters, to fell, and to form by pattern moulds, live oak and cedar, in the states of Georgia and Carolinas, for the Naval Armament. Persons willing to engage, are desired to apply to*
JEDIDIAH HUNTINGTON, *Agent.*
New-London, *June 23, 1794.*

26 June 1794

Notices from the New London Connecticut Gazette

Marine List,
Kept by THOMAS POOL, *at the* CITY COFFEE-HOUSE

THURSDAY, SEPT. 18. Pleasant morning, wind S.W.
Arrived, brig Revival, N. Palmer, from Bassaterre, Guadaloupe, via Turk's-Island, 17 days passage.
FRIDAY 19. Pleasant morning, wind N.b.E. P. M. S.W.
Sailed, Packet David & Jot, Wm. Harris, for New-York.
SATURDAY 20. Pleasant morning, wind S.
Arrived, brig Julia, Griffith, in 20 days from Port-au-Prince; left there, brig Lucy, M'Neal, to sail in 6 days if he could get men, one man dead—the rest all sick. Left at Laiquaha, schooner ——, Trowbridge, New-Haven, to sail in 8 days;—superfine Baltimore flour, by the single barrel, 6 dollars—and every other kind of produce in proportion. Extremely sickly in Port-au-Prince.
Arrived, schooner Lucy, Baily, in 21 days from Port-au-Prince—8 days before Capt. Baily left there, Capt. Angell, of this port, was at the Mole, Hispaniola, hearty and well. Left at Port-au-Prince, sloop Mary, Tatton, of New-Haven—sold his stock at the Mole.
SUNDAY 21. Fine cool morning, wind N.W.
Arrived, Packet Lady Washington, Colver, from New-York.
MONDAY 22. Pleasant morning, wind N.W. P. M. W.N.W.
TUESDAY 23. Sail'd, sloop ——, Noyes, for Savanna, with 90 men on board, bound to the river St. Mary's, to cut timber for the ships ordered by Congress.
WEDNESDAY 24. Pleasant cool morning, wind N.b.E.
Sailed, Packet June, R. Niles, for New-York.
Packet Betsey, E. Chappel, for ditto.

25 September 1794

Marine List,
Kept by THOMAS POOL, *at the* CITY COFFEE-HOUSE.

THURSDAY JUNE 11. Fine pleasant morning, wind S.S.W.
FRIDAY 12. Pleasant morning, wind E.N.E. P. M. E.
Arrived, packet David & Jot, Wm. Harris, from New-York.
SATURDAY 13. Pleasant morning, wind N.W. 10 A.M. S.W.
Sailed, brig Samuel, S. Stillman,—brig Aurora, Wadsworth,—and sloop Nancy, I. Chapman,—for West Indies.
SUNDAY 14. Cool morning, wind N.E.
MONDAY 15. Pleasant morning, wind S.W.
Sailed, brig Friendship, A. Pride, for Liverpool.
Arrived, packet Lady Washington, Colver, from New-York.
TUESDAY 16. Pleasant morning, wind W.S.W.
Arrived, schooner Metomkin, Thompson, from Richmond, Virginia, via New-York, who informs that on Sunday last, a ship belonging to Philadelphia was boarded by Admiral Murray's squadron in the latitude of Sandy Hook, stripped of her people, and had two men put on board her, one being sick and the other good for nothing. The ship was obliged to put into New-York, not having hands sufficient to conduct her to Philadelphia. Captain Thompson further informs, that there was a report in New-York on Sunday last, " That his Britannic Majesty had issued orders to his commanders to take all American vessels bound to France."
Arrived, brig Polly, E. Griffing, from New-York.
Sloop Diamond, Churchill, in 35 hours from Boston,—came passengers, a number of wood cutters and carpenters from Georgia.
WEDNESDAY 17. Pleasant morning, wind N.E.
Sailed, packet Betsey, E. Chappel, for New-York.

18 June 1795

seen 10 fair days since I left you . . . the whole country is almost under water and if the rains continue it will be impossible almost to get the timber for where the live Oak grows is all low Land and Swampy in a dry time, but there never was so much rain known in this Country. . . .[12]

The first week in September, property owners signed agreements in Savannah with Joseph Clay and the Collector of Customs, John Habersham, stipulating a rate of sixpence Georgia money per foot of live oak to be cut by the government and hauled to navigable vessels of eleven feet draft by the contractors. On 3 October Tench Coxe, Commissioner of Revenues, notified Captain John Barry of the brig *Schuylkill*'s imminent departure for St. Simons Island. Barry's instructions for the voyage were to ascertain progress of the work force, dispatch whatever timber was ready for Philadelphia, procure another vessel for shipping additional timber, and consult with customs and other officials in Savannah and possibly Charleston. All public property aboard the brig was to be in his care, "especially the oxen and horses, which are of the utmost importance."[13]

Arriving at Gascoigne Bluff, St. Simons, on 14 October, Barry reported that he found Morgan "with two boys Sick and not a man with him nor a stick of wood cut; the 15th the Revenue cutter arrived from Savannah with a part of the utensils for Cutting timber part of the moulds and . . . provisions."[14]

Humphreys had estimated that fifty-five men working twenty-four days a month could cut the timber necessary for one frigate in two months' time, but he failed to consider the obstacles. Morgan had no illusions; on 21 October he wrote Humphreys, "you have not told me how large to side the timber nor do I know how much timber and Rum you have allowed, these Moulds frighten me they are so large & they will be hard to be got"; everything, in fact, seemed to be going badly. "I have had no hands but negroes and have been all but dead since the 4th of September, I lost a fine lad, an apprentice last Saturday with fever, I have it now, everybody is sick." Then, thoroughly exasperated, he added, "if I am to stay her[e] till all the timber is cut I shall be dead. . . . I cannot stand it, you say that if I was there I should be mortified, if you was here you would curse live Oak."[15]

Within a week of Barry's arrival and at his urging, they managed to rent sixteen slaves from two local planters and, with oxen and horses, began cutting a road through the woods. Long delayed by their apprehension about the climate, eighty-one men finally arrived from New London on 22 October. They immediately set about building their shelters, and the next day started felling trees.[16]

Agitated at having received no news, Coxe wrote to Habersham, Clay, and Morgan on 18 October that vessels were being readied to load timber, but they needed information concerning amount of timber and location of loading; ". . . we are extremely embarrassed for want . . . of information."[17] A few days later he wrote again to inform Morgan that the brig *Anna* of Philadelphia was bound for St. Simons; with Morgan's men numbering one hundred and five there should be no problems since he had been given the authority to obtain as many "as he saw fit."[18]

By 18 December 1794, a welcomed cargo of live oak arrived at the Philadelphia yard. Its quality, wrote Humphreys, was "greatly superior to any in Europe & the best That ever came to this place."[19]Although this was encouraging news, within two weeks Morgan wrote to John Barry:

> Comodor Sir in your Leter from Savanah you promised me that you would see that I should Com from heair But I now begin to think that I shall be planted heair the feveuorer has fel in to all my Lims and I can not walk you will see by the Leters to Mr Cox What a State the Bisness is in all the fin oxen that you Brought is dead Save 4—and have not been abel to hall a Long stick this month till with in a fue days past for god Sack dont Send no More. . . .[20]

By the time spring approached, some of the northern carpenters had died, others had deserted, and only three who were capable of selecting and moulding the timber could be persuaded to remain and continue working with the slaves.

All in all, it was a cruel time for Morgan and his men. Hauling enormously heavy timbers from swamps with oxen and carts was never easy; after unusually heavy rainfall, it was nearly impossible. Among the vessels that set sail to transport the live oak, one large schooner bound for New York was lost off Cape Hatteras with her entire cargo, and several men who made the first voyage encountered such hardship and sickness that they refused to go back. Nevertheless, the War Department judged it "practicable to procure the whole of the live oak timber by the month of May 1796."[21]

Because no replacement had been found for Morgan and it was imperative to keep the operation alive, he was informed by the War Department in July 1795 that his services in Georgia were indispensable; he was expected to continue there until all necessary timber had been forwarded. Only then could he report for duty in Virginia.[22] Meanwhile, Josiah Fox replaced him as constructor at the Gosport yard.

Morgan's reaction to this directive can be imagined. While the mercury may not actually soar to a hundred degrees every day of the week, the high temperature and humidity of coastal Georgia in summer saps vitality, and lassitude can take hold for endless days and nights; afternoons are punctuated with violent thundershowers; the vast populations of mosquitoes, "chiggers," and ticks are voracious; and the swamps and woods are alive with venomous reptiles. Somehow Morgan survived the season.

By early November James Hackett, the naval constructor at Portsmouth, New Hampshire, who was impatiently awaiting his live oak, received word from the War Department that it was too expensive to send "people from your part of the country to cut the Timber as Negroes can be obtained in Georgia who are good workmen with the axe at a vastly cheaper rate, and Mr Morgan reports their efficiency is very satisfactory." Hackett was free to send one man, but the War Department made it clear that since Morgan was superintending "the whole of that Business your Foreman must be under his orders."[23]

Regular delivery of the timber was one problem, but its disposition was another. Typically, too many knees or futtocks in one yard and too few in another meant transferring the essential pieces. This was both time-consuming and expensive. As a remedy Humphreys requested each of the constructors to make a detailed inventory of their stock to aid in marking shipments from Georgia.

But arrival of the proper pieces did not insure satisfaction. A few days after Christmas 1795, Humphreys wrote Morgan to thank him for a box of oranges, but vigorously complained that they were "so sowered by the most infamous Stem Piece you sent that their Flavor is lost. I am sure you must have never seen it, for the most ignorant negro you have employed would have had sufficient understanding to know it would not do." Humphreys claimed that if the necessary rising and other timber arrived from Morgan on the next load he could "proceed on with a degree of Spirit, otherwise I shall soon be obliged to discharge the Hands." He included instructions about beveling and siding the timber and ended incisively with, "I expect to raise my Stem & Stern this Week weather permitting but not with your Stem."[24]

Throughout 1795, delivery of live oak continued to be slow, thus impeding progress on the frigates. In June, dismayed by the reports, Secretary of War Timothy Pickering wrote, "Had the difficulties of getting the live oak been foreseen—had it been known that full and regular supplies for two only, could be kept up—certainly, the carrying forward of six frigates at the same time, would not have been attempted."[25] He recommended that delivery of supplies for only two of the frigates be kept up and the work on their completion be continued. Unforeseen difficulties slowed progress and increased expenses. Some of the moulds were destroyed by fire, and a number of large timbers that were prepared for the frigates proved to be defective. By December, among the six yards involved, New York had received only a third of the necessary timber and the other five yards had received two thirds of their requirements. Meanwhile, negotiations were under way to effect a treaty with the Dey of Algiers, "the most restless and impatient man in the world."[26]

Finally, in the spring of 1796 after the Dey had extorted a million dollars in tribute in exchange for the free movement of

American merchant vessels, the treaty was signed and ratified. According to the Act of 1794 that created the navy, all work on the frigates should have been suspended. However, President Washington was firmly convinced that the public loss would be considerable, and saw to it that a supplementary act was passed by Congress to permit work to proceed on the three frigates nearest completion.[27]

This did not automatically solve the timber problem. Almost 1,000 pieces of live oak were required for each vessel, and predictions were gloomy that enough would ever be received in the yards. Delivery continued to be sporadic. In January the schooner *Rachell*, bound for Baltimore, was blown off course to Martha's Vineyard. In March Captain Truxtun, who was supervising the construction of *Constellation*, wrote Fox that although 98 pieces of live oak had arrived and another cargo was expected daily, he doubted that Morgan was properly exerting himself.[28] By late August only 41 frames for *Constitution* had been built, and the live-oak stock was depleted in Boston. Colonel Claghorne felt impelled to visit Philadelphia, where he persuaded the Secretary of War to transfer essential timber from Portsmouth to Boston; by December the supply was sufficient.[29] By February 1797 more timber became available, and two sloops were directed to three landings of the Morel family on Ossabaw Island to collect 1,003 pieces of live oak totaling 19,110 cubic feet.[30]

Finally, in 1797, three agonizing years after passage of the act authorizing their construction, the first three frigates were launched: the 44-gun *United States* on 10 May at Philadelphia, the 38-gun *Constellation* on 7 September at Baltimore, and the 44-gun *Constitution* on 21 October at Boston. Work on the other vessels—*Congress*, *Chesapeake*, and *President*—was not resumed until the following year when difficulties with France reached the boiling point.[31]

Having successfully overthrown British authority, many Americans were sympathetic with the revolution that overthrew the French monarchy in 1789. But sentiments soon shifted as France took up arms once more against England, and American

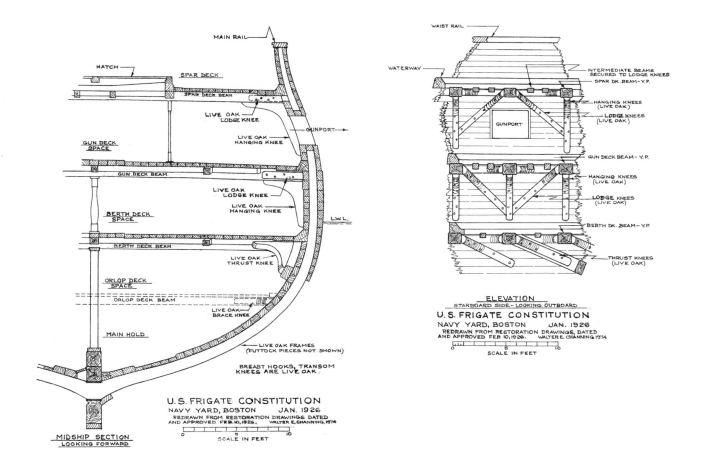

MIDSHIP SECTION
LOOKING FORWARD

U. S. FRIGATE CONSTITUTION
NAVY YARD, BOSTON   JAN. 1926
REDRAWN FROM RESTORATION DRAWINGS DATED
AND APPROVED FEB. 10, 1926.   WALTER E. CHANNING, 1974
SCALE IN FEET

ELEVATION
STARBOARD SIDE - LOOKING OUTBOARD
U. S. FRIGATE CONSTITUTION
NAVY YARD, BOSTON   JAN. 1926
REDRAWN FROM RESTORATION DRAWINGS, DATED
AND APPROVED FEB 10, 1926.   WALTER E. CHANNING, 1974
SCALE IN FEET

efforts to remain neutral and continue trading with both nations proved untenable.

The signing of Jay's Treaty in 1794 staved off war with Britain, but annoyed her old enemy, France. The XYZ affair, a French attempt to negotiate secret terms with three American commissioners sent to Paris by President Adams (including proposed payment to France of a quarter of a million dollars in bribes), was rejected out of hand. The result was an undeclared naval war with France in 1798, as Americans rallied around the popular slogan, "Millions for defense, but not a cent for tribute." During the spring and summer, Congress passed acts to consolidate the national defense, including creation of the Navy Department, appointment of a Secretary of the Navy, and appropriation of funds for building additional warships.[32] American success against French vessels on the high seas dramatically proved the worth of the new United States Navy. Despite the extraordinary difficulties and hardships accompanying the procurement of timber needed for building these fighting ships, naval officials continued to insist that live oak was indispensable. Their concern over assuring its supply in sufficient quantities was intensified by the gnawing fear that England and other maritime nations would soon recognize its value and grab the readily available supply for themselves.[33]

In addition, the invention of Eli Whitney's cotton gin in 1794, which revolutionized the course of Southern agriculture, was already seriously affecting the forests. Heedless of our nation's maritime needs, coastal planters were eagerly girding and "deadening" trees, then burning over their land to clear it for the planting of profitable Sea Island cotton. An exception was George Gibbs, an enterprising citizen of Wilmington, North Carolina, who envisioned profiting from both timber and cotton. Arriving in St. Marys, Georgia, with sixty-eight slaves in 1799, he filed with county officials an affidavit claiming the slaves were "not intended for Sale but [were] for the Purpose of Establishing a Cotton Plantation and to cut live oak."[34]

Although the trees grew profusely along our southern Atlantic coastal plain, the supply was still limited to what could be obtained under contract with property owners, mostly in the Carolinas and Georgia. In 1803 the Louisiana Purchase added the present states of Louisiana, Mississippi, and Alabama to the Union, but timber in these regions was not surveyed or examined for nearly two decades. Besides, the navy was too small to protect American merchant vessels shipping timber in Florida waters and the Gulf of Mexico. It was not until the cession of East Florida to the United States by Spain in 1819 that the federal government could designate thousands of acres as timber reserves for naval use.

Meanwhile, the need for live-oak timber remained a pressing issue. With great urgency, Secretary of the Navy Stoddert recom-

mended to Congress the advantages of preserving the timberlands. In response, Congress passed an act in February 1799
authorizing payment not to exceed $200,000 for "the purchase of
growing or other timber, or of lands on which timber is growing,
suitable for the Navy."[35] As a result, two Georgia islands became
our first federally owned timber reserves—Grover Island, comprising 350 acres in Camden County, was purchased in December
1799 for the sum of $7,500; and in April 1800, Blackbeard Island
in McIntosh County, with about 1,600 acres, was obtained at a
cost of $15,000.[36]

The Act of 1799 also provided for further naval construction.
Contracts were signed with Phineas Miller of Cumberland Island,
Georgia, to supply live-oak frames for six 74-gun ships of the line,
and with Colonel Thomas Shubrick of Bulls Island, South Carolina, to supply frames for two 74s. The price was set at 75 cents
per cubic foot; the timber had to be "good merchantable live oak,
free from sap, or other defect . . . & shall not exceed the Mould by
more than one Inch in Breadth, Thickness or Length," otherwise
excess freight would be charged the supplier at the rate of 50 cents
per cubic foot. Vessels of 150 tons burthen were to load and carry
it from the landings; they could draw no more than twelve feet of
water when loaded.[37]

Learning to organize and carry out any large-scale operation
by experience can be painful. As Savannah's Navy agent Ebenezer
Jackson wrote to Secretary Stoddert,

> No one in the outset of the business could possibly forsee the great
> difficulties which have arisen in the execution of a contract so ex-
> tensive. No person in this Country, before the experiment was
> made, had any doubt of there being in Georgia alone Timbers suffi-
> cient for twenty ships of the line, [but] . . . the truth is otherwise.[38]

Phineas Miller, the Yale-educated tutor of Nathanael and
Catherine Greene's children, and their close friend and adviser, is
best remembered as Eli Whitney's business partner, and specifi-
cally for his efforts to help market the cotton gin, which Whitney
invented at the Greene plantation. When Miller married Greene's

Advertisement appearing in the
Newburyport Herald, *8 October 1799*

35

From the Columbian Museum & Savannah Advertiser, *4 April 1800*

widow in 1796, he assumed the burden of untangling the family's complex finances. Although he anticipated, as Greene had before him, that selling live oak would be profitable, soon he was plunged into the vicissitudes of an overwhelming obligation to the government. In June 1800 he wrote to Shubrick, "The further I advance in this purplexing contract for Timber, the greater do I find the difficulty the expense & the disappointment." He was "fully convinced," too, that Secretary Stoddert "has not the most distant idea of the trouble we meet with. . . ."[39]

By 21 June, Miller's men had hauled two thousand pieces of live oak to various landings, and he expected them to haul another thousand in a month or six weeks. For this purpose he employed "between fifty and sixty well Broken oxen which are constantly fed with grain," and noted that he would "be obliged to increase the number to an hundred by the next fall."[40] Monthly expenses were close to $5,000, and only two carpenters out of the thirty-six hired were competent to mould the timber properly. By July his advance from the government had been spent, he was forced to borrow money at a premium, and could foresee only ruin unless relief was forthcoming to defray operating expenses.

There were other problems. The quantity of timber in Georgia was less than a fourth of what had been estimated by government agents, and "the report which was procured by Genl. Greene & several other Persons at the close of the American War, with a view to supply the Naval Powers of Europe with this species of Timber, extended the Error in a ten fold Proportion."[41] Another problem lay in "reducing timber rough in the woods to such exactness of shape & dimensions as is required" by the naval constructors. Jackson informed the Secretary of the Navy that:

> Mr. Miller's exertions have astonished me; he was obliged to send on to the Eastern States where he engaged upwards of three hundred prime Workmen; who were sent out to this Country to cut the Ship-Timber at great expense; this would have been the smallest part of the difficulty, could timber have been found within the Compass of fifty Miles; but instead of that Mr. Miller has been obliged to cut his timber in Florida and on all the Coast of Georgia, and far into South-Carolina, at fifty or sixty different landing

TABLE 1 Some Expenses Incurred by Colonel Thomas Shubrick in Procuring Live Oak Frames for a 74-Gun Ship of the Line in 1799–1800

Passage for 65 men from Massachusetts at $15	$ 975.00
Paid for their advertising and other expenses in Boston and Newburyport	11.82
Total for Board & Lodging of the men at 64 cents pr. day	7133.67
Passage money for 51 men, to return home, at $12 each	612.00
2 grind stones cranks	17.50
1 doz X cut Saw files & ½ doz Whip saw	3.00
4 cross cut Saws and files	26.15
4 Squares, and 2 marking irons	3.07
Dr. Irvine, attending McGilvray and Warner, while sick	51.75
2 pair Wheels	134.52
Blacksmiths work at wheels and for 950 lb. Iron	203.35
163 feet Oak plank for Blacksmith	23.28
3 grind Stones	12.03
1 ton coals $1	15.00
Medicines	1.16

SOURCE: RG45, File AC, Box 10, National Archives.

Places; at all . . . he has been obliged to make encampments for his Workmen, cut New Roads for hauling the Timber to a landing, then transporting the Moulds, Provisions, Oxen, and Wheels from Landing to Landing; a distance of nearly two hundred Miles. . . . Such a Contract would have ruined almost any other Man. . . . Knowing as much of the nature of the business as I now do, I certainly would refuse the Contract at one dollar twenty-five Cents pr. Cubical foot.[42]

For Colonel Shubrick, the contract was ruinous. Poorly trained local labor forced him to employ; and pay round-trip expenses for, sixty-five ship carpenters from Newburyport, Massachusetts, and to engage nineteen other men and rent a number of slaves. It only added to his woes when five shipwrights died on the job.

With forty black carpenters and sixty shipwrights constantly employed, Shubrick found he was unable to complete on schedule one frame of a 74-gun vessel because of "the immense labor required." So much of the timber on Bulls Island was rotten that he could eventually supply only two-thirds of one ship's frame. He offered to forfeit his bond of $10,000, but was persuaded to persevere and complete the contract as best he could with a verbal assurance of government compensation for additional timber. In the end he spent $22,000 and received only $17,000 from the government for 1050 pieces of live oak estimated at 50,000 cubic feet. Years later a good deal of that still lay on the ground. After Shubrick's death in 1812 the facts pertaining to his contract were brought out in a court case involving his heirs, his creditors, and the government; in 1825 his son and executor, Lieutenant Edward Shubrick of the United States Navy, was still applying for money due from the 1799 contract.[43]

The spring of 1801 was a trying time for the conscientious Navy agent Ebenezer Jackson, as he harried others to get on with their jobs in proper fashion. After chartering several galleys to transport live oak to the navy yards, he discovered one captain had overdrawn rations, could not account for the deficiency, failed to discharge his crew when ordered, and then landed in jail for debt. Two unsatisfactory crews had to be discharged, one of them for mutinous conduct.[44]

Jackson was responsible for keeping accounts of all payments made for naval provisions and services in his area as well as the advances made to Shubrick and Miller. He regularly submitted expenses to the Collector of the Port, and regularly pleaded with the Secretary of the Navy to obtain authorization from the Secretary of the Treasury so that regular remittances could be made in cash.

By the end of March he was agonizing over the timber, and prodding the twenty-three-year-old inspector Samuel Humphreys to "push the business of inspection [for] . . . the Vessels will soon come crowding in upon you"; indeed, the barque *Atlantic* was

WANTED to CHARTER, Suitable Veffels to tranfport Live Oak Timber, from Georgia to Norfolk, City of Wafhington, Philadelphia, New-York, Bofton and Portfmouth, (N. H.); for which a liberal price per cubical foot will be paid for Freight; the price of Freight muft be regulated according to the diftance, and the difficulty of the different loading places. Veffels in Charlefton that are for Charter, for this employ, muft call in at Tybee, when the captain or owner may go up to Savannah in their boats and fix the terms and place of loading, with the fubfcriber, without any unneceffary delay.

E. Jackfon,
Broughton-ftreet, oppofite the Poft. Office, Savannah.
March 31.   60

From the Charleston, South Carolina, City-Gazette and Daily Advertiser, 2 April 1801 scheduled to load timber at Honey Creek on St. Simons in a few days.[45] Jackson urgently requested periodic reports of the amount of timber inspected and measured so that he could advertise for additional charter vessels, reminding the inspector that delays in loading would cost the government $25 per day demurrage.

Concerned about his son's health, Joshua Humphreys also urged Samuel to hire additional inspectors to insure that the process could be completed before the dreaded fever season. He insisted that his son not remain in Georgia past mid-July, for "I see no necessity for you running the risk of your life."[46] By mid-May it was certain that a quantity of live oak would have to remain at the landings. This perturbed Jackson, for "to leave the Timber here a whole Summer exposed to the excessive heat of the sun & the effects of frequent Showers & occasional heavy dews, will nearly ruin it."[47] Although fire was a constant danger, he had no alternative but to recommend that the wood be covered with brush to prevent it from drying out too quickly.

This, then, is a fair sample of what went on for three years. As the Quasi-War with France wound down, the navy was reorganized and plans for naval construction were abandoned under the Act of 3 March 1801.[48] Within a few months the thirty-nine-year-old Miller died, still far from successful in any of the endeavors he so courageously attempted.

Since the methods used to fell live oaks and to mould and haul the timber for shipbuilding had been well established a hundred years before the Shubrick and Miller agreements were signed with the navy, one can reasonably question why it suddenly seemed so difficult. The key lies in John Morgan's reaction during the 1794–96 season; the moulds were so long that they frightened him. The largest ship completed had been the 74-gun *America* constructed during the Revolutionary War by Colonel James Hackett in Portsmouth, New Hampshire. Apparently, the ship was constructed of familiar northern timber; Hackett commented to Secretary of War Pickering in May 1795 that "building ships of live oak timber with us has never been practiced," and admitted that he did not know "the nature or durability of it."[49] The frigates and 74s authorized by Congress in 1794 and 1799 required

Preparation for WAR to defend Commerce.

Building the 36-gun live-oak frigate
Philadelphia *to aid in the war against*
Tripoli. *Launched from the city of her*
name in 1799, she became part of the
Mediterranean blockading fleet in
1803. Unfortunately she struck a
reef while chasing an enemy cruiser,
ran aground, and was captured by
Tripolitan gunboat crews. In a daring
night raid on 16 February 1804, led
by Lieutenant Stephen Decatur of
Enterprize, *about seventy-four*
American officers and men set fire to
Philadelphia, *escaping unharmed.*
Destroying the frigate successfully
prevented its being used by the enemy
against American naval vessels.

the largest quantity of massive live oaks ever used in this country.
Trees of the appropriate dimensions were difficult to find, and
often those cut down had to be rejected as unfit. Some measure of
the difficulty can be garnered from a letter written by Shubrick to
Stoddert in February of 1800:

> I neglected to mention in my last that the deficiency of pieces of
> timber there stated was owing to the prodigious number of trees
> that proved rotten upon being cut down but which could not be
> discovered to be so until they were felled. It appears that when the
> live oak tree begins to decay the part first affected is the tap root &
> the decay extending upwards destroys the heart of the timber with-
> out its exhibiting any external marks of being defective which
> makes it impossible to estimate with any degree of accuracy the
> quantity of timber contained in any given number of trees or any
> number of acres of timberland.
>
> My foreman informed me that he felled ten trees out of which
> he expected to have gotten as many floor timbers but six of them

40

proved so entirely decayed as not to be applied to any part of this frame—one tree that he expected to have got the main transom from as it girted twenty four feet at the butt & would have squared full 22 inches to the extent of thirty six feet we found in the same situation when cut down—

These defective trees not only misguide us in our calculations but greatly retard our progress & occasion a great loss both of labor & time.[50]

With the end of America's Quasi-War with France and the advent of Thomas Jefferson's administration in 1801, the policies of which ran counter to development of the sea-going navy, all major construction as well as urgent requirements for live oak came to an end. Instead of frigates, Jefferson favored the construction of gunboats, sixty-nine of which were built during the succeeding six years, although none reached the Mediterranean. In May 1801 the Pasha of Tripoli declared war on the United States; the war lasted until a vigorous blockade of the Tripolitan coast precipitated a peace treaty in June 1805. By 1807 all four of the Barbary powers had been subdued.[51]

During the summer of 1811, Governor of the Louisiana Territory William C. C. Claiborne advised Secretary of the Navy Paul Hamilton to direct a competent and confidential officer to visit those regions where the best ships' timber was located and report to the Navy Department its potential with a view toward reserving considerable acreage for public use. He called special attention to Louisiana lands bordering Lakes Maurepas, Pontchartrain, and Borgne, where timber was of the best quality, declaring "there is perhaps no District in the United States where as good Materials for Ship Building are to be found, or . . . prepared at a lesser expense."[52] Claiborne's sensible suggestion was disregarded, as another armed conflict with the British gathered momentum and finally erupted.

The War of 1812 was a costly demonstration that military preparation, when inadequate and lacking in solid public support, could result in near disaster. Thanks to experience gained by veteran American naval officers during the Tripolitan War of 1801–05, and their well-built fighting ships and competent crews, some

Constitution *and* Guerriere, *19 August 1812*

Wasp *and* Frolic, *18 October 1812*

Constitution *with* Cyane *and* Levant, *20 February 1815*

Because on-the-spot battle shots were not possible until the advent of modern photography, the public waited weeks or months for publication of illustrations depicting victories. Details were often inaccurate in stylized woodcuts such as these, but they nevertheless engendered feelings of ardent patriotism.

outstanding naval victories were achieved in the early months. Lieutenant Christopher Claxton of the Royal Navy was candid in his admiration for the United States Navy's 44-gun ships:

> American frigates, in point of size and crews, and consequently in the most important essentials for an effective man of war, are superior to us [sic]. Latterly, we have built a few Frigates on an equality with them: —but they were all a day after the fair. At the commencement of the war, we had not a single ship [of] one [gun] deck in the Navy, fit to cope with their three largest frigates—the *President, Constitution,* and *United States*.[53]

At the beginning of 1813, Congress authorized construction of new men of war; at the same time British forces blockaded our major ports from the Chesapeake and Delaware bays southward. Sea battles nearly ceased, and commerce and shipping were closed off. As Secretary of the Navy William J. Jones later indicated, such circumstances prevented awarding any contracts for live oak.[54]

In August 1814 British troops under Rear Admiral Sir George Cockburn marched into Washington, where they deliberately burned the White House and other public buildings partly in retaliation for American destruction of York and Newark. Under orders from Secretary Jones, American forces proceeded to destroy the Washington Navy Yard. They burned 15,000 cubic feet of live-oak timber, the nearly completed 44-gun frigate *Columbia*, and the 16-gun sloop of war *Argus,* both with frames of live oak, both still on the stocks.[55]

Moving along the Southern seaboard, Cockburn's detachments created panic as they plundered and occupied the coastal plantations. Slaves and cotton were not their only bounty. Occupying Cumberland Island in Georgia during December 1814, they cut "a quantity of live-oak timber" and loaded it aboard the Bermuda-bound British ship *Rolla,* which embarked in 1815, nearly a month after ratification of the Treaty of Ghent ended the war.[56] Such high-handed action emphasized the vulnerability of the nation's timber and underscored the need to safeguard it from being usurped by foreign powers. The need for a strong navy was also underscored when the Dey of Algiers, dissatisfied with the amount of his tribute, declared war on the United States in March 1815 after seizing American vessels. In May, with a fleet of ten ships, Captain Stephen Decatur sailed from New York for the Mediterranean. There he captured an Algerine frigate and a gunboat, then sailed into the harbor of Algiers. On 30 June he obtained a treaty in which the Dey renounced tribute, interference with American commerce, and ransom for all captives. American naval superiority was effective in bringing about the end of all payments of tribute to the other Barbary powers by 1816.

Chapter 3

Rampant "Oak Mania"

*During my residence here for the last eight
months . . . a fortnight has scarcely elapsed without the departure from this port of Vessels loaded
with* Cedar & Live-Oak *timber believed by everyone to be cut upon the publick lands, nay in many
instances* known *to be, but as the most respectable
mercantile houses here engage in such shipments—
no one is willing to become Informer. . . .*

> *William F. Steele, U. S. Attorney for West
> Florida in Pensacola, 1823*

As the War of 1812 was ending, Secretary of the Navy Jones delivered a vigorous plea to the Senate that it secure for government
use "all the valuable species of oak which is found only on the
southern seashore"; the act appropriating funds for naval timber
directed that a survey be undertaken in 1815–17 to determine the
quantity of available timber from the Carolinas to Alabama.[1]

From the viewpoint of a modern timber cruiser, whose job is
to determine the number of board feet of timber in a specified
forest area, the twelve-page survey prepared by Thomas M.
Newell and Abraham Thomas was useless. Often imprecise and
contradictory, it was an unsatisfactory and unreliable guide. As far
as North Carolina live oak was concerned, Smiths Island was the
only place surveyed. It had been culled and had only three hundred sound trees remaining; the rest were rotten or fit only for
firewood. In South Carolina, Bulls Island could supply frames for
three sloops of war, and some timber was available on Hilton
Head, Daufuskie, and Hunting islands, the latter of which had a
good landing with ten feet of water.

Thomas reported that although the Georgia islands nearest
Savannah (such as Wassaw and Ossabaw) had once been well tim-
bered, valuable trees remaining were scattered and therefore undesirable. Newell, on the other hand, thought Ossabaw had excellent quality timber sufficient for frames of two 74s and several

American axemen sketched by Joshua Shaw, ca. 1810–25

frigates. He also claimed Sapelo had "a considerable quantity of the best timber for frigates" and two good ten- and twelve-foot landings; Thomas reported it had already been culled and cleared. Cumberland Island, according to Thomas, had quantities of large-growth timber and thriving forests of young oak; Newell claimed former contractors had cut off all the large trees and that frames for only two sloops were available.[2]

At least they were in general agreement on Blackbeard. It abounded "with large timber as well as small and never having been culled may by cutting out from time to time be kept in a constant state of improvement, as a nursery." Flats of a thousand feet could load at different places, roads could be opened within two to three miles of landings, and it had the best pasturage for a few head of oxen. Even though expenses would be great, they believed it was necessary to obtain timber on the island because large old trees were on the decline and were "constantly injured by Huntsmens fires, which likewise destroys the young ones."[3]

45

So Blackbeard it was for E. & T. Swift of Falmouth, Massachusetts, and Joseph Grice of Philadelphia, who sent gangs to cut live oak in the autumn of 1816. The timber was to meet naval requirements for building eight new 74s (making a total of nine) and nine new 44s (making a total of twelve) authorized by an act of 1816 for the gradual improvement of the navy.[4] A group of live oakers from Philadelphia returned to the island in 1817 and were disappointed to find much less timber than officials had led them to expect, yet another example of the inadequacies of evaluating and reporting on standing trees.

The timber survey of 1815 indicated that Louisiana was a potential source for excellent live oak, but more data were needed. On 1 March 1817 an act was passed authorizing the Secretary of the Navy to appoint agents and a surveyor to explore and select lands bearing live oak and red cedar sufficient for naval purposes.[5] The president had authority to reserve any that was selected, and there were penalties to discourage illegal cutting.

The following year President James Monroe appointed James Leander Cathcart and James Hutton as Navy Department agents along with John Landreth, a surveyor, to make the Louisiana expedition. They embarked on the schooner *Nonsuch*, accompanied by a Navy Lieutenant and several armed men. The expedition lasted from January 1818 to mid-April 1819. Daily journals kept by all three men provide fascinating details of the journey, which took them through the forests, bayous, swamps, and creeks of the state's southern region, at times a tortuous course.[6] They went up the River Teche to St. Martinville; back down to Belle Isle; over to the islands in Lakes Chetimaches, Palourde, and Chico; and finally to New Orleans. They found quantities of excellent live oak located with easy access to lakes and rivers leading to the Mississippi. At the request of a naval official, they also examined red-cedar timber on the Alabama River before returning to Washington. Only once, at Bryant's plantation (currently Morgan City), did they find live oak being prepared to fill a naval contract. Edward Livingston had nearly a hundred pieces hewn, and the group was particularly impressed by a single, forty-cubic-foot timber.[7]

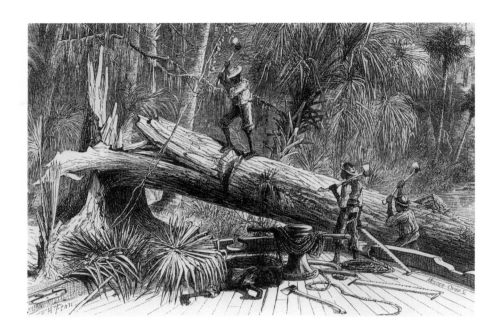

Clearing a slight obstruction in the river

Efforts to purchase supplies from local citizens were discouraging. Little variety was available and Cathcart found prices inordinately high. On the River Teche, near what is now Patterson, they noted a good stand of live oak that the owners would give merely in exchange for clearing the land. However, "if the United States were to order the purchase they would not fail to demand an exorbitant price . . . for patriotism is a plant which does not grow in this climate, & Uncle Sam is consider'd fair game!",[8] a statement reminiscent of the perfidiousness discerned by Bernard Romans some forty-odd years earlier.

The wilderness of Louisiana was a haven for bald eagles and huge flocks of pelicans and gulls. At times, Cathcart's party came upon a hundred alligators congregated in one place, some of them twelve to fourteen feet long. Fortunately all reptiles were in "a torpid state," but at night the men were aware of "panthers" (cougars), wildcats, and raccoons. Fish were plentiful, and Landreth found the islands beautiful, a "constant habitation of the Red Bird and Mocking Bird whose united harmony gives a continual delight

47

Bath

Shipbuilding on the Kennebec River in Bath, Maine. In 1819, before the treaty with Spain was ratified ceding Florida to the United States, Green and Emerson of Bath were sending live oakers south. During the 1821–22 season, working under master carpenter John Bosworth, they cut timber along the Georgia-Florida coast at Cumberland Island, St. Marys, St. Augustine, and New Smyrna.

to the Ear."[9] But for all its beauties, the area imposed afflictions too; it was a portent for future live oakers when Cathcart bemoaned the many days he suffered the enervating effects of diarrhea brought on "by drinking the waters of the Mississippi," and reported that even in mid-January the men were tortured by swarming mosquitoes that left them "spoted like Leopards & bleeding at every pore, notwithstanding we used every precaution in our power to evade the depredations of those noxious insects."[10]

The immediate result of their expedition was a presidential order reserving the 19,000 acres on Commissioners, Cypress, and Six islands on Lake Chetimaches. The islands contained about 37,000 live oaks of various sizes, all of them fit for naval purposes, although many were difficult or impossible to approach.[11] Even a decade later, the Navy had cut none of them, for Louisiana's importance was overshadowed by Florida's cession in 1819, finally ratified by treaty in 1821. Huge areas of these newly acquired, rich live-oak lands were set aside for naval use and by 1868 the public reserves totaled nearly 268,000 acres in the states of Florida, Alabama, Mississippi, and Louisiana.[12] By this means the government tried to ensure its supply of quality timber, but was hampered by both the settling of complicated Spanish title claims on the part of American citizens and the hardships of surveyors. Inadequate protection against widespread illegal cutting was to be a plague for decades.

In the course of the early nineteenth century, two concepts emerged to govern the utilization of naval-timber resources: one was to reserve the vast live-oak forests as public lands, enact trespass laws to prevent pillage, and appoint agents to provide surveillance; the other was to develop live-oak nurseries on publicly owned land and cut the timber on a sustained-yield basis. Although Ebenezer Jackson had suggested transplanting and caring for trees on Blackbeard Island as early as 1801, and developing nurseries had again been suggested in 1815, the first course was initially the more popular one; many officials believed that cultivating trees represented an absurd expense, considering the nation's "inexhaustable" supply of timber. It required presidential influence—the intelligence and farsightedness of John Quincy Adams—to make the public aware of the lasting benefits of conservation.

A plan to develop nurseries was actually precipitated by the continual disappearance of naval timber that began on a large scale soon after Florida was ceded to the United States. In February 1822 "at least 300 hands" were discovered illegally cutting live oak and cedar along the St. Johns River up to thirty miles from their base in the village of Pablo; scarcely a fortnight passed without vessels sailing out of Pensacola loaded with timber stolen from public lands.[13] Government officials were bombarded with reports of the pillage, but there was nothing to stop the unscrupulous, both American and foreign, from taking what they wanted. A congressional act was passed in 1822 to help safeguard the public lands of Florida.[14]

In 1826 Secretary of the Navy Samuel L. Southard sent an agent to examine the southern Atlantic coast, and his dispatches from Florida were jolting. More than half of the accessible timber along the coast had disappeared; a mile south of Jacksonville on the St. Johns River and its tributaries, live oak was stripped up to fifteen miles inland, and the port collector estimated that in the previous six to eight years some two million cubic feet had been illegally taken and probably "consumed abroad."[15]

Southard made his report to Congress, which passed a resolution providing for more effective preservation of live-oak timber on public lands, and the possibility of forming plantations for the rearing of live oak. The resulting Timber Trespass Act of 1827 empowered the government to withhold red-cedar and live-oak lands from public sale, to impose penalties for the unauthorized removal of timber, and to establish a live-oak nursery or plantation.[16]

President Adams, already a serious student of horticulture, was enthusiastic about the idea of nurseries; his close friend John M. White, Florida's territorial delegate, introduced a congressional resolution establishing a site at Deer Point on the Santa Rosa Peninsula.[17] Ideally located between Santa Rosa Sound and Pensacola Bay, most of the 3,000 acres were already publicly owned. In addition, the acreage was surrounded by water, allowing easy removal of timber, and it was conveniently near the Pensacola Navy Yard.

Although some of the land was owned by White, most of it was the property of Henry Marie Brackenridge, an author and the district judge for West Florida. He was agreeable to selling his tract to the government and, in the course of the negotiations, offered to superintend the live-oak plantation without stipend, except for expenses, since he felt the privilege would be sufficient compensation. Brackenridge crystallized his ideas about developing the plantation while experimenting with fruit trees on Deer Point, and at the request of Secretary Southard he prepared a report on live oak that is among the earliest serious works on forestry written by an American.[18]

The live oak, wrote the judge, is "one of the most valuable timber trees our country produces, and is unequalled for the frames of vessels"; nor is there any wood superior "in strength, bouyancy, and durability." He was greatly concerned that its future was in jeopardy, citing in support of his pessimism the French botanist Michaux, who believed that in fifty to ninety years the valuable timber tree would vanish because of the limited quantity and great demand.[19]

To Brackenridge, live oak had "the appearance of a large apple, or pear tree, [with a] . . . spreading picturesque top, and delicate olive shaped leaves, of a deep shining green . . . ; one of the most magnificent and delightful shade trees in the world." Unlike the common oak, he noted, it was not found in extensive forests, for "it loves solitary, and detached situations, . . . requires a free circulation of air, and must have ample space to extend its prodigious horizontal branches." In fact, he had once measured a seventy-five-foot limb that was growing so low he could reach it from the ground.[20]

The tree "rarely attains its full size anywhere except on the margins of rivers, and on the shores of the bays and sounds, and on the edge of open ponds." "But," he continued, "in order to form their curious and valuable crooks, so much esteemed for knees, or futtocks, breasthooks of upper deck, top timber, and bow timber etc. it will be an advantage to grow [them] so much closer, in order to form longer and larger bodies."[21]

If grown from acorns, the trees would require fifty to sixty years to mature sufficiently for naval purposes. But Brackenridge thought this method of propagation was unnecessary; instead, he suggested permitting stumps of old trees to send up their vigorous shoots, which would reach maturity in a third the time required by the parent stem. He also advocated transplanting young trees, for he was acquainted with no forest tree that improved more quickly than live oak.

Brackenridge was not surprised that handsome young specimens fared so poorly in Pensacola's public square and navy yard, because they had been planted too deeply, with little root and no water. Good care of the trees involved freeing the root from bark and litter to prevent rot and discourage forest fires. Removal of decaying lower limbs could contribute to preserving the trunks. By judicious pruning the trees could be made to assume almost any shape; this would check horizontal branching and result in the longer, straighter trunks so essential for stern posts and certain other "great timbers." Brackenridge related the astonishment of an old Spanish shipwright who saw the cultured live oaks after being absent from the area for fifteen years. The man was amazed "at the appearance of the large live Oaks here, which he told me, within his recollection had almost been stripped naked of limbs, for crooks, but they had since formed others of such a size, as scarcely to show where they had been cut. The dead trunk of a Live Oak will stand half a century without decay. . . ."[22]

In the second part of his report, Brackenridge made four proposals for organizing the reservation in terms of land use, experimentation, labor, equipment, and salaries:

1. Give the four hundred trees already growing in the area proper care by cutting away all pine, water oaks, and suckers. These could provide a quantity of firewood for the navy yard. Fell some of the largest live oaks, cut them to moulds, and store in navy sheds where they would last "for a hundred years, without any other inconvenience, than that of becoming so hard as to break the tools of the workmen."
2. Transplant, when conditions are favorable, some four thousand young trees, four to twelve inches in diameter, "which with proper care may be fit for use in ten or fifteen years."
3. Cultivate ten thousand young trees, two or more inches in diameter, having the advantage of old roots, clearing a few yards around each or opening wide avenues to provide sufficient air and room for excellent growth.
4. Experimentally set out one thousand to three thousand trees "in open savanas" annually adding up to five thousand more, giving careful attention to their cultivation.[23]

Brackenridge suggested that for a small compensation, two or three poor families could be induced to settle on the land already cleared to act as keepers and help prevent fires. The danger of forest fire, he emphasized, should not be underestimated, for crews of boats passing to and from the Choctawhatchee River often camped there, leaving their fires burning, as did the few Indian families who hunted on the peninsula.

For the first year's expense, the judge proposed an appropriation of $4,000 for twenty laborers (at $15 each per month); $1,000 for rations, cart, oxen, boats, and tools; $400 for a superintendent's salary; $500 for the overseer's salary; and a few hundred dollars for temporary buildings to be used as living quarters, storehouses, etc. Annual expenses would amount to little more than $10,000; when compared to the value of the timber already available for naval use, this expenditure would be money well spent.

Convinced by the report, Adams approved the appointment of Brackenridge as superintendent in July 1828 (although Southard's letter of appointment was not sent until December). But the president did insist that acorns be planted on several hundred acres so "that their growth to maturity may be observed, and perhaps a better knowledge of them be obtained. My passion is for a hard, heavy, long-lived wood, to be raised from the nut or seed—requiring a century to come to maturity."[24]

In two months' time the judge employed fifteen laborers to clear and replant young trees, to build facilities, and to clear roads for firebreaks; however, the project was doomed in its infancy by the president's political opponents. Unfortunately, the Santa Rosa experiment was conceived near the end of Adam's only term in office, and it failed to survive the bitter campaign of 1828 and subsequent political upheavals in Florida during Andrew Jackson's administration. Ammunition first came in the form of a letter to the new Secretary of the Navy, John Branch, written by a disgruntled former naval employee who had been fired by Southard. His letter claimed that federal funds had been misused for private benefit, and hinted that the entire live-oak project was a fraud. Eager to attack the former administration, Branch suspended the Deer Point operation until a Navy commission could investigate, and during the interim he enlisted the support of Amos Kendall, a Navy official, who helped him confuse the issue for the benefit of Congress.[25]

Even though no evidence of either misspent funds or fraud could be found, Branch threatened to suspend all financial support when the fiscal year ended in January 1831. He charged Adams with overstepping his authority in permitting trees to be planted at Santa Rosa, and he hinted that personal gain for certain individuals had been the former president's motive. Adams lashed back at the "malicious pleasure" Branch enjoyed in "destroying everything of which I planted the germ," and concluded that the Deer Point experiment now enjoyed "a condition as flourishing

53

as possible and more than a hundred thousand live oaks are growing upon it. All is to be abandoned to the stolid ignorance and stupid malignity of John Branch and his filthy subaltern, Amos Kendall."[26]

By the time Branch was relieved of his post in May 1831, the Santa Rosa nursery was in a state of neglect, although Secretary of the Navy Levi Woodbury did grant Brackenridge his request for $300 in wages for an overseer and some laborers. In January 1832 when his term as judge of West Florida expired it was no surprise when no reappointment was forthcoming; he was as much a victim of Jacksonian politics as was his noble experiment. Shortly afterward, the Santa Rosa lands were transferred to the administration of the navy-yard commander, under whose direction the project eventually perished.[27]

In theory, the United States had a virtual monopoly on the world's supply of live oak; most of it was publicly owned by 1831. But as Europe's timber resources steadily shrank, American live oak became a commodity more and more coveted by Britain, France, Spain, the Netherlands, and Denmark. Even Czar Alexander I of Russia showed interest by ordering several barrels of acorns to plant in the Crimea. The congressional acts of 1817, 1822, and 1831 were all designed to safeguard the needs of American naval and merchant vessels by imposing fines and imprisonment on those found guilty of illegally cutting or removing timber on the public domain.[28] Between 1817 and the end of 1831 the government spent a paltry $3,500 a year to prevent trespass on these lands, to have surveys prepared, and to support the Santa Rosa project. The country was, as a result, ill-prepared to protect itself against continual plunder of its timber; in December 1832, as directed by the House of Representatives, Secretary of the Navy Woodbury presented a lengthy "Historical Statement" with facts and figures to prove it. Recommending that the Navy Department continue to obtain live oak of the best quality, he confirmed that:

[The wood is] superior in strength, resistance, and hardness to the celebrated British oak that forms "the wooden walls" of England. It

Live Oak Timber for sale on Cumberland Island.
THE proprietor of this Timer wishing to clear the lands on which it stands, will dispose of it on very reasonable terms. It is believed the frames of a frigate and sloop of war & about thirty thousand feet of Timber suitable for merchant vessels, might readily be obtained here. For further particulars apply to Messrs. Bayard & Hunter at Savannah or to   P. M. NIGHTINGALE,
oct 18   On the premises.

Advertisement appearing in the Georgian, 18 October 1832

is, when used for frames, much more durable that that, or even cedar, which the ancients called "the everlasting wood," and in some qualities surpasses the teak of India, which is confessedly the best timber for the greatest number or variety of naval purposes that the research of man has yet discovered. [But it] would not, with profit, bear the long transportation to this country, as it will not from India to England, except when made up into vessels, and earning freight.[29]

He stated that with only 144,655 publicly owned live-oak trees and fewer than 10,000 trees on private lands suitable for shipbuilding, a serious shortage existed. Some large trees grew three to an acre, and in any case no more than twenty to thirty per acre should be left to mature. However, seldom were even half that number to be found, since many young saplings died. With annual demands at 62,286 cubic feet, and calculating 50 cubic feet per tree, the annual requirement was 1,245 live-oak trees; at an average tree age of seventy-five years the annual acreage requirement would be 4,640. If only two trees were available per acre and each was a hundred years old, the annual requirement would be 62,286 acres. Taking into consideration fire, depredation, injury, and

TABLE 2   Approximate Requirements of Live Oak Timber for Frames of Naval Vessels

Type of Vessel	Cubic Feet of Live Oak	Number of Live Oak Trees
Ship of the line	34,000	680
Frigate		
First Class	23,000	460
Second Class	18,000	360
Sloop	8,000	160
Schooner	1,800	36

SOURCE: *American State Papers, Naval Affairs*, 4:192.

other contingencies, Woodbury suggested that it would be judicious to reserve at least 160,000 acres of live oak.[30]

Woodbury acknowledged that "imperfect examination" of lands in Florida, Alabama, Mississippi, and Louisiana had resulted in ignorance of what timber grew where and what had been cut on both public and private lands in the years following their examination in 1819 and 1827. This had "led to a new system of districts and agents, whose chief duties were to make a further and full examination and report on the whole live oak timber which might be found still to remain on lands belonging to the public. . . ."[31]

Under this "new system" (authorized by his predecessor, John Branch) the entire area of Florida and the Gulf coast territory as far as the Louisiana–Texas border was divided into seven districts. Each district had its own agent, whose duties were clearly stated. They were to:

1. Make public their appointment and the provisions of the trespass laws, report trespassers to the United States Attorney, and cooperate in their prosecution.
2. Obtain surveyor's maps and examine all the red-cedar and live-oak lands to locate private holdings and to mark areas worthy of government reservation and report these to the land office.
3. Evaluate the nature of the soil; the possibility of navigation by water; the quality of existing roads to landings or the feasibility of building new roads; the depth of water at landings; the distance required before timber could be taken aboard vessels "drawing not less than ten feet of water"; and any obstacles in the way of getting the timber to these vessels.
4. "Keep always in view that the protection of Government lands from pillage and injury, is the first great object to be attended to, and that the selection of lands containing valuable Navy Timber . . . is the next important point of duty . . . to discharge."
5. Dispatch regular, confidential progress reports to the Navy.

Compensation was an annual salary of $1,800 plus $1.25 per day

Occupational hazard of the timber agent

for expenses, including a horse, and $26 per month for an assistant.[32]

Actually, it was ludicrous to believe that seven men could effectively cover an estimated 3,000 miles of coastline (with all its inlets and bays) and also scrutinize the interior. No matter how diligently they labored, the task far exceeded their capacities. As Kephart pointed out, this work was "in a wilderness area of inter-mixed swamps and high ground cut up by countless lakes and meandering streams that made overland travel a nightmare."[33] One agent reminded the Navy secretary that summer was a par-ticularly poor time to penetrate thickets and underbrush of live-oak hummocks, because the heat was intense, the snakes and rep-tiles were abundant, and the men refused to work.

In 1831 three small Baltimore-built schooners were pur-chased by the Navy for patrolling the coast from Florida to the Louisiana-Texas border to apprehend poachers. The 50-ton *Spark* was assigned to the Atlantic coast; *Ariel* (48 tons) cruised in the Gulf of Mexico between Cape Sable and the Perdido River; and *Sylph* (41 tons) covered the waters between the Perdido and Sabine rivers. Each was armed with one gun.[34] The only surviving log is that of *Spark*, and it reveals a disappointing ten-month cruise lasting from mid-June 1831 until late April of the following year. She embarked from the Washington Navy Yard under the command of Lieutenant William P. Piercy, whose complement in-cluded a midshipman, eight seamen, and two boys. They were be-set by gales and foul weather and ran aground twice. Seven of the crew deserted ship, but were finally replaced by five new crew members. In nearly a year at sea, they sighted and boarded only one vessel loaded with live oak, the American schooner *Argo*, bound for the navy yard at Charlestown, Massachusetts. Appar-ently, her cargo was legal.[35]

The schooner *Sylph* suffered a harsh fate. She departed Pen-sacola in July, and was assumed lost with all hands sometime dur-ing the great hurricane of 1831. Developing in the Caribbean, its savage winds pounded Barbados on the night of 10–11 August, killing over 1500 people; it then ripped across Haiti, Cuba, Ma-

LIVE OAK TIMBER.

NAVY COMMISSIONER'S OFFICE,
18th July 1832.

THE Commissioner's of the Navy will receive Proposals until the 15th September next, for furnishing Live Oak Timber, cut to moulds (which they will furnish) for one frigate and one sloop of war, with 3000 feet of promiscuous timber cut to dimensions for the frigate, and 1000 feet for the sloop of war. The timber must be cut from trees grown in situations within the influence of marine air, and not more at farthest than 25 miles from the sea. The frigate frame and promiscuous timber to be delivered at the Navy Yard Washington, and that for the sloop at the Navy Yard Portsmouth, N. H. on or before the 31st December, 1833.

Persons offering will state their prices per cubic foot for the frame and promiscuous timber seperately. Bond with two or more sufficient securities for the faithful performance of the contract, will be required, and as additional and collateral security, ten per centum on the amount of each delivery will be retained until the contract is completed to the entire satisfaction of the Commissioners, unless otherwise specially authorized by the Board. In all deliveries of timber, a due proportion of the most difficult parts of the frame must be delivered, otherwise it shall be at the option of the Commissioners to withhold such further amount, in addition to the ten per cent. as they may judge expedient to secure the public interest, until such difficult proportion shall be delivered.

Persons offering must state their residence and the names and residence of their securities. Any bid not made in conformity with this advertisement, or that may not be received within the time herein limited for receiving offers, will not be considered.   July 25.

From the Providence (Rhode Island) Republican Herald, 28 July 1832. Appearing in newspapers of nine states and the District of Columbia, this notice alerted northern contractors and owners of southern timberland that another season of live oaking would soon begin.

tanzas, and Dry Tortugas, and by the 16th was crossing the Gulf of Mexico. On the 29th its devastating effects on land and at sea were felt as far west as New Orleans and central Louisiana.[36]

After a trial of one year's duration, the ambitious experiment of patrolling the Florida and Louisiana coastal waters was abandoned; the two remaining schooners, *Ariel* and *Spark*, were decommissioned and sold.[37] As one critic remarked, to succeed in suppressing "oak running" along the labyrinthine southern coast with "a marine force . . . would have called for well nigh the combined navies of the world."[38]

When hostilities with the Florida Seminoles erupted during the 1830s, all surveys for naval timber had to be suspended, and work by the live oakers curtailed; an exception was William Acken, who doggedly persisted near St. Marks in the spring of 1839. His crew was twice attacked by Indians, and one of his men and two of the Indians were killed. "We are now," he wrote, "busy shipping timber at the hazard of our lives. There is no knowing what a day may bring forth."[39]

As long as live oak was used in shipbuilding, the overwhelming problem was stopping the poachers who threatened to denude the public preserve of trees. A letter written in 1841 spelled out the government agent's difficulty. He must "be constantly on the alert, and should visit in person the spot on which they are cutting, to determine whether the land be public, or of a doubtful title, &c., for it is impossible to seize the timber unless he can prove that it is the growth of lands belonging to the United States; and to do this he must see the very stump from which it was taken.[40]

The agents employed could not possibly perform these duties successfully, and both the administration and Congress publicly acknowledged this during the 1840s. It would have required a concerted effort by a modern amphibious force with a sophisticated means of surveillance to thwart the "bands of lawless thieves" that daily invaded the southern coast to purloin timber. As it was, the small government force that tried to penetrate the interior on foot and horseback had a slim chance of apprehending

A temporary palmetto lean-to, easily constructed and hastily abandoned—the perfect shelter for illegal cut-and-run live-oak gangs.

anyone, much less obtaining proof of the theft—particularly in areas where the inhabitants were unwilling to act as informants. Given these circumstances, it is not surprising that the agents were held in "the most supreme contempt" by those they pursued.[41]

The method frequently used in stealing much-prized timber from public lands was practiced repeatedly, until it became common knowledge:

> A person who calls himself a "sub-contractor" arrives here from the north with laborers, tools, and provisions. He goes to the woods and hunts up a piece of public land well stocked with live oak. He then hires some miserable creature (a free negro or an Indian answers all his purposes) to go on to that section and build himself a cabin, and claim the land, or rather the right to the land by pre-emption. This settler then sells the sub-contractor all the live oak on his land, for which he receives seven or eight cents per foot; and this is the share the settler receives for his part of the transaction. The timber is then cut according to the patterns and models brought out, and shipped to the navy-yards, where the Government pays . . . from $1 to $2 per foot.[42]

The "settler," tired of his squatter's rights, moved on to another live-oak grove (known in Louisiana as a *chenier*) where he repeated the process. Meanwhile, the "sub-contractor" was reasonably safe from prosecution and, if worse came to worst, could depart in haste with his portable equipment—with no one the wiser. In terms of risk it seemed worthwhile, since the clear profit from spending two to four weeks at live oaking was estimated at no less than $1500.

Violations against these unprotected and unguarded lands were not perpetrated merely by small-time entrepreneurs; live oaking had become big business and some of the largest shipbuilding firms were involved. One irate informer claimed in 1841 that Samuel Grice and William Aiken of Philadelphia, Dennis and John Vermillion and William N. Joy of Norfolk, Thomas Vaughan of Baltimore, and William Deal of Portsmouth, New Hampshire, had all "knowingly cut" trees on government land for several years. They had groups of thirty and forty men working, and sent hundreds of schooners laden with live oak northward. In January 1837 at least 200 vessels left the Atchafalaya River loaded with approximately 700,000 cubic feet of timber, probably three quarters of which was taken from government land; its value was estimated at a million dollars. During the winter season of 1840–41, about 60 schooners and brigs filled with timber left the Atchafalaya, carrying away approximately 180,000 cubic feet of live oak. Much of what was stolen went to private shipyards, but a great deal was sold to the navy yards, resulting in the government's paying for its own trees.[43]

Herman Thompson, a shipwright from Kensington at Philadelphia, wrote to Secretary of the Navy Abel P. Upshur concerning his experience with the Grices. He had signed on as second foreman of a gang going to Louisiana in 1841. They cut 2,500 feet of timber and were paid for their labor. Shortly afterward, the Grices:

> . . . induced several of the men belonging to the gang to squat and take possession of the public land, which contained some of the best groves of live oak in that section of the country. These very contractors, after the men had taken possession, bought or contracted to buy, which they never paid for, a certain quantity of feet standing . . . [and] knew very well they were buying that which belonged to the Government, and were committing a fraud by so doing; and at the same time turn round and sell the very timber which belongs to the United States at an exorbitant price to the Government.[44]

Balie Peyton, U.S. District Attorney for the Eastern District of Louisiana, wrote to President Tyler that Grice had "cut and carried off more timber than any hundred men in Louisiana."[45]

Agent Hezekiah L. Thistle of Florida, small of stature and prickly as his name, "an instrument of tyranny, possessed of old-fashioned ideas of honesty and of the bowels to back them up . . . characterized the live oak 'business' of the day as 'crooked as Captain Cook's voyage around the world.'" He was vigilant in apprehending offenders, remarking (perhaps with some irony) that one of them "thought it hard" to be prevented from removing timber from public lands "as he had always done."[46]

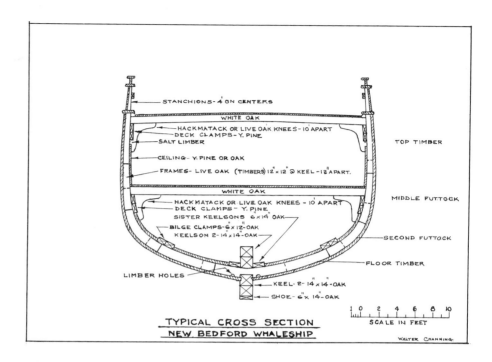

TYPICAL CROSS SECTION
NEW BEDFORD WHALESHIP

Typical cross-section of a New Bedford whaleship

TABLE 3   Density and Specific Gravity of Some North American Wood Commonly Used in Shipbuilding

Type of Wood	Specific Gravity	Density in Pounds per Cubic Foot
Red cedar	.44	41.1
Yellow pine (short leaf)	.47	44.0
Pitch pine	.47	43.9
Tamarack (hackmatack)	.49	45.8
White oak	.60	56.1
Live oak	.80	74.9
Water	1.00	62.4

Specific gravity values are based on oven dry weight and green volume; density values are for green timber with 50% moisture. Calculations based on data in *Wood Handbook. Wood as an Engineering Material.* USDA Agriculture Handbook No. 72, revised 1974.

In 1843 when the brig *Nimrod* was seized near New Smyrna with seventy-six pieces of live oak cut by Palmer & Ferris and destined for the Gosport Navy Yard, Thistle was on hand to testify. The case *United States* v. *brig Nimrod, Palmer and Thomas Smith, master, claimants* was heard before Judge Isaac H. Bronson at the District of East Florida Superior Court in April. The judge decreed the brig was to be forfeited, together with sixty-six pieces of timber determined to have been cut on public land, after delivery to the Gosport Yard. This was big news in St. Augustine; the local press devoted three full columns to the court's opinion.[47]

The outcome so enraged the claimants that Darius Ferris, described as a powerfully athletic young man well over six feet tall, violently attacked and severely injured the older Thistle. Backing Ferris was "a guard of Live oakers" and two friends who prevented interference from the agent's would-be defenders. This onslaught only strengthened Thistle's indomitable spirit and resoluteness in performing his duty to safeguard the public timberlands. Angry Florida citizens, incensed over the malicious assault on Thistle, wrote to Secretary of the Navy Abel P. Upshur, claiming it demonstrated both the inherent danger to any timber agent assiduous in his duty and the ease by which "desperados" such as Ferris could bribe or intimidate a weak-willed agent to violate his oath of office.[48]

As one agent asserted, it was extremely difficult to obtain sufficient evidence to punish offenders. Distinguishing between private and public lands was often impossible for agents, and the existing laws had no clout in places where district courts and district attorneys were located a hundred miles or more from the illegal operations. Starting out through the wilds of Louisiana to make a complaint, for example, was unthinkable. Throughout the 1840s and 1850s, until the Civil War, "oak mania" was rampant and literally volumes of letters were sent to officials in Washington protesting plunder of the public domain.[49] These resulted in a series of investigations and the subsequent passage of stiff laws to stop the pillage, but Congress, not for the last time, was penurious when it came to allocating funds to enforce the statutes effectively.

Packet ship Isaac Webb *of New York. The rise in commerce that followed the War of 1812 resulted in a demand for more ships; a mania for speed resulted in design and construction of fast packets and clippers for transporting goods and passengers to Europe, to China, and later to the gold fields of California. Packets were ships sailing on a regular schedule, regardless of weather conditions, with or without cargo and passengers. This concept was initiated when the Liverpool-bound* James Monroe *left New York harbor on 5 January 1818 at precisely 10 A.M.—the beginning of what became the celebrated Black Ball Line. The ships were driven unmercifully to meet announced schedules; "quick passages" meant fame for sea captains, profit for owners, and "hell for the crew."*

When this picture appeared in Gleason's Pictorial in 1851, the packet had made the New York to Liverpool trip in seventeen days. Built the preceding year by William H. Webb and named for his father, she belonged to the Black Ball Line. The caption in Gleason's read: "Her timbers are of live oak, locust and cedar, and she is most throughly put together . . . a splendid specimen of maritime beauty." With three full decks, her length was 188 feet; her breadth, 40 feet; and her depth of hold, 22 feet. In 1881 she foundered in the mid-Atlantic, carrying a cargo of iron rails.

The situation deteriorated further during the 1870s. A dozen political appointees acted as timber agents in Florida, drawing annual salaries of $480 to $1000, while residing up to a hundred miles away from the timber reservations for which they were responsible and on which they never set foot. Needless to say, depredation continued in the forests.

Beginning in the 1840s steam-powered vessels began replacing sailing ships, and another drastic alteration in ship construction—combined with the astounding events of 8 and 9 March 1862—set in motion the ultimate abandonment of live oak for naval use. When the ironclad steam ram *Virginia* (formerly the screw frigate *Merrimack*) destroyed the frigates *Cumberland* and *Congress* and then battled the ironclad *Monitor* to a draw, the era of sailing men of war was as good as over, as the Navy turned to metal ships driven by screw propellers. The change-over was not, in fact, immediate; the technology and skilled labor force required to produce and shape vast quantities of iron plates, rolled angles, bulb plates, etc., were yet to be developed. Therefore, the construction and repair of wooden ships continued for a number of years, although the ironclads and a looming timber shortage signaled their oncoming demise.

Joshua Humphreys once estimated that when cut to moulds only about one quarter of a tree trunk was used.[50] Nevertheless, cutting to moulds to save excess freight charges was standard practice. There were other wasteful habits. In the 1830s John James Audubon lamented that because live oakers were unable to detect in standing trees either disease or "windshakes" (longitudinal cracks presumed to be caused by the wind), they felled worthless trees; in so doing, they knocked down and destroyed a great many healthy young specimens leaving abandoned trunks strewn about the woods. He predicted that "before long a good-sized live oak will be so valuable, that its owner will exact an enormous price for it, even while it yet stands in the wood."[51]

As pointed out in a naval engineer's report of 1843, the expense of ships' timber was, in large measure, dependent on the distance it had to be hauled. As the easily accessible live oak was cut and contractors were forced into the interior, costs soared. At the end of the Civil War, consumption of timber had become so great that future supplies were in jeopardy. "From navy-yards to coopershops, from railroads to street alleys, and from bridge-building to shingle-making, there is no quarter given to the oak and no peace to the pine."[52] Contractors were encouraged to saw timber with steam-operated equipment in the shipyards, rather than hew it by hand in the forests. With judicious power-cutting, chips and blocks that would otherwise be left to rot on the forest floor could be salvaged in large, single pieces and put to good use. The difficulty lay in altering the well-established habits of hewers as well as contractors.[53]

By 1867 the price of live oak on the New York market was in fact quadruple that of white oak. Rough-squared, it was fetching $2 per cubic foot as compared to 50¢ for white oak; a single live-oak knee sided at 13 inches was $25 as compared to $13 for one of hackmatack; and 14-inch live-oak knees had no rivals at $35 each.[54]

The congressional acts of 1882 and 1883 providing for the construction of steel cruisers finally hastened the end of the Navy's wooden fighting ships and, consequently, its voracious requirements for live-oak timber. In fact, framing for two ships of

Amid flags and cheering crowds, the 130-ton, four-masted schooner Mary L. Newhall *was launched from the Houghton yard at Bath, Maine, in December 1904—length 209.1 feet, breadth 40.2 feet, and depth 21.6 feet. Built at a cost of $70,000, her entire frame was constructed of 40-year-old live oak purchased from surplus stock at the navy yard in Kittery. The wood's long underwater storage in a special timber dock obviated the necessity for preserving it with salt. The builder obtained an A-1 classification for a period of sixteen years, one year longer than was customary for wooden ships at the time. Bound from Port Tampa to Philadelphia and overloaded with phosphate rock,* Newhall *foundered in heavy seas 200 miles northwest of Bermuda in February 1908.*

the line was dissembled in late 1883 and the wood used for other purposes. No part of the annual appropriation for naval construction and repair was to be "applied to the repairs of any wooden ship when the estimated cost of such repair shall exceed thirty percent of the estimated cost of a new ship of the same size and like material."[55] This was, in effect, the end of live oaking except for one brief postscript. During World War I several small craft were contracted to be built at Brunswick, Georgia, presumably for naval use. Charles C. Stebbins of nearby Darien signed an agreement with William Downey to "supply all the live oak knees [he] could get."[56] These were cut on Stebbins' property near Eulonia by local labor, hauled out with timber carts, and shipped by rail to Brunswick. Very likely it was the last time live oak was cut for naval use anywhere in that vicinity.

This was not, however, the last time the Navy made use of its live oak. For the 1927–31 restoration of USS *Constitution*, hundreds of tons of live-oak timber were transported to Boston by rail from the Pensacola Naval Air Station where it had been stored underwater prior to the Civil War. Some of it was retained for repair of the frigate into the 1960s, but most of the reserve timber was shipped by barge from Boston to the Portsmouth (New Hampshire) Navy Yard for storage in the Ice Pond.

In 1945 two sample pieces were lifted from the ooze for testing to establish whether it could be used by the Navy for purposes other than ship repair. But when they tried it at the sawmill, the "saw was severely damaged, millworkers were nauseated by the stench and the Master Joiner stated (with certain pertinent and pithy comment) that the job could not be undertaken under any circumstances." In 1957, the Navy ordered another investigation of its live oak; some of the hundred-year-old timber was cut, but within hours it split, checked, and cracked. "Pieces were sawed, planed, turned, and soaked in linseed oil, . . . [but] as it dried it became hard with more tool damage . . . Its stench was even riper than before and the comments more pithy."[57] Now officially abandoned, the live oak remains "as is" and "where is" underwater at Portsmouth, no longer fit for renewal of any wooden ship.[58]

Constitution *under repair at the old Philadelphia Navy Yard in 1873. For ballistic purposes, an inch and a quarter was the average spacing of her live-oak frames and this is clearly shown where the outer planking has been removed. According to tradition, during her battle with* Guerriere *on 19 August 1812, a Yankee seaman observed British shot bouncing off* Constitution's *hull and exclaimed, "Huzza! Her sides are made of iron!"—hence the name "Old Ironsides." (Length 204 feet, breadth 43.5 feet, depth 22.5 feet.)*

A massive 24-foot-long piece of live oak from the Pensacola shipment. It measured 32 inches across the center, 32½ inches at one end. Weight is calculated in tons.

Nine hundred tons of live oak were needed to replace all below-deck stanchions, all stern cant timbers, the bitts, waterways, after deadwood, the counter timbers, and the outer stern post. Mast steps, a number of the breasthooks, all second futtocks, many third futtocks, some knees, certain framing for the gun ports, and portions of the quarter-deck galleys were all replaced with new live oak. To aid in preservation, heavy brush coats of creosote were applied, and feed salt packed between the frames. The quality of both timber and workmanship was evident when most of this renewed live oak was found still to be in good condition forty years later.

A new 6-ton, 28-foot live-oak stem piece for Constitution *being set in place with a steam-operated crane at the Boston Navy Yard on 17 July 1928. Hewn out with broadaxes and scarfed in three places, it was made by Samuel H. Barnes and Henry Littlefield.*

During Constitution's *1927–31 restoration, Lieutenant John A. Lord of the United States Navy personally inspected pine and oak timber from Maine to Florida, handpicked civilian shipwrights skilled in wooden shipbuilding, and vigilantly supervised all the work. Live-oak timber sent from the Pensacola Naval Air Station was an important component, but after about seventy years of underwater storage it was "nearly like concrete," and hewing it with broadaxes was initially a trying experience for most of the men. They found their tools had to be sharpened every thirty minutes to an hour, instead of the more usual once a day. "At first it was like chopping at a truck tire, my axe just*

bounced off," recalled Sam Barnes, "but we all soon got the knack."

The use of unseasoned timber was a principal cause of dry-rot spores spreading throughout a wooden ship. Seasoning removed the sap, and proper air seasoning had to be slow in order to dry the wood evenly, thus making it more durable. Drying the wood too rapidly caused it to twist and check; therefore, it was desirable to fell trees in winter when the sap was down. If shipments to the yards were delayed, timber was often submerged in water until it could be removed for air-drying in sheds. Live oak was stored under water to prevent hardening and to keep it in workable condition.

Installing new live-oak cant frames aboard Constitution *in April 1927*

Wide spacing of frames on the steam merchant vessel John G. Christopher *contrasts with that of* Constitution. *Built in 1891 at Wilmington, Delaware,* Christopher *was renamed* Winyah *in 1895. (Length 200 feet, breadth 38 feet, depth 17.5 feet.)*

One hundred and thirty-four years after her launching, U.S.S. Constitution *visited Georgia, and Savannah artist Christopher Murphy captured this moment on Visitor's Day in December 1931. She is now permanently moored in Boston Harbor, where her Navy crew, dressed in 1812 uniforms, conduct visitors through the ship daily. The nearby U.S.S.* Constitution *Museum has exhibits and research facilities. Etching in possession of the author.*

Chapter 4

The Live-Oaking Swift Family

*Our men have been quite contented and happy
throughout the passage our Boats came safe and in
fact we have not lost a straw—*

Oliver C. Swift, South Carolina, 1825

Although live oak probably was seldom found in New England
shipyards prior to the Revolutionary War, when trade was resumed after the peace and our commercial fleets began sailing the
world over, Yankee tradesmen began using it to prolong the life of
their ships. Because of its great expense, live oak had to be justi-
fied in terms of profit; it had to enhance the strength and durability of whaleships, merchants, and packets, but at the same
time allow for their increased size and speed.

The term *live-oak ship* is misleading; actually mixtures of
hard and soft woods were used in ship construction. For example,
Joshua Humphreys claimed a vessel in Philadelphia was called
"cedar and live oak, although her floor and raising timbers and
the first futtocks [were] of white oak."[1] The whaleship *Oneida*,
launched in 1832 at New Bedford, was described in one breath as
"built of live-oak, stanchions locust, ceiling and deck frames of
yellow pine, outboard planking white oak."[2] Probably her futtocks, keel, keelson, and knees were live oak.

The wood, however, was not universally favored. Some regarded it as too costly, too difficult to work, too heavy, and too
easily split when spikes were used; but none denied that live-oak
frames endured. Among giants in shipbuilding who did use it
were William Doughty and Son of Georgetown, D.C., the Grices
of Philadelphia, and Henry Eckford and the Webbs of New York.

69

The timbers of a ship.

A *Stern Post*

B *Deadwood*

C *Keel*

D *Quarter Timber*

E *Transom Beam*

F *Stem*

G *Futtocks (frames)*

H *Battens*

J *Breasthook*

K *Knighthead*

L *Treenails*

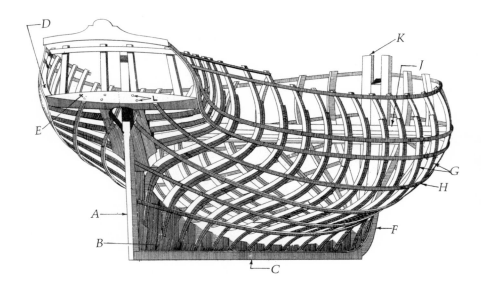

Eckford had a small coasting vessel that he used frequently in transporting timber from the South. In 1805 he built the 427-ton *Beaver* for John Jacob Astor's fur trade, and her live-oak frame was said to have been reused forty years later in another vessel for the same owner. The last ship Eckford constructed was a corvette sold to the Sultan of Turkey in 1831. It was hailed as "a beautiful specimen of naval architecture," built "of our unrivalled live oak."[3]

Between 1845 and 1860, that brief period of the clipper ships, premium-built carriers engaged in a booming trade with California and China, bringing rewards of high profit to merchants and fame to their hard-driving sea captains. Southern timber played an important role in those "thoroughbred racers of the sea," and their names often reflected the emphasis on speed and strength: *Flying Cloud, Hurricane, Telegraph, Gladiator, Intrepid, Undaunted,* and *Challenger.*

In August 1849 the 1050-ton *Oriental,* "a splendid vessel for the China trade," was launched in New York. "A copper-bottomed, two-decked ship, she was 175 feet in length, 30 feet in breadth of beam, 21 feet in depth of hold and was constructed

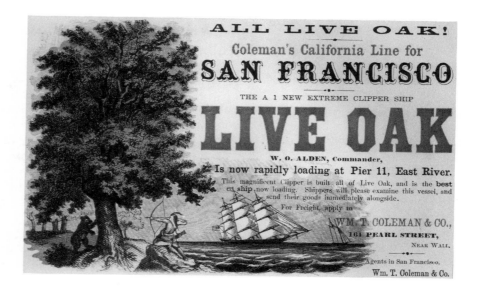

with white oak, live oak, locust and cedar."[4] In a record eighty-one days, she made the trip from New York around the Horn to Hong Kong. The *N. B. Palmer*, constructed of the same timber and named in honor of *Oriental*'s captain, was launched two years later. The quality of the workmanship and raw materials of these vessels was of paramount importance to their owners.

> [N]ever in the history of the world . . . have ships been rigged so heavily or driven so relentlessly as were American clippers in the early California trade. One has only to read the details of construction to know that in their day better ships were not built. Many a "soft wood" ship was oak or better from shoe to broad teak rail, while few clippers had less durable stuff than the heavy hard pine of Georgia with generous white and live oak timbers at the critical points. Far weaker ships came through without a mark, but they never had to beat past St. Diego against gales of hurricane force. The wracking below and the wreckage aloft were not the result of faulty construction, but of the conditions under which these ships sailed in the hard journey around the Horn.[5]

Among early New England shipbuilders who ventured to try live oak were William Rotch & Sons, a Quaker whaling family of

Nantucket and New Bedford. They began the experiment in late November 1791, when William Rotch, Jr., directed Zacchariah Hillman to:

> proceed with Capt. Robert Macy to such parts of Georgia as may be thought best or other parts of the Southern States . . . procuring in the best manner by Cutting, Sawing, Hewing or otherwise such parts of the frames for two Ships as will be hereafter described agreeable to dimentions & Moulds deld thee, all of the best Live Oak & red ceder—having regard to the places that it be where vessels can easily command it to take it on board, thy judgement must be used as to the sizes of the timber to have it hewed as near as will answer on acct of the freight. . . . .If more help is want'g thou must hire it.[6]

Hillman was expected to acquaint himself with "the customs of the country & not be imposed upon." Any excess timber was to be sold on the Savannah and Charleston markets. A contract was signed between Rotch and the four men who would accompany Hillman to "dilligently assist in cutting, hewing or sawing," and they were expected to discharge their duties faithfully as "honest & industrious labourers." All tools and provisions would be supplied by Rotch & Sons; wages would be paid from the time they set sail in New Bedford until their return. One of the men received $9 a month and the others $6. All four were given advances.[7]

Colonel George Claghorne, a master shipwright who was also a friend and neighbor of the Rotches, evidently was employed to start building the two ships as soon as the live oak arrived. Later he would construct the frigate *Constitution* in Boston.

In a letter to his uncle dated May 1792, William Rotch, Jr., reported on the winter in Georgia, where they had "cut the most material parts of a ship timber of live oak for two ships. It will cost us more than thrice the common timber. We shall also send to North Carolina for cedar for top timbers. These ships we mean only to frame and timber, and let them stand to season one year."[8] Possibly the *Barclay*, which they launched in 1793, was a live-oak whaleship.

Little additional information is available concerning the use of live oak by New Englanders prior to the War of 1812. Nearly total destruction of their whaling fleet during that unfortunate war prompted an active period of shipbuilding. During the 1820s and 1830s successful whaling voyages provided incentive as well as money for bigger and better vessels, and new live-oak ships soon became important news. When the sons of Zacchariah Hillman, who operated the J. and Z. Hillman Shipyard in Mattapoisett, launched the 600-ton Liverpool packet *George Washington* in 1831, she was described as "built entirely of live oak." The following year they finished the 460-ton *Horatio*, "a beautiful live oak ship," and in 1834 the *William Hamilton*, "a splendid ship . . . built of live oak."[9] Other vessels similarly described were also sent down the ways in Falmouth.

One interesting aspect of the postwar boom in shipbuilding was the continuing demand for proficient Northern shipwrights whose reputations were well established along the Atlantic seaboard. Southern forests were replete with timber, but skilled labor had always been in short supply, and it became a common practice to offer temporary employment in the South to Northern carpenters. They not only cut the timber, they built and repaired the sailing vessels. Boston-born-and-bred Ebenezer Coffin paid the passage of nine shipwrights from New York to his plantation on St. Helena Island, South Carolina, in 1816. They worked for two months, assisted by Coffin's slaves, spending part of their time cutting and making live-oak frames.[10]

Some of these craftsmen traveled alone, probably starting out as live oakers and then picking up other jobs during a dull winter season in the North. For example, Jonathan Handy of Sippican Village in the town of Rochester, Massachusetts, labored in the Carolinas and Georgia almost every winter for thirty years at the urging of various employers—a testimony to his competence as a master shipwright. The German-born Savannah shipbuilder Henry F. Willink wrote to Handy in 1841:

> I thought you would of Ben hire be fore this as I am waiting tetotaly with my ways for you and I hope you will come on as soon as conveniently. I have stopd all hands about three weeks a goe and I aint a going to commence on it again un till you com on. Please Let me Know how soon you can come. . . .[11]

Henry Yonge to Jonathan Handy in Savannah, Georgia,
26 December 1839

Darien [Georgia] Decr 26, 1839

Mr J. Handy—

D Sir,

*We have got Mr Spaldings permission to cut Live Oak on
Sapello, and if you make up your mind to come on we will commence at once— Let me hear from you—*

*Your Obdt Servt
Henry Yonge*

care Capt Blankinship

In 1836 Handy's daily wage at home in Massachusetts was
$1.92; in Savannah, it ranged from $3 a day to $19 a week, and
with a family to support the extra dollars were important. He bore
the expense of room, board, and laundry, but life in Darien or
Savannah was considerably more comfortable than a winter of
camping out in the woods.[12]

Foremost among the Massachusetts shipbuilders who engaged in live oaking were the Swifts of Cape Cod and New Bedford. Their enterprise was initiated by the astute Elijah Swift, son
of a Falmouth family and by trade a carpenter. His wife died in
1803 when he was in his late twenties and already the father of
three young children; five months later he married Hannah Lawrence, a step that would change the course of his career.

Elijah's brother-in-law, Thomas Lawrence, was in the business of supplying precut lumber for houses in the South (a fore-
runner of modern prefabricated buildings). Each fall, Falmouth
vessels transported the carpenters, mechanics, and necessary ma-

Elijah Swift (1774–1852)

Thomas Swift (1785–1857)

terials to Georgia and the Carolinas for the winter house building activity. In spring these same schooners were chartered to carry cotton, rice, molasses, and sugar to New England, and the passengers included the Cape Cod home builders returning to tend their farms and to fish.

Soon after his second marriage, Elijah Swift began spending winters in South Carolina, learning about its resources, building houses, and operating a store. The embargo on trade during the War of 1812 interrupted these annual trips. According to family legend, Elijah was so irked by this and by the British destruction of Falmouth ships at Wareham in 1814 that he vowed the enemy "should never keep him from the high seas."[13] Laying the keel of the 50-ton *Status Ante-Bellum* in the yard of his house on Main Street in Falmouth, he had the completed schooner drawn by oxen to the water and managed to outmaneuver the blockade for a successful voyage.

The resumption of our naval shipbuilding following the war gave Elijah and his brother Thomas the perfect opportunity to initiate a new business. In 1816 they signed contracts with the Navy to furnish live-oak timber for two 74-gun vessels at $1.55 per cubic foot, deliverable in twenty-four months; one set of frames was to go directly to any of the navy yards, and the other set to Philadelphia. That autumn their live-oaking work on Blackbeard Island marked the beginning of what became a million-dollar business for the family, and during the next few years they successfully competed for contracts with firms from Maine to Louisiana. All of this meant winter employment for hundreds of shipwrights in the towns of southern Massachusetts.[14]

The following agreement, signed by Ephraim Hathaway in 1818, is typical of the labor contracts the Swifts used for decades:

Memorandum of an Agreement made and concluded between E. & T. Swift on the one part and Ephraim Hathaway on the other part:
Whereas the said Ephraim Hathaway doth agree with the said E. & T. Swift to go with them to Carolina or Georgia to work for them at getting live oak Ship Timber for Twenty Six dollars per month and find himself in necessary tools and bedding and to work for them until the last of May if they wish and the said E. & T.

Swift agree to pay the said Ephraim Hathaway Twenty Six dollars per month and find him in wholesome provisions from the time the said Ephraim sails from Falmouth for the southward and until he is discharged there (sickness excepted) and provide him a passage off and pay him his wages that may be due when he is discharged in Carolina or Georgia and likewise to put him on wages when he arrives on the spot where the timber is to be got and his tools landed.

The parties bind each other in the penal sum of Two Hundred dollars to perform the above contract.

N.B. The said Ephraim Hathaway agrees to be ready to sail from Falmouth on or about the 20th day of October next.

In witness thereof We Set our hands and seals at Berkley this 22nd day of September 1818.

[Signed] Ephraim Hathaway

signed and sealed in the presence of Samuel Tobey, 2nd.[15]

In 1825 Elijah's son Oliver C. Swift went South to superintend the season's cutting operation. Some of the perennial difficulties—the death of valuable oxen, competition for available timber, and delays in obtaining cash for expenses—are discussed in his surviving letters (see Appendix).[16]

In those days no national banking system existed; each private bank printed its own money, and a draft from one section of the country was viewed with suspicion in every other. Eight hundred miles from home, Oliver might just as well have been halfway around the globe. Each transaction required payment of a brokerage fee, two endorsements by local citizens, and a ten-day waiting period. Understandably, property owners wanted cash payment for cutting rights, having learned the hard way that any other arrangement could mean financial loss.

As the whaling industry boomed in the 1820s, Elijah Swift was among the first to recognize Falmouth's potential as a challenge to Nantucket and New Bedford. By 1827 his contracts were bringing $1.75 per cubic foot for live oak, and it was clear that all timber not sufficiently large for the Navy could be put to good use at home.

With his usual foresight, Elijah built Falmouth's first shipyard and wharves, the Bar Neck Wharf Company, located on the site of the present Woods Hole Oceanographic Institute. He then

Oliver Cromwell Swift (1797–1874)

PÊCHE A LA BALEINE

The Swifts' live-oak whaleship Uncas *on a whaling voyage at the Cape of Good Hope. She was launched in 1828 at Falmouth, Massachusetts.*

proceeded to build his own whaleships and coastal schooners. It was from his yard that Swift's first live-oak whaleship, *Uncas,* was launched in 1828. This was followed by the "large and elegant" *Awashonks* in 1830, "built entirely of live oak." The ship *Bartholomew Gosnold,* built for Ward Parker, was constructed of live oak, as was *Hobomok,* built for the Swifts at Mattapoisett; both were sent down the ways in 1832. At this same time Elijah and his son Oliver owned Falmouth's largest salt works. The family rode high on waves of prosperity; the economic depression of 1837 seems to have affected them little.[17]

John C. Jenkins, brother-in-law of Oliver C. Swift, became a close associate, superintending the O. C. Swift & Company affairs in South Carolina during 1841 and 1842. A charter agreement for freighting timber northward is included in one of his letters.[18] At least some of the live oak and mixed timber (both softwood and hardwood) was cut with the expectation of selling it to the Navy. Thomas Swift's idea of sticking the government "hard for a price" has a familiar ring.

77

The Swift enterprise was a family affair. Reuben Swift (1780–1843) moved across Buzzards Bay to New Bedford to become a partner with his brother Elijah, forming the E. & R. Swift Company, which flourished during the 1830s. As the demand for Carolina and Georgia timber threatened to deplete supplies, the vast live-oak lands of Florida beckoned, and the Swifts started a huge operation on its east coast. They purchased several thousand acres between St. Augustine and the present Cape Canaveral at what is now New Smyrna, Daytona Beach, and Ormond. In 1834 Congress appropriated $11,000 for constructing a lighthouse at Mosquito Inlet (now Ponce de Leon Inlet), principally to aid brigs and large schooners passing over the bar to load live oak.[19]

Oak Hill, near Point Orange, was once Live Oak Hill; Shipyard Island, opposite Turtle Mound on the Indian River, is said to have been one of the Swift sites; Live Oak Landing, a mile-and-a-half-long strip north of Ponce de Leon Inlet, was a depot for timber awaiting shipment. Along the Halifax River's west bank, landings for loading were once in evidence, left over from the days when the Swifts reigned as "Live Oak Barons of Florida."[20]

According to Hebel, as many as five hundred live oakers journeyed south each fall to man the Swift camps. In spring, as they were leaving for the trip north, the back-country settlers near the St. Johns River would buy up all the remaining supplies, for nothing more would be arriving until October brought the Swift labor force back to Florida. When the Seminole Wars finally ended in the 1840s, these camps became more or less permanent installations, and a number of men moved their families south.[21]

In the early 1900s some of the old Florida residents recalled seeing remnants of Swift-built docks and two sunken barges in the mud of Smith Creek north of the Tomoka River. These measured 75 by 25 by 3½ feet and may have been similar to the one in Clement Nye Swift's painting (page 86). In Daytona one elderly gentleman recalled scenes of his boyhood in which as many as seven schooners lay off Live Oak Point awaiting their cargoes, and timber was piled at the wharfside "as high as a two-story house."[22] Ballast from New England vessels collected at such a

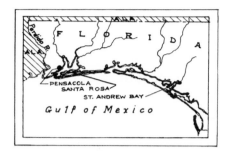

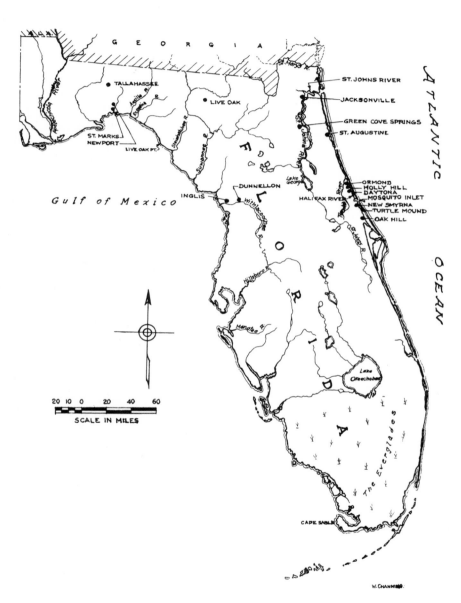

rate that it was supposed to have formed an island in the nearby
river, and huge timbers hewn by hand are still occasionally turned
up at construction sites. At Daytona Beach, city crews excavating
for a storm drain at First Avenue and North Beach Street uncov-
ered a massive hewn timber in April 1963. Local historians specu-
lated that it was left behind by Swift gangs who initially opened
up First Avenue for hauling live oak and cedar to landings from
the back country.

It all seems long ago, but Hugh Langdale of Newport, Florida,
still tells of hearing old timers in years past talk about the
Northerners who came down to cut timber on the Aucilla River.
"They hewed it, put it on lighter barges up to St. Marks, then
loaded it onto schooners. From a fishing boat where it's forty feet
deep at 'Spanish Hole' I have myself seen pieces of timber down
there in the water with the shapes cut out for ships' ribs."[23]

Two of Reuben Swift's sons also joined the business.
Rhodolphus Nye Swift spent two seasons in the South with his
father and Uncle Elijah, and then at seventeen shipped out on the
whaling bark *Canton*. Later he became master of the whaleship
Lancaster, and then in 1853 returned to the live-oak trade. His
brother, William Cole Nye Swift, entered Brown University at sixteen, but left the following year because of ill health. Accepting a
partnership from his father in E. & R. Swift Company in 1835, he
began by superintending the live oaking on Ossabaw Island, eventually becoming the firm's purchasing agent. On a trip south in
1838 he took passage aboard the ill-fated steamer *Pulaski* and was
among those who survived the terrible boiler explosion. By the
early 1840s, William C. N. Swift had bought into a profitable
whaling business, which was later greatly increased by the estate
of his father-in-law, who owned a large interest in whaleships.
Obed Nye Swift, Rhodolphus's son, was the third generation of
the New Bedford family to be involved with live oaking. They all
divided their time between the office in New Bedford, their
homes in nearby Acushnet village, and the South.[24]

Although decades of experience prepared two generations of
this family to handle the myriad problems attendant upon obtaining timber from live-oak country, a vexing new problem arose in

William Cole Nye Swift (1815–1892)

Rhodolphus Nye Swift (1810–1901)

1844 when they found themselves grappling with accusations of complicity in a fraudulent government contract.

On 22 March of that year, a lawyer and partisan of President John Tyler, James C. Zabriskie of New Jersey, applied directly to the chief executive for a contract to furnish live-oak timber for "an unnamed friend." President Tyler directed Zabriskie to inquire of acting Secretary of the Navy Lewis Warrington concerning the necessity for timber; on so doing, Zabriskie learned of the availability of a large quantity of live oak in various shapes and sizes (known as "promiscuous" timber), but no contract could be obtained without complying with the Act of 3 March 1843 that required advertisements for all prospective purchases by the Navy.[25] When Zabriskie boldly informed the president on the following day that timber was needed, Tyler immediately wrote to the Bureau of Construction, Equipment and Repairs:

> Let J. C. Zabriskie have a contract for 25,000 feet of promiscuous live oak, to be delivered at Norfolk or New York, within 18 months, at the price paid for the last purchase.
> [signed] John Tyler.[26]

Zabriskie delivered the order to his friend Borden M. Voorhees, chief clerk of the Bureau of Construction (but temporarily the acting chief), who assigned it to W. C. N. Swift of New Bedford, Massachusetts. On 4 April, Swift signed the contract to procure "at his own risk and expense" the live oak from "lands situated no more than 25 miles from the sea . . . suitable for ships of the line, sea steamers, and sloops of war and frigates" at $1.25 per cubic foot. He departed immediately for Florida to procure the timber.

On 17 April, the day after Commodore C. Morris became Chief of the Bureau of Construction, chief clerk Voorhees requested an official execution of Swift's contract. Morris, on learning that appropriations for live oak were exhausted and the law ignored requiring advertisement for such proposals, refused to sign the papers and so informed the new Secretary of the Navy, John Y. Mason.

After nearly nine months of refusing requests to validate the contract or to forward a copy to Swift in New Bedford, Mason outlined the Navy Department's unresolved dilemma and asked the president for guidance. Tyler responded on 27 January 1845, noting that when the timber was requested there had been only an acting Secretary of the Navy and an acting Chief of the Bureau of Construction. Therefore, he had expedited the order for timber with assurances that Zabriskie was a man of "the highest respectability," and Secretary of the Navy Warrington had himself praised Swift as a "faithful man who . . . has given entire satisfaction to the department." On the matter of payment, the president advised taking no steps contrary to law.[27]

The entire affair mushroomed into a scandal the following day when a letter written by Eugene McDonnell, a former Navy Department employee, was read before the House of Representatives. Claiming that Voorhees's death in September relieved him of maintaining silence, McDonnell divulged details of a conversation in which Voorhees told of a bargain between Zabriskie and Swift to obtain a live-oak timber contract in return for a bribe of $10,000. Reportedly, when Zabriskie first applied to Tyler for the contract, he had reminded the president of sacrifices he had made on his behalf during the election; Zabriskie also claimed that he was "completely out of pocket," and would be "irretrievably ruined" if he did not receive the contract. On hearing of the success of this subterfuge, Swift allegedly reduced his payment to $4000, which Zabriskie refused to accept. Voorhees then "stole a march on Zabriskie, called upon the purchaser, at Gadsby's Hotel, delivered him the papers, and pocketed the $8000." Of this amount he kept $4000, "a perquisite of office," and gave $4000 to the infuriated Zabriskie.[28]

In light of these extraordinary accusations, the House passed a resolution on 31 January directing the House Committee on the Expenditures of the Navy Department to investigate the matter, flinging open the gates of inquiry for a brief twenty days before their adjournment. After obtaining conflicting testimony and depositions from witnesses and examining available documents, the committee minced no words in admonishing the president for granting an "irregular, illegal, and improper Contract." They puzzled over his motivation; they could appreciate an inducement to express gratitude for political services, but this had been stoutly denied by Zabriskie. They felt strongly that Voorhees had "betrayed his trust and violated his duty" in obtaining and selling the order for a contract, and they rebuked Zabriskie for defrauding the government.[29]

Two men who could have enlightened the committee were unavailable: Voorhees because of his death a few months previously, and Swift because his refusal to supply an affidavit stating his involvement arrived just as the 28th Congress was adjourning, all too late for him to be called as a witness. As the investigation unfolded, the committee discovered that another contract was granted to W. C. N. Swift in July 1843 while David Henshaw was Secretary of the Navy and Captain Beverley Kennon was Chief of the Bureau of Construction. It had been for 20,000 cubic feet of live oak; no advertisements for proposals had been submitted and no bids had been received.[30]

At the end of its investigation, the committee resolved to abrogate and annul the 1844 contract, and recommended that Congress undertake a full and perfect examination of the matter. Their report was read and tabled. A new administration was sworn into office on 4 March 1845 and the 29th Congress, preoccupied with numerous problems including events leading to the Mexican War of 1846–48, quite understandably neglected to reopen hearings. The matter lay dormant and the short-lived tempest had no intimidating effect on William C. N. Swift, an aggressive entrepreneur who sailed away for a year's stay abroad, where he evidently arranged to furnish spars for the British government. Zabriskie, it seems, found in California a milieu well suited for developing his talents in the practice of law, specializing in land litigation.[31]

Apparently until the mid-1850s, William C. N. Swift made a number of trips to Europe obtaining orders for timber from both the French and Dutch governments; in this country he continued securing Navy Department contracts for live oak, which in 1857 alone totaled $232,940.[32]

The Swift family of Falmouth prospered in the mid-nineteenth century, and by the time Oliver C. Swift's young son Elijah

Elijah Swift, Jr. (1831–1906)

came along, they could offer him the advantages of schooling at Phillips Andover Academy and Harvard College. Upon graduation from Harvard in 1852, he worked for an import firm in Boston, then made his European grand tour in 1855. He spent the following winter near Charleston, overseeing the cutting of live oak and for several years was junior partner with his cousin John Jenkins 2d in the firm of J. & E. Swift, spending much of his time working in Florida.[33]

In 1857 W. C. N. Swift signed contracts with the Navy Department to supply 150,000 cubic feet of live-oak timber, creating a tremendously active period for the family business, including the Falmouth branch.[34] That August, the New Bedford *Daily Evening Standard* called attention to an ingenious Swift innovation:

> **NEW STEAMER TUG BOAT—***A steamer is being built for the Messrs. Swift Brothers, of this city, near the foot of Hillman street, by John Delano. After being built, she is to be taken apart and shipped for Florida, where the Messers Swift are extensively engaged in getting out live oak for ship timber. The steamer is intended to tow the timber down the river to the place of shipment. Her dimensions are 90 feet long on deck, 21 feet beam, and 30 feet extreme width outside of guards, 5 feet deep with a flat bottom, and sharp at both ends. She is to be a side wheel, and to have two high pressure engines of 22 horse power each.*[35]

During the first week of October, the Boston *Herald* reprinted an interesting New Bedford item—the brig *Galveston* was loading at George Howland's wharf destined for Florida's Aucilla River and was "taking along the little steamer which we have before noticed with a gang of about fifty men as hewers and choppers. Other vessels will shortly be despatched with gangs of workmen both for Florida and Louisiana."[36]

On 20 October 1857, young Elijah Swift set out from Falmouth for what he described as a wretched eight-day journey by carriage, rail, steamer, stagecoach, and wagon to "the land of Hog meat & Hommony." His destination was Tallahassee, where he and cousin Rhodolphus were to meet with wealthy landowners regarding cutting rights. Elijah then traveled the twenty-one miles to St. Marks by train (a two-hour trip), and by carriage to the store of Daniel Ladd in Newport, where he purchased supplies for the winter. His short journal of that memorable Florida trip chronicles with good humor the conditions endured by mid-nineteenth-century overland travelers.[37]

When war was declared in 1861, Elijah used his "coolness and spunk" to save himself from being hung as a Yankee, and escaped on the last boat out of Florida. The following spring a Union naval officer aboard the steamer *Henry Andrews* discovered some 40,000 feet of live oak and 2,000 feet of red cedar ready for shipment about four miles north of Mosquito Inlet on the Halifax River. It was "apparently well cared for, being covered with palmetto leaves and mud to protect it from the sun."[38] Assurances by Samuel F. DuPont, Flag Officer of the South Atlantic Blockading Squadron, to Secretary of the Navy Gideon Welles that it would be strictly guarded for Mr. Elijah Swift were short lived; an estimated $50,000 worth was burned in a single day by Southerners protesting the federal blockade.

This unfriendly act may have precipitated Elijah's joining the Union Army as quartermaster for three years' service. A Harvard classmate sent his recommendation, claiming Elijah's lack of military experience would be offset by his Florida live-oaking experience that required him to superintend "gangs of 50 or 100 men in forests and up rivers removed from ordinary modes of transportation,—to provide his own wagons and lighters on the spot, to build his own roads and bridges, to catch his half-tamed cattle, tie their tails together, and accustom them to the yoke,—in fact to manage the entire life, sustenance and movements of bodies of men carrying on a logging business in a wild country."[39] In 1862 Elijah enlisted as a sergeant in the 38th Regiment, Massachusetts Volunteer Infantry, and was mustered out in 1865 as a first lieutenant.

One of the Swift family's live-oaking operations along the Florida coast probably in the late 1860s, the only known contemporary illustration of a live-oak camp. From an oil painting by Clement Nye Swift (1843–1917), son of Rhodolphus Nye and Sylvia (Nye) Swift.

Following the war, Oliver C. Swift lost a good deal of his Florida property in local courts to others claiming title. In the meantime, Elijah had left Falmouth to join an uncle in Wisconsin, where he enjoyed a successful career in lumbering. With no one to take over his business affairs, Oliver retired from the live-oak trade, but continued as president of the Falmouth National Bank until his death.[40] It was not quite the end of live oaking—the New Bedford cousins were still hiring "Hewers and Choppers to go South" until the mid-1870s—but the halcyon days were over.[41]

Pounding Live Oak[42]

1   *One day as I was travelling, I happened to think*
My pockets were empty, I can't get a drink;
I am an old bummer, completely dead broke,
And I've nothing to do but go pounding live oak.
    Derry down, down, down, derry down.

2   *I started at once for to see Captain Swift,*
To see and find out would he give me a lift;
He viewed me all over from top unto toe;
Says he, 'You're the boy that live-oaking must go.'
    Derry down, down, down, derry down.

3 *Then he drew up the papers which both of us signed,*
To keep and fulfill, if we both felt inclined;
But the very best wages that he could afford,
Was twenty-five dollars a month and my board.
  Derry down, down, down, derry down.

4 *He bade me get ready without more delay,*
As the schooner set sail on the very next day.
We landed on the wharf, some eighty or more
Poor miserable wretches, being tired of the shore.
  Derry down, down, down, derry down.

5 . . . .
 . . . .
With two pints of whiskey, some tobacco and a spoon,
I was ready to set sail for Mosquito Lagoon.
  Derry down, down, down, derry down.

6 *Bluff was the game that we played every night,*
And in it Charles Douglass he took great delight;
He won my tobacco, while others cracked jokes,
Says he, 'You'll get more while you're pounding live oak.'
  Derry down, down, down, derry down.

7 *Pounding live oak is nothing like fun,*
Especially the dry ones will make the sweat run;
It will make your axes glitter and smoke,
You'll need iron handles to pound this live oak.
  Derry down, down, down, derry down.

8 *Instead of the woods on a lighter I went,*
I thought it much better to my poor heart's content;
All day with a pole in my hand I would poke,
Till I wished that the Devil had all the live oak.
  Derry down, down, down, derry down.

9 *It's mosquitoes by day and minges by night,*
The sandflies and beagles they bother me quite;
And if [ever] at home my head I do poke,
To Hell I'll kick Swift and his cursed live oak.
  Derry down, down, down, derry down.

Chapter 5

Shipwrights, Shipyards, and Live Oakers

A ship . . . is a distinguished master of human skill. To build and manage so stupendous a vessel as a first rate ship of the line, gives us a very high notion of the power of the human mind.

William Henry Pyne, 1806

For the most part those who went live oaking were craftsmen proficient in the shipbuilding trades; they had little in common with ordinary loggers who manned the northern lumber camps. Just why their particular experience and skills were needed in the South becomes clear when one considers that eighteen tons of blueprint paper were used during construction of the great steel battleship U.S.S. *Missouri,* while the live-oak ships were once built without any detailed specifications. To produce a large wooden structure that could stay afloat, withstand the rigors of stormy seas, and accommodate its crew and sometimes hundreds of fighting men was essential; to be able to design it and put it together by "rule of thumb" seems altogether impossible. Yet from early times a combination of tradition, experience, and skill made this possible. Shipbuilding was an art.

Many early ship designer-builders created the vessel in their minds, made drawings called *draughts* on paper, and then transcribed draughts to full-scale chalk drawings on a smooth floor. By 1790, according to Griffiths, the lift-type half model, that "ensign of mechanical genius," was developed in America; with this accomplishment, draughts became obsolete.[1]

The half model was composed of a large block of laminated layers of wood called *lifts* which were usually three to six feet long. The layers sometimes alternated cedar with pine, and were

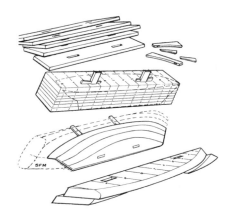

Lift-type half model. Half models were often broken up for kindling or disposed of in some other way after the lofting was completed. Today they are prized by collectors as the only surviving "plans" of many a vessel long since gone.

Discussing the half model

held together with dowels or keys. From the lift, designers carved a model of half the hull from bow to stern, with each line of the future ship carried out in miniature, taking into consideration the displacement of water. The designer first had to form the stem and waterline to offer "the least possible resistance to the water . . . and at the same time have great buoyancy," then the water line had to "run with perfect smoothness the entire length of the ship, thereby insuring free action of the rudder and good steerage. In the attainment of these ends . . . all the science of the naval architect [was] lavished."[2]

The half model was then subjected to the scrutiny of all who had an interest in the vessel. Walter E. Channing, who grew up in New Bedford, remembered when ship owners, sea captains, and shipbuilders all gathered to discuss the merits of a model's design, suggest alterations, and debate what had gone wrong during the last great storm at sea so that mistakes in design would not be repeated.[3]

As soon as the model "looked right" to all concerned, it was given to the loftsman, who produced the patterns or *moulds*. His place of business was the mould loft, a well-lighted room with a smooth and even wooden floor. With care he separated all lifts of the model, then "took off the lines" by tracing them on paper. After making careful measurements, these lines were expanded to full-size chalk drawings on the floor. This was called "laying down the ship." For the first, or *sheer* drawing, he made the sheer plan, then the half-breadth plan, and finally the body plan. The following excerpt provides one of the simplest explanations of how these drawings came about.

[I]magine yourself called on at dinner to dissever a turkey without being posted in the ways of carving. As you will naturally do the thing wrong, allow me to suggest that on the first slash of the knife you will divide Mr. Turkey in two parts, from the neck to the pope's nose. That is the Sheer Plan. Or, as there is more than one way to do the thing wrong, we will suppose that you see fit to divide the bird by cutting him in two parts, equidistant between those extremes of its person mentioned above. This would be the Body Plan; while by laying it upon the side and slicing it through lengthwise, you will get the Half-Breadth Plan.[4]

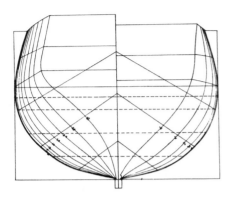

Body Plan

Lines of the United States Frigate
Philadelphia

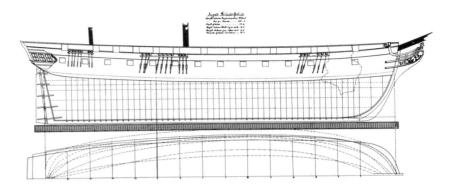

Sheer Plan and Half-Breadth Plan

The loftsman traced the great curved lines of these plans ac-
curately on the loft floor by using long, flexible strips of wood
held in place with awls. When the ship was "laid down," the loftsman stood at one end of his huge drawing, appraised the chalked
offsets, and then with suitable gestures and comments had his
assistants "fair it up"—perhaps an inch here, an inch there—until
the lines suited him.

Once he was satisfied that all lines were "fair," the moulds
could be made. These were constructed of thin wooden battens of
half- or quarter-inch stock, placed over the drawings, and again
held in place with awls stuck in the loft floor until the joints
could be tacked together. A collection of numbered moulds were
used in the forest to help determine which trees should be felled.
According to Griffiths, so-called "skeleton moulds" were taken
south to the live-oak areas. Moulds were also used as templates to
score the hewing line on squared-off logs and as guides in the selection of timber already stockpiled in the shipyard.

Some ships were simply constructed by eye, without benefit
of drafting or models, and the results could be rather strange. The
Mattapoisett-built 448-ton whaler *Trident* of 1828 was so "out of
true" that she always carried 150 extra oil barrels on one side
of her keel; sailors claimed that she was "logy on one tack, but
sailed like mischief on the other." One crooked sloop was nick-
named *Bowline*, and a local owner was "put in a towering passion

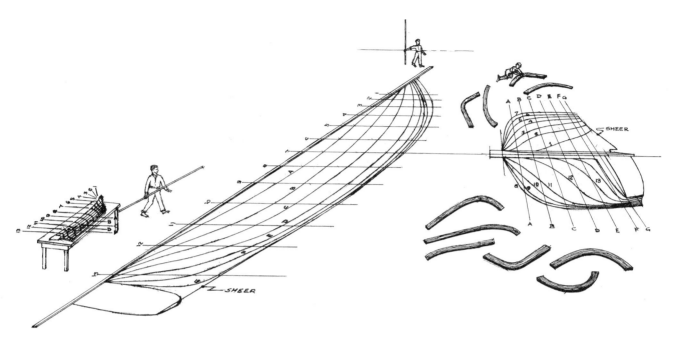

"Laying down" a small vessel in the mould loft. The vertical lines and station numbers aid the loftsman in marking his reference points on the grid he draws on the loft floor.

by being told that his starboard bow was all on one side."[5] Good half models and good lofting were clearly advantageous.

For six days out of seven, turmoil, noise, and hard labor defined life in the old shipyards. Rum drinking was customary. Hewers "beat out" the timbers for frames; dubbers trimmed them with the adze so the planks would "lie fair" against frames; and plankers followed dubbers, putting on each "streak" or strip of planking around the hull. These were whipsawed by hand over pits, until steam mills came into use. All day some of the men bored holes for treenails (wooden pegs usually called "trunnels") with the auger "literally fighting it into the hard wood after using a gouge and mallet to start it." Some carried pails of pitch, and caulkers pounded in the oakum with their special mallets and irons; blacksmiths turned out iron fittings, and teamsters drove the oxen that carted timber and lifted tackles. Many workers were stoop-shouldered from a lifetime of swinging the broadaxe. When somebody yelled "Frame-up!," all hands stopped to help raise a frame on the keel.

"Beating out" timbers with broadaxes in the shipyard while children collect baskets of wood chips to take home for kindling

Masters of the tools were legendary, and it was said that a good hewer could easily split any timber by following a pencil line with the broadaxe. There is an old story about a crowd that gathered one day for a launching in Maine. As some trunnels were being made a young dandy came along, removed his kid gloves, laid them on the block, and placed one end of an unshaped peg on top. As the astonished crowd watched, he easily hewed a perfectly tapered trunnel with the broadaxe, with no damage to his gloves.

Whether it was laying the keel, setting in a stem piece or sternpost, making frames, laying decks, or launching the vessel, experience was the shipwright's teacher. He developed his craft through years of work alongside masters of the art; precision instruments were not a part of his equipment. Every man had to be a specialist, an expert at his job, and one could reasonably say that a shipwright had brains in his hands.

Decades ago, Marion Nicholl Rawson wrote down a conversation she overheard in a Maine shipyard. Working a foot apart, two men shouted above their hammering as they fitted planking over a frame. Anyone familiar with "down-East" speech can almost hear them now:

> "How's that goin', Freddie?"
> "Good." The first three planks had slipped into place with little trouble but the fourth one was acting up, refusing to snuggle.
> "How's that, Freddie?"
> Quite seriously: "I could crawl through, Ralph."
> "How's it now, Freddie?"
> "There's an eighth of an inch, Ralph, sternward," came the answer from a few inches away, but over the planking. More hammering and urging.
> "I got a strain on it now, Freddie," and the hammer came down with short quick strokes. "How's it now?"
> "It's slippin', Ralph. Good!" A few more strokes and then a cry rang out . . . "Wood on wood, Ralph, wood'n wood." The plank had gone home against its neighbor at last.
> "She sets all right does she, Freddie?"[6]

Some shipwrights remained in the same yard for forty, fifty, or sixty years by choice; they felt a loyalty both to their associates

Four ships on the stocks at East Boston in 1855

and the yard. Dana Story claims that animosity among the men rarely erupted, for the rigorous "life of toil created a kind of brotherhood which tended to emphasize the lighter side of life whenever possible."[7] Sam Barnes spoke of the keen competition between yards in the same town, each group working hard to launch their vessel first. If a man disliked his companions, he left and got employment elsewhere.[8] One shipwright admitted that certain hard feelings surfaced from time to time, but since there were no policemen and no court house or jail in the village, "if a man and me had trouble we'd go out behind the barn and fight it out."[9]

Today the term *gang* can have ominous connotations, but among ship carpenters then it simply identified an employer; one belonged to the "Miller gang" or the "Rogers gang," depending on the shipyard owner's name. The gang represented "a sort of informal fraternal association having a common cause—the building of a good vessel and the making of a living while doing it."[10] It was only natural, then, that a group of men going south would

93

refer to themselves as a "live-oak gang," since any one group was most likely made up of men from various yards.

As technology advanced during the nineteenth century, steam-operated equipment gradually replaced some of the ox- and manpower in shipyards, and age-old customs began to change. Working hours were shortened, and rum drinking was abolished.

Traditionally, workday hours were determined by daylight hours, but wages were computed by the day. This meant that laborers received the same pay for a long day in summer and a short day in winter. In 1830 workers at a South Street shipyard in New York City were raised from $9 a week to $10.50, but they struck for a ten-hour day, rejecting a small pay increase to keep on at the old hours.[11] During the next three decades other yards followed their lead, and in 1860 the Washington Navy Yard adopted the ten-hour day.

A rum or "grog" ration was once as much a part of the routine as the long hours, and almost everyone—the clergy, shopkeepers, lawyers, field hands, and seamen—imbibed. New England's "triangle trade," which transported rum to Africa, slaves to the West Indies, and molasses back home for distillation of more rum, made it easily available and cheap. Dram shops and groggeries flourished in every town and village. It was purported to keep one warm in winter, cool in summer, and dry when it rained. Hospitality dictated that alcohol in some form be offered at christenings, weddings, funerals, corn huskings, barn raisings, ship launchings, town meetings, and the ordinations and installations of ministers. In short, whether rejoicing with friends or consoling them, custom demanded that it be served.[12]

In shipyards the shout "Grog-O" at 11 A.M. gave men strength until the dinner horn sounded, and at 4 P.M. it signaled a welcomed respite for jaded, sweating souls. William Hutchinson Rowe mentioned that sometimes at dawn on sharp, frosty New England mornings the gang congregated at the shipyard store and were served out their portions. The formula was a tumbler of rum and two of water, sometimes with molasses, the "long sweetening." Repeated twice more during the day, this scheduled pause

Sharpening axes in the shipyard

Straight to the grog shop for "a glass of liquid fire and distilled damnation"

A TREATISE ON DRUNKENNESS

Drunkenness expels Reason, drowns the Memory, defaces Beauty, diminishes Strength, inflames the Blood, causes internal, external, and incurable Wounds . . . is a Witch to the Senses, a Devil to the Soul, a Thief to the Purse, the Beggar's companion, a Wife's Wo, and Children's Sorrow . . . the Picture of a Beast and Self Murderer, who drinks to other's Good Health, and Robs himself of his own.

Paxton's Philadelphia Directory, *1818*

for rum celebrated some special occasion—raising a sternpost or fastening the final plank.[13]

As the number of distilleries rapidly increased following the Revolutionary War, so did the number of drunkards, weeping women, and starving children. In the early 1800s some local societies were organized to encourage temperance, but "alcoholic poisoning" grew to be "an evil of wide extent."[14] During the decade beginning in 1820, per capita consumption of beer increased to 28 gallons; per capita consumption of distilled spirits rose to a record high of 9.5 gallons.[15]

In 1826 the Reverend Lyman Beecher delivered his famous six sermons in Boston, emphatically stating that the "daily use of ardent spirits, in any form or in any degree, is intemperance."[16] Stimulated by Beecher and others, the American Society for the Promotion of Temperance was formed as a national organization in 1826 and shared with the new weekly *National Philanthropist* a common theme: "Moderate Drinking is the Downhill Road to Intemperance and Drunkenness."[17] As the religious and moralist movement spread, sin was equated with drunkenness; the concept of alcoholism as a disease was ignored. For a million followers, total abstinence became the watchword. In tracts, poems,

95

and songs, at meetings and church services, appeals were made to workers in all facets of American life to renounce spirituous liquors. Children, joining the Cold Water Army and Band of Hope, urged family members to "sign the pledge."[18]

Attempts to abolish grog in the shipyards set off indignant reactions, even walkouts; the anger was sometimes assuaged by offering all hands the cost of rum instead of the ration itself, a victory for the "tea-totalers." By 1830 temperance societies numbered over 1000, and when the first-rate 400-ton ship *New Orleans* was launched at Bath that year, the local press acclaimed she was "built without the use of any ardent spirits —which was not only in accordance with the wishes of the workmen but much to their satisfaction and comfort."[19]

Pressured by the temperance movement and by debates in Congress over whether or not to end both spirit rations and flogging in the Navy, the old custom of serving rum in the shipyards gave way as many states adopted prohibition laws in the mid-nineteenth century. In 1862 Congress passed an act to end forever the spirit ration aboard vessels-of-war except for medical purposes.[20]

Since the maritime requirements for live-oak timber called for cutting it in winter while the sap was down, the labor force was recruited each fall in northeastern shipbuilding communities. With newspapers advertising "Hewers and Choppers Wanted to work at getting Live Oak Timber," one can envision lively arguments around the family hearth concerning the merits of going or staying home. Because of severe weather, shipyards were less active during part of the New England winter, but so was almost everything else; and because so little seasonal work was available to the men in shipbuilding trades, many felt they had no choice but to go south. For others, the seasonal migration was routine; for young men it was a chance to see new country, and it offered the prospect of returning with cash in their pockets. In addition, absence from home for months at a time was a fact of life among families in those coastal towns native to so many seamen.

The contracts were nonnegotiable; signing on meant agreeing to abide by all terms. Employers carried on, blissfully free of such notions as social security, minimum wages, fair-employment

HEWERS & CHOPPERS WANTED.
WANTED to go South, a number of men to work at procuring Live Oak Timber. Apply to
oct 21 1w   O. N. SWIFT, 56 Fifth st,

From the New Bedford Mercury,
29 October 1841

Waiting to sign the contract

Nineteen-year-old Wilson Barstow, one of eight children, obtained his stepmother's permission to go live oaking in 1855.

practices, health insurance, and withholding tax. During the 1850s the Swift Brothers had a simple, straightforward agreement that they no doubt expected to use—and did—for years without alteration (see page 99.) The only change occurred following the Civil War, when all references to slaves were deleted.[21]

In the fall of 1855, the Swifts arranged for nearly a hundred men "to go South and to work for them at getting Live Oak Timber, or to do such other work as they may require." One each came from Bangor, Maine, and distant Ireland; all the others were from New Bedford and the nearby towns of Plymouth, Westport, Mattapoisett, Dartmouth, Fairhaven, Fall River, Sippican, Freetown, Somerset, Berkley, and Lakeville. The Swifts wanted no runaways on their hands, and cautiously avoided employing minors without permission from parents or guardians. Of the several young boys who were hired, each presented a statement certifying full permission had been granted for him ". . . to go South with Messrs. Swift Brothers and to receive his pay himself." One of these statements reads: "Benjamin D. Simmons of Somerset will be twenty-one years old in February and will bring permission from his father before he leaves."[22] Large families counted as a blessing the absence of one more mouth to feed in the winter.

Among the ninety-one men and boys who signed agreements in 1855, the jobs of seventy-eight were specified. Monthly wages varied, the lowest being $10 paid to one of the nine boys who was to do odd jobs or start learning to handle an axe. Seventeen ordinary choppers received $15 and $18; twenty-three narrow axemen, $15 and $18; twenty-two hewers, from $23 to $28; and the liner, $26. There were two cooks at $21 and $25; two blacksmiths at $20 and $23; a road cutter at $19; and two teamsters at $20. Seven flatboatmen were paid $18 and $19, and the captain received $40.[23]

The following is the text of a holograph contract of Ezra Burbank (1802–1879), who was foreman of a Swift Brothers live-oak gang in Attakapas, Louisiana, in 1857–58. At a hundred dollars a month, he was paid twice as much as a general in the United States Army.

[Massachusetts]
New Bedford   Sept 7/ '57

This Memdum of agreement made this day as above, by and between Ezra Burbank of Matapoisett and Swift Brothers of New Bedford Mass. Witnesseth that the said Ezra Burbanks agrees to go South as foreman of a gang of Man to work at getting Live Oak timber to use his best exertions at all times for their interest whilst in their employment, to be ready to sail when the vessel is ready, and work until the gang is discharged.

And the said Swift Brothers on their part agree to pay to the said Burbank at the rate of ($100) One hundred dollars pr Calender Month sickness or other enabilities excepted, wages to commence on the fifteenth day after he leaves here in the vessal for the South. The said Swift Brothers further agree to find him a passage off and him in 'provisions' while there & pay him off when discharged, the parties hereby affix ther Signatures to the above agreement

[signed] Ezra Burbank
[signed] Swift Brothers

Live-oaking contract between Swift Brothers of New Bedford and Seth G. Mendall of Sippican, Massachusetts, 1855.

Hewer

This Agreement, made this *Twenty Sixth* day of *September* in the year of our Lord one thousand eight hundred and fifty-five, by and between SWIFT BROTHERS, of New Bedford, in the State of Massachusetts, on the one part, and *Seth G. Mendall* of *Sippican* in the State of *Massachusetts* on the other part.

WITNESSETH, That the said *Mendall* agrees with the said SWIFT BROTHERS to go South, and to work for them at getting Live Oak Timber, or to do such other work as they may require—and to submit to such by-laws and regulations as may be deemed necessary by said SWIFT BROTHERS, and their Foreman—to promote good order and a proper feeling in the gang, and to find himself in necessary tools and bedding—(all baggage and tools to be carried in a bag, no chest or box being allowed,)—and to work for the said SWIFT BROTHERS, until the last day of May next ensuing, if they require it. It is further understood and agreed, that if the said *Mendall* should not, in the opinion of the Foreman of the gang, prove competent to perform his duty, or for any reason does not perform it, the said SWIFT BROTHERS shall have the right to lower his wages or discharge him. The said *Mendall* further agrees that he will have no intercourse, trade or traffic with any of the slaves where he may be located, without permission of the proprietor thereof. He also agrees that upon no account or pretext whatever will he bring to the house or place where he may be located, any ardent spirits—and it is understood that any instance of intoxication will be a violation of this contract.

The said SWIFT BROTHERS on their part agree to pay said *Mendall* provided he continues to work as before specified, to the satisfaction of the Foreman of the gang, at the rate of *(28) twenty eight* dollars per calendar month, (sickness or other inability excepted)—wages to commence when he arrives where the timber is to be cut and his tools landed, and to be paid off when discharged. They further agree to procure him a passage off, and to find him in wholesome provisions from the time he sails from New Bedford until discharged. No ardent spirit allowed.

The parties bind themselves each to the other in the penal sum of Two Hundred Dollars to perform the above contract. The said *Mendall* agrees to be ready to sail from New Bedford the *Twenty third* day of *October next*

In Witness Whereof, we hereunto set our hands and seals, at *New Bedford* the day and year above written.

Signed, sealed and delivered }
in presence of }

Seth G Mendall

John Armstrong   *Swift Brothers*

All of them were bound, at a penalty of $200, to abide by all terms of the agreement. There was no portal-to-portal pay and no workmen's compensation to cover injury or illness; a day's pay for a day's labor was the practice. Wages commenced after the men reached their destination and unloaded all tools; they were paid at the season's end. Each man supplied his own tools and bedding and each was guaranteed passage south and food from the time of sailing until discharge. Any instance of intoxication voided the contract.

A number of these agreements bear such handwritten notations as "first Rate," "Good," "Fair," "A1," "Isnt ferst rate," "Pretty good man," and "2d Rate"; some have unexplained single or double cross marks that are not in lieu of signatures. On Henry Graves's agreement, the notation suggests that he evidently had last-minute second thoughts about the whole thing; the only comment on his contract is "Gon Whaling."[24]

Foremen signed separate contracts with the Swifts, agreeing to exert themselves "at all times for their interest whilst in their employment, to be ready to sail when the vessel is ready, and work until the gang is discharged." At $100 a month, they were the highest paid employees.[25]

No two voyages were exactly alike, and what lay in store was unpredictable. Autumn was hurricane season, so any ocean voyage could easily become perilous. However, if fair weather and food rations held out, the journey often proved to be a relaxing cruise of a week or more, with time to enjoy the company of friends. Live oakers were merely passengers; crew members did the work.

Jacob W. Chase spent several seasons down South as an employee of the Swifts, and he kept detailed notes of his 1857 trip to Louisiana. At the wharf in New Bedford on 21 October a big crowd gathered to watch as the schooner *Charles R. Vickery*, chartered to transport the live oakers, was readied to set sail. Last goodbyes were said, the captain finally gave orders to cast off, and they were under way. For some it was not the first time; a good many were acquainted, and they looked forward to the voyage. Things went well until eighteen days out of New Bedford off the Florida coast, when:

> [We] noticed a small cloud far to the north. The captain regarded it for a moment. . . . "That cloud," he said, "looks as if it were loaded to the muzzle with trouble and we had better prepare for a squall." Everyone was ordered to scoot for cover, and once down in the hold,

Louisiana

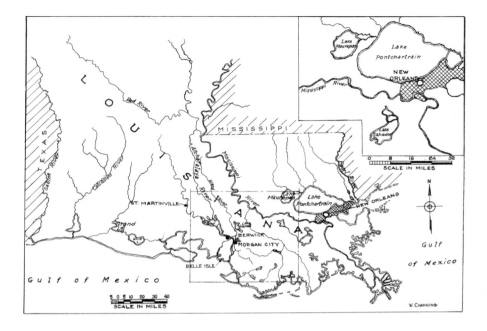

hatches were boarded down. The wind blew a veritable hurricane. It threatened to carry away the sails, and members of the crew had the boats ready for lowering. Down in the hold with the hatches clamped on tight it was sickening and nearly all of us were glad when word came that the captain wanted some assistance on deck if there were any sailors among us. Nearly all of us were sailors for the nonce. There were too many volunteers to suit the skipper and after he failed in his efforts to persuade some of the men to return to the hold, he had the crew make fast a rope to the fore-mast, and to this we clung while the *Vickery* was tossed and rolled about like a chip on the tempestuous sea.[26]

The stench in those ever-rotting wooden vessels was bad enough in fair weather but dreadful when the hatches were secured against a storm. The combination of foul bilge water, seasick landlubbers, fumes from human and animal excrement, un-washed passengers, lack of ventilation, and nearly total darkness would convince almost everyone that the greatest chance for sur-vival lay on deck.[27]

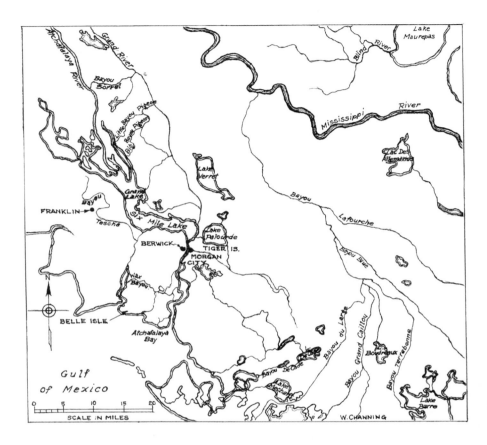

Attakapas region of Louisiana

Happily, the gale lasted only three hours and none aboard *Vickery* sustained injury, although some of the live oakers were "considerably upset in consequence of the experience." For the next two days they enjoyed good sailing, and reached the Mississippi without further mishap. At the mouth of the Atchafalaya River, while waiting for high tide to carry them over the sandbar, they were attracted to oyster reefs and gathered a large supply "to break the monotony of the ship's menu." Progressing only about two miles each time the tide took them over a bar, they used one of the long intervals to visit a plantation where they saw cane grinding and vats of boiling juice in the sugarhouse. From there the group walked five miles into Berwick, where they posted letters home and picked up mail.[28]

Returning that evening from town, a few of the men stopped by the plantation again to speak with the owner and his overseer. Suddenly several slave women "bolted out of one of the shacks emitting terrifying screams." Intoxicated from a bout of drinking in town, one of their shipmates had wandered into the outbuilding and appropriated the overseer's coat. When pursued he threw it into a sugar field, then denied charges of stealing. "There were some words and it began to look serious when the overseer pulled a revolver and leveling it . . . threatened to send a bullet through him. In the meantime quite a crowd of live oakers had gathered, and we took sides with our companion for if he did attempt to steal the coat it was because he was intoxicated. We could overlook it but the overseer couldn't." Finally the overseer agreed to dismiss the incident if the crew took their mate back to the ship with a guarantee he would not return to the plantation. "We tried to get the fellow into a boat but he balked, and while we were arguing with him he darted into a sugar field nearby and disappeared. We never saw or heard from him . . . what became of him I do not know."[29]

After they reboarded, the schooner *Vickery* moved slowly upstream with the tides, past Berwick and Bradshaw on opposite banks. Eventually they came to Grand Lake "through a bayou so narrow in some places that the over-hanging trees caught on our rigging. About two miles up we anchored. A few miles beyond was where we were going to camp. The gang which left New Bedford a week ahead of us in the schooner *George C. Gibbs* was there several days in advance of us and had built their camps."[30]

On reaching their destination, *Vickery*'s gang was divided in half, each with its own foreman, and the two groups set out in boats to select campsites. One group pitched camp on the Bayou "Horse," while the other chose a place on the Bayou "Jackass" eight miles up the lake. As the voyage ended, so did the holiday spirit; the men knew they were facing five months' hard labor with living conditions that would often turn their thoughts to family and friends back home.

Forty Years A Live Oaker

Beginning at the age of nineteen, Barnabas Hiller recorded six inter-mittent live-oaking voyages in his grist-mill account book between 1819 and 1837. These two letters attest to the fact that he also went in 1841 and was still working at live oaking just after his fifty-ninth birthday in April 1859.

Barnabas Hiller to his brother, Nathaniel Hiller, in Mattapoisett, Massachusetts, 26 December 1841

Bulls Island [South Carolina] December 26 1841

Dear Brother Nathaniel Hiller

I am glad to inform you that I am well & harty in hopes you are all the same, we had a vary good passage out here of 6 days only have ben at work 6 weeks with 50 men all lived in one hous untill yesterday I mooved on the North end of the Island about 5 miles with 14 men I expect we shall find work on this Island about 2 weeks longer then we shal moov to Georgia about 20 miles abov Darien whare the Swifts think thay hav timber anuf to last the remaining part of the season Bulls Island is about 20 miles north east from Charleston SC

the wether has ben quite worm for the most part of the time as yett tho it is much cooler today last night was the coldest night we hav had & it is cold this evening I think it will freez again tonight. We hav now a vary comfortable hows with 2 fine rooms which is much better [t]han our own hous—I hav had but one letter from home dated Nov 26th which I received December 6th

if you can I wish to get board logs a nuf for me to mak two or three thousand common inclosing boards and saw them & 2 or 3 logs for jois 10 & 16 ft long, if you cant get them your self I wish you to gett some body to do it if you can gett the loggs as I note on the other side I should like to hav them cut between the little field and the olde slow & swamp first the rest where you think best if you gett a man to do it I wish you to mark the trees and see to it & I will satisfy you for your trouble. if you can gett 7 or 8 thousand of shingles sawed for me I wish you to do that allso—

I should be glad to hav a letter from you in answer to this and giv me the current news of Rochester.

it is getting late in the evening & my feet are geting cold & I cant think of any more so I will close my fue scrols & go to bed if you can find it out I shall be glad   In answer to this direct to me at Darien Geo in care of O. N. Swift & Co

this is from your respectful brother Barnabas Hiller

Barnabas Hiller (1800–1875), of "Rocky Nook" in Marion, was a typical live oaker from southern Massachusetts. He was a surveyor, justice of the peace, sometime live oaker, and part-owner of a saw and grist mill. Remembered as a quiet man and kind neighbor, "Uncle Barney" was highly regarded in the community.

Barnabus Hiller to his brother Nathaniel Hiller in Mattapoisett, Massachusetts, 17 April 1859

at Spruce Creek New Smyrna [Florida] April 17th 1859

Brother Nathaniel

I improov this sunday evening to wright to let you know that we are all well and good cheer I recieved your letter last thursday as to shingles tell Job & Isaac if thay lik to tak half the shingles I lik for them to doo so but if thay rather not I will take them and I will pay them for sawing when I gett home I want you to tak them up some whare toos the bundles and cover them up so that thay may not rott or gett some one elce to doo it if you cant & I will pay the bills when I gett home
Nathaniel has ben troubled some with a lame side a while back & Calvin Dexter too but thay are both better now Ephraim Dexter cut his leg just below his knee he has ben laid up two weeks but thinks he can work again tomorrow I expect we shall be discharged in a week or ten days all except anuf to doo the teeming which is 3 or 4 weeks behind that is this gang or Hillers gang as they call it the wether for 3 or 4 weeks has been quite worm until last night we had a thunder storm which cleared & cooled the Air. this evening it is quite cool for this country it is getting late so I must bid you good night

Barnabas Hiller

Chapter 6

Yankees Go South to Work

Trouble springs from idleness . . . .

Benjamin Franklin, 1758

Unloading *Vickery* meant transferring all the equipment—timber carts, oxen, tools, cooking pots, and food—onto lighters or scows; longboats from the schooners were also used occasionally. Depending on how far out the schooner was anchored, the distance to shore could be several miles, and once they reached a landing everything had to be unloaded and stowed. The shelters they made were put together in that time-honored fashion used by Indians, colonists, and present-day campers:

> We got busy with our axes and it was not long before we had poles for the framework of our huts cut and in position. Great palmetto leaves which are water proof were bound together and used for the roof and sides, and in short order we had some comfortable and spacious houses in our little settlement in the wilderness of Louisiana. The camps were large enough to accommodate eight men, a cook and caretaker comfortably. With each house there was a cook house, a store shed and a covered place where we were to dine. We needed no shelter because of the temperature, but the roof of our camp had to be substantial to keep out the water. There was considerable rain. The straw mattresses we had on the *Vickery* were brought to the camps and we slept comfortably.[1]

Getting oxen to and from the South could be a tricky business. In 1841 Alex Libby went from Warren, Maine, to Virginia for timber and reported to J. H. Counce on just how he fared:

A simple, palmetto-covered shanty

When we came from Thomaston I did not know any thing about carying oxen to sea. You know they was not cleated nor any thing else. It was very rough when we went out. About dark she began to pitch very bad & all very sick; no one on deck except the capt. & myself. The oxen began to fall down. I did not know what to do, but I turned to and cleated them as soon as I could. After that they never fell once. The of[f] one never eat any thing for 4 days, neither lay down for 92 hours. When we lay two I thought it was all day with him, but he is as smart as ever today.[2]

In order to get the beasts ashore, the men had to lower them in a sling over the side into a boat, and Alex took this responsibility seriously:

If I recollect wright, you told me before I left home not to throw them overboard if we could get them to shore without. We took them in a ferry boat. I was standing by yours with their heads to the mast of the boat while they got the others in; but through carelessness they threw one of theirs over & come very near drown him.[3]

Ferrying cattle

When oxen were set down in the hold of a vessel with head, tail, and belly guyed and feet hobbled, they were reasonably safe unless a storm hit; then they could easily fall and break a leg. It was best to adjust a piece of canvas under their bellies and suspend it with a heavy loop of rope from blocks; as the ship rolled, the rope would slip through the block, keeping the oxen more or less upright.

When the camp was all in order, the men got down to work. In a few days, Jacob Chase recalled, "things were working systematically and we were making the chips fly." He worked so well, in fact, that within a few weeks he was promoted from narrow axeman to hewer.[4]

Because green live oak is so much heavier than water, it could not be floated downstream. From the spot where it fell and was hewn, all of it had to be hauled to a landing by oxen and "big wheels." For this reason, the first job of swampers was to clear trails and roads; the first job of choppers was to cut oaks nearest the landing. As the most readily available timber was cleared, the men began working back into the woods, eventually walking several miles away from camp to find suitable trees.

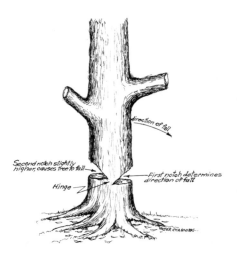

Choppers can, if skillful, lay a tree, in falling with sufficient accuracy to hit and drive a stake into the ground.

John S. Springer, 1856

Tracts of the richest land supporting hardwoods, known as *hummocks* or *hammocks*, are elevated slightly above nearby swamps, in contrast to the flat barrens where tall pines dominate, and undergrowth is a mixture of low bushes, grasses, and palmettos. Pine barrens are covered with water during rainy seasons, but the sandy soil is parched in summer and fall when stagnant ponds attract cattle and wild game. Once after walking for miles through a barren in Florida, John J. Audubon came to a dark hummock of live oak. He described it as a refreshing place where "the air feels cooler and more salubrious, the song of numerous birds delights . . . , the flowers become larger and brighter, and a grateful fragrance is diffused around. Overhead festoons of innumerable vines, jessamines, and bigonías, link each tree with those around it. . . ."[5]

Into this luxuriant and peaceful jungle came some live oakers to prepare timbers for a man of war. They exchanged greetings with Audubon and he stayed to watch them work.

Here two have stationed themselves on the opposite sides of the trunk of a noble and venerable live-oak. Their keen-edged and well-tempered axes seem to make no impression on it, so small are the chips that drop at each blow around the mossy and wide-spreading roots. There, one is ascending the stem of another, of which, in its fall, the arms have struck among the tangled tops of the neighbouring trees. See how cautiously he proceeds, barefooted, and with a handkerchief round his head. Now he has climbed to the height of about forty feet from the ground; he stops, and squaring himself with the trunk on which he so boldly stands, he wields with sinewy arms his trusty blade, the repeated blows of which, although the tree be as tough as it is large, will soon sever it in two. He has changed sides, and his back is turned . . . . The trunk now remains connected by only a thin strip of wood. He places his feet on the part which is lodged, and shakes it with all his might. Now swings the huge log under his leaps, now it suddenly gives way, and as it strikes upon the ground its echoes are repeated through the hummock, and every wild turkey within hearing utters his gobble of recognition. The wood-cutter, however, remains collected and composed; but the next moment, he throws his axe to the ground, and, assisted by the nearest grape-vine, slides down and reaches the earth in an instant.[6]

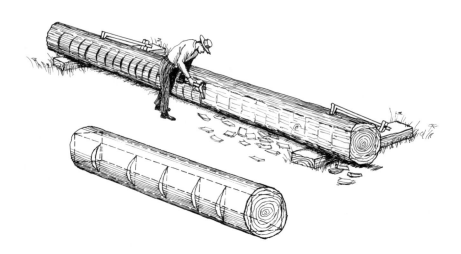

Hewing to the line to square off a piece of timber

Hewing out a knee

One type of race knife used to mark the hewing line on a piece of timber and to outline the moulds

Several of the men examined the prostrate trunk, then cut it at both extremities "to enable them to judge if the tree has been attacked by white rot . . . if not, and it is free of injury or 'wind shakes,' while there is no appearance of the sap having already ascended, and its pores are altogether sound, they proceed to take its measurement." This was done with the aid of moulds "like fragments of the skeleton of a ship."[7]

When the choppers had removed undesirable limbs, a hewer took over. After marking a line on the timber from end to end with a race knife, he stood on top of the log and scored it vertically or diagonally, using an overhead swing of a long-handled felling axe. Back on the ground he exchanged this tool for a broadaxe and, standing against the log, he hewed to the line, moving backward. A timber was "squared off" when all four sides were hewn. Using the mould as a pattern, he traced its outline with a race knife and proceeded to hew out a knee, part of a frame, or some other piece of the ship.

As hewn timber and sticks of red cedar were carted to landings, the superintendent inspected, recorded, and numbered each piece; the timber inspector then examined, measured, and approved them, and they were loaded onto scows for transfer to the waiting schooners. Finally, when the hold was filled to capacity,

Timber scribe or race knife. Since ink or chalk marks on timber were easily obliterated, this tool was used to inscribe tally marks or numerals by woodsmen, carpenters, and coopers. The fixed iron prong was pressed vertically into the wood, becoming the center of a circle gouged out by the knife-edged hook. The scoop fixed to the prong cut hollow channels to form the Roman numerals I, V, or X.

the vessel sailed north to the shipyards, leaving behind the gang to continue its labors.

Whether the men were clearing roads, felling trees, removing branches, or hewing great timbers, their only tool was a simple axe. Making axes was a special skill; they were developed first by blacksmiths, later produced in forges and manufactured on a large scale beginning in 1826 by a firm in South Canton, Connecticut. Axes have two parts: the head or *poll*, which has an eye into which the handle or *helve* is fitted; and the cutting edge or *bit*. Steel of the proper temper must be used for the bit; otherwise, it breaks when too hard and curls when too soft. The live oakers usually purchased their axe heads, but carved their own handles. As Samuel Barnes pointed out, "No self-respecting hewer would buy a factory-made helve even if it was available."[8] Hickory and hard maple were best, and each man carved his axe helve to fit his height, his manner of working, and his particular job; there was no standard pattern. Collections of old axes yield a variety of weights, sizes, and shapes of helves and heads.

The felling or narrow axe they used was single-bitted, the sides slightly concave, smooth, or beveled. The helve was straight. Its weight depended on the type of work to be done and on individual preference, but three and a quarter to four pounds was average. Its main purposes were for felling trees, swamping underbrush, and making logs. Double-bitted axes seem to have been introduced in America about 1850 in Pennsylvania. Although they had the advantage of staying sharp twice as long as the conventional type, they did not become popular for another ten or twenty years because they were considered dangerous; they could badly wound a man's back.

All the work of hand-hewing timber was done with broad-axes. Because their poles are heavy and square, they generally have a reversible bit—that is, they can be used by either a right-handed or left-handed hewer, depending on which way the helve is wedged into the eye. The head's inner face is flat and the outer side slightly concave, with a cutting bevel of half to three-quarters of an inch. Heads generally weigh from six to nine pounds; helves

15			16			17			18		
	Cubic ft. in. pt.	Superfi. ft. in.		Cubic ft. in. pt.	Superfi. ft. in.		Cubic ft. in. pt.	Superfi. ft. in.		Cubic ft. in. pt.	Superfi. ft. in.
15	23 5	281 3	16	26 8 0	320 0	17	30 1 3	361 3	18	33 9 0	405 0
16	25 0 0	300 0	17	28 4 0	340 0	18	31 10 6	382 6	19	35 7 6	427 6
17	26 6 9	318 9	18	30 0 0	360 0	19	33 7 9	403 9	20	37 6 0	450 0
18	28 1 6	337 6	19	31 8 0	380 0	20	35 5 0	425 0	21	39 4 6	472 6
19	29 8 3	356 3	20	33 4 0	400 0	21	37 2 3	446 3	22	41 3 0	495 0
20	31 3 0	375 0	21	35 0 0	420 0	22	38 11 6	467 6	23	43 1 6	517 6
21	32 9 9	393 9	22	36 8 0	440 0	23	40 8 9	488 9	24	45 0 0	540 0
22	34 4 6	412 6	23	38 4 0	460 0	24	42 6 0	510 0	25	46 10 6	562 6
23	35 11 3	431 3	24	40 0 0	480 0	25	44 3 3	531 3	26	48 9 0	585 0
24	37 6 0	450 0	25	41 8 0	500 0	26	46 0 6	552 6	27	50 7 6	607 6
25	39 0 9	468 9	26	43 4 0	520 0	27	47 9 9	573 9	28	52 6 0	630 0
26	40 7 6	487 6	27	45 0 0	540 0	28	49 7 0	595 0	29	54 4 6	652 6
27	42 2 3	506 3	28	46 8 0	560 0	29	51 4 3	616 3	30	56 3 0	675 0
28	43 9 0	525 0	29	48 4 0	580 0	30	53 1 6	637 6	31	58 1 6	697 6
29	45 3 9	543 9	30	50 0 0	600 0	31	54 10 9	658 9	32	60 0 0	720 0
30	46 10 6	562 6	31	51 8 0	620 0	32	56 8 0	680 0	33	61 10 6	742 6
31	48 5 3	581 3	32	53 4 0	640 0	33	58 5 3	701 3	34	63 9 0	765 0
32	50 0 0	600 0	33	55 0 0	660 0	34	60 2 6	722 6	35	65 7 6	787 6
33	51 6 9	618 9	34	56 8 0	680 0	35	61 11 9	743 9	36	67 6 0	810 0
34	53 1 6	637 6	35	58 4 0	700 0	36	63 9 0	765 0	37	69 4 6	832 6
35	54 8 3	656 3	36	60 0 0	720 0	37	65 6 3	786 3	38	71 3 0	855 0
36	56 3 0	675 0	37	61 8 0	740 0	38	67 3 6	807 6	39	73 1 6	877 6
37	57 9 9	693 9	38	63 4 0	760 0	39	69 0 9	828 9	40	75 0 0	900 0
38	59 4 6	712 6	39	65 0 0	780 0	40	70 10 0	850 0	41	76 10 6	922 6
39	60 11 3	731 3	40	66 8 0	800 0	41	72 7 3	871 3	42	78 9 0	945 0
40	62 6 0	750 0	41	68 4 0	820 0	42	74 4 6	892 6	43	80 7 6	967 6
41	64 0 9	768 9	42	70 0 0	840 0	43	76 1 9	913 9	44	82 6 0	990 0
42	65 7 6	787 6	43	71 8 0	860 0	44	77 11 0	935 0	45	84 4 6	1012 6
43	67 2 3	806 3	44	73 4 0	880 0	45	79 8 3	956 3	46	86 3 0	1035 0
44	68 9 0	825 0	45	75 0 0	900 0	46	81 5 6	977 6	47	88 1 6	1057 6
45	70 3 9	843 9	46	76 8 0	920 0	47	83 2 9	998 9	48	90 0 0	1080 0
46	71 10 6	862 6	47	78 4 0	940 0	48	85 0 0	1020 0	49	91 10 6	1102 6
47	73 5 3	881 3	48	80 0 0	960 0	49	86 9 3	1041 3	50	93 9 0	1125 0
48	75 0 0	900 0	49	81 8 0	980 0	50	88 6 6	1062 6			
49	76 6 9	918 9	50	83 4 0	1000 0						
50	78 1 6	937 6									

Tables in Peter Guillet's Timber Merchant's Guide *eliminated time-consuming calculations for superintendents, timber inspectors, and measurers. A hewn stick measuring 30 feet long, 15 by 16 inches across equals 50 cubic feet or 600 board feet of timber. The following is Guillet's formula for arriving at these figures:*

$$
\begin{array}{r}
15 \text{ in.} \\
\times\ 16 \text{ in.} \\
\hline
90 \\
15 \\
\hline
240 \text{ in.} \\
\times\ 30 \text{ ft.} \\
\hline
12\ )\ 7200 \\
\hline
12\ )\ 600 \text{ board ft. (superficial ft.)} \\
\hline
50 \text{ cu. ft.}
\end{array}
$$

Polygonal log measures, marked with varying scales, were also used to determine length and diameter of timber and to calculate the number of cubic feet in a given piece.

vary in length and shape, but all are curved so the user can hew at the proper angle and avoid scraping his knuckles.

From each camp the superintendents sent in periodic reports to shipyard offices or Navy Board Commissioners indicating the quantity of moulded timber on hand, and the number of "sticks rolled up" ready for shipment. "Sticks" are felled trees with branches removed. They can measure over a hundred feet in length and weigh more than a ton.

The hauling was done with a vehicle variously called a timber cart, logging cart, big wheels, logging wheels, balance wheels, or merely "a set of wheels." These were taken south each fall by the live oakers, and when dismantled they were relatively easy to transport on schooners.

Made of wood, these carts were a simple device for lifting and moving heavy objects over bad roads. The huge wooden wheels had a diameter of seven to twelve feet; they were bound with iron tires six to eight inches wide, and the pair were connected with a single axle. It required less labor and time to raise objects under this high axle than it did to load onto the top of conventional wagons.

The carts are of ancient origin, and were used throughout Europe. From early times in America they were essential for clearing farm land, for carrying stone in quarries, and for hauling loads from forests to and around the shipyards. When thousands of pieces of live oak for frigates were demanded in 1794, it was logical to take timber carts to Georgia for the job, since the men were accustomed to using them in shipyards.

Carts that were too small may have been one of John T. Morgan's problems in Georgia during the 1794−96 seasons. Wheels and axles surely had to be increased in size to bear the extraordinary weight of the enormous green live-oak timbers and to provide sufficient bearing surface for hauling them out of swamps, through tangled masses of undergrowth, and through the deep sand of primitive roads and trails.

The principle involved in loading one of these carts was simple. Attached to the wooden bed over the axle were a pole and a

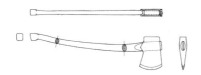

Chopping or felling axe

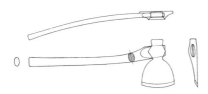

Broadaxes. Each shipwright carved out the helve and whittled it to suit himself.

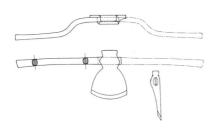

Most broadaxes were easily converted for use by right- or left-handed hewers.

tongue, to which chains were fastened. The teamster had his cart pulled alongside the stick at an angle and "jumped it" with one wheel, to straddle the stick. Then he positioned the cart a few inches behind the balance point. "This was tricky," claimed one teamster, "but an experienced man could judge it pretty well the first time." The cart was then tilted backward, and the teamster passed a strong, heavy chain under the stick and hooked it to the pole. As the tongue was pulled forward and down by the oxen, it acted as a lever, hoisting the stick under the axle and swinging it off the ground. A second chain secured it to the tongue. With the heavy butt end of the stick forward, the pull on the animals was uniform. If a cart fell on its side while "jumping" a stick, the driver simply used his oxen to right the cart and then began all over again. The principle involved in releasing a load was even more straightforward: "Just unhook the chain and git outta th' way." It all sounds simple, but it required patience as well as skill, and good temper helped.[9]

Hauling out a stick from several miles in the forest to the landing was laborious work that could take the better part of a day, but as a South Georgia man commented, "Course it was slow but there wasn't nobody in a hurry."[10] Nobody, that is, except the superintendent and his employer.

Driving one of those carts was a hazardous occupation. They were unwieldy vehicles, and they could be killers. A Florida logging man explained: "Sometimes the tongue gets away when lifted upright and falls over backward. At that time the driver is in double danger. If the tongue doesn't get him, when the axle turns upside [down] the linchpins fall out letting the wheels fall off."[11] No one could expect to escape serious injury or death if one of these immense wheels crushed him, but when accidents happened on the job they were usually considered the victim's own fault for being careless.

As late as the 1930s some two-wheeled carts with teams of draft animals were seen in parts of southern Georgia hauling great long sticks of pine to the sawmills.[12] Nowadays it seems remarkable that a lone man could have been responsible for lifting one of those forest giants off the ground, when one observes the exces-

Small carts could be maneuvered into position with manpower, but heavy wheels ten to twelve feet in diameter required the draft power of animals.

sive amount of labor and power equipment now "required" to perform much simpler tasks.

"Skidding" timber meant raising the long sticks butt end first under the axle and dragging them behind the cart. This could be damaging to roads, but in live-oak country such damage did not matter; the trails cleared out for hauling were not public thoroughfares, and were abandoned once the timber had been removed. Up to fourteen oxen would be used in skidding, the number depending on the weight of the stick, the distance to be covered, and conditions of the road or trail.

"Snaking" was the method employed to drag timber out of the forest using oxen but no timber cart. It was recommended only for short distances—a few hundred feet through thick undergrowth, or over crude trails where only large obstacles had been removed—until a better road was reached, where the timber could be hauled or skidded. Snaking required a strong yoke with rings attached. A draft chain was attached to rings on the yokes of each pair of oxen; then a choker chain, 12 to 16 feet long, was attached to the draft chains. One end of the choker was put around the forward end of the stick, looped through the draft chain, then wrapped around the stick several times. As the oxen moved forward, the choker tightened and was thereby prevented from slipping off the stick. Sometimes a choker-hook was attached to the end of the choker chain. After the chain was

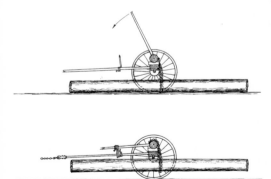

Raising a stick for hauling

Skidding timber

Hauling with big wheels

wrapped around the stick several times, the hook was put through a link of chain to hold it in place. Both methods were readily adjustable to any size stick.

No matter which method was used to pull out timber, oxen were essential. They were used extensively as beasts of burden in England for hundreds of years before being introduced into the American colonies during the seventeenth century. They were ideal for pioneer farmers. Steady at the yoke and sure-footed in rough soil and hilly country, they had tremendous draft power and were indispensable in helping clear the wilderness of trees, roots, stumps, and boulders. They cultivated with the plow, crushed stone, moved houses, cleared snow-filled roads, and pulled the family cart to Sunday meeting in town and to haying fields at harvest time. Buck, Broad, and Bright were—and still are—favorite names for oxen.

The animals were easy to keep, requiring only one feeding a day if they were turned out for grazing at night, and their necessary equipment was inexpensive and simple. With good care the homemade yokes and bows lasted for decades. When their hauling days were over, oxen were fattened and butchered, thus supplying meat; powder horns; leather for leggings, shoes, chair bottoms, and knapsacks; tough ligaments for thongs; tallow for candles; and other necessities.

In the early nineteenth century, as prosperity increased and speed became of greater concern, horses began replacing the economical oxen; but the change-over was gradual. For example, the shipbuilding and farming community of Ipswich, Massachusetts, which claimed some five hundred families in 1831, recorded a total of 404 oxen and only 187 horses.[13]

Snaking timber

A good deal of controversy can be generated about the best method of training oxen. Often, training begins when they are two or three months old. Care is first given to matching a pair in size, color, and temperament. Then, with a rope tied around their horns, the calves are led up and down a path as they learn their names, the voice commands of "gee gee" (turn right) and "haw haw" (turn left), and eventually to back up and move forward. At the same time they are broken to small yokes. At six months the steers are castrated; this results, as they grow, in heavier hindquarters and greater weight than bulls of the same age and breed. At the age of two years, the oxen are hitched to a cart or wagon for regular work and become "half-handy"; by three years they are "handy," and by the fourth year they are capable of doing farm work. They are at their peak of usefulness at the age of five to ten years.

Poorly trained oxen establish bad habits; they can unexpectedly bolt and run "like deer—bucking and flinging their heels in the air."[14] Intelligent oxen learning at the hands of competent trainers and serving good masters are gentle and develop qualities of patience, endurance, and fidelity. For that reason, masters who persist in treating them poorly have always been regarded with disdain as being either foolish or ignorant.

When driving his cattle, the teamster usually walks alongside the left or "nigh" ox; the one to the right is the "off" ox. Frequently worked in teams of three to five yokes, the front, lighter pair are called "leaders," while the rear heaviest pair are the "wheelers." They can be directed over rough ground and around

A perfectly balanced load. As Lewis F. Allen commented in 1868, "A team of well grown, well matched, and well trained oxen, is a noble sight, and everyone who owns them, and properly values them, feels an honest pride in their possession."

sizable obstructions with ease, merely by giving verbal commands or lightly using a goad or whip. New England teamsters commonly used goads instead of whips, driving the oxen by nudging them high on the shoulder. Isaac Stephenson described the goad as a stick about four feet long, approximately five-eighths of an inch at the larger end and half an inch at the lower end, which had a half-inch-long brad.[15]

In New England shipyards, oxen were the traditional dray animals, performing all those functions of lifting and hauling that were later to be done by cranes and tractors. With block and tackle they loaded vessels; with two-wheeled carts they hauled or skidded timbers from one end of the yard to another. Because their hooves are cloven, they avoid getting stuck in wet, muddy places; they were ideal animals for the forest and swamp work of the live-oak gangs. Their imperturbable nature was an asset in forests where wildlife could easily be a distraction.

About 1855 the Swifts contracted to cut timber (allegedly for the French government) along the Altamaha River in Georgia, using their own gang and equipment. They set about working "in a manner unfamiliar to the local inhabitants," exercising "extreme care" to avoid damaging the wood. Sometimes the men used fourteen yoke of oxen and two carts at a time to haul a single stick. One observer was impressed with their efficiency:

> The drivers used goads and the oxen were not whipped at all. Those faithful beasts were given four quarts of cracked corn with their forage every night. Sanitary measures prevailed around the camps

and everything was done with precision and order. The drivers were as expert as the cutters. Before a piece of timber was hoisted up under a cart it was wrapped with dressed raw hides in order to keep the chains from cutting into the wood . . . . Everything was done with Yankee ingenuity and system.[16]

To prevent illness it was as important to avoid overtaxing the oxen as it was to provide them with proper food, for they could not work strenuously every day for months subsisting entirely on hay or the rough vegetation growing near the camp. Their diet had to be supplemented with enough concentrated food to provide the essential protein, carbohydrates, and fat supplied by such grains as corn, oats, and barley.

Oxen, like all cattle, are ruminants and can consume more food at one time than horses or mules. According to figures computed at the turn of the century, the daily rations for oxen in a Louisiana logging operation amounted to 26 pounds of corn (nearly 15 quarts) and 14 pounds of hay. This is probably more than cattle were fed in live-oak camps, since they were smaller animals. Still, the quantity of feed needed was formidable. No wonder Phineas Miller was so perturbed at facing the daily expense of feeding one hundred oxen on Cumberland Island. By the mid-1850s a single order of "good Eastern hay" for oxen in a Louisiana live-oak camp amounted to thirty tons.

The live oakers' preference for oxen continued even after horses gained popularity as draft animals in New England and mules became widely used in southern lumber camps. Horses were too nervous for the job; mules habitually panicked when their feet mired in the swamps. Besides, oxen could endure pulling heavy loads day after day better than other draft animals, and they were also less susceptible to disease.

Considering their usefulness and all the training and care that went into a good team, it is easy to see why their welfare was a matter of great concern. Replacing an ox at camp involved considerably more than simply buying another animal from some local planter. Finding another available, well-trained ox could be time-consuming, if not impossible. A damaged cart could be repaired by the blacksmith, but illness, injury, or death of valuable steers was serious and could mean sending to the North. Delays were costly.

A teamster had the most demanding job of all in a New England logging camp, and his routine could not have been any easier down South. He was the last to turn in at night and, along with the cook, the first to arise. Claiming his daily attention was every hoof, shoe, yoke, hauling wheel, and chain. The following excerpt expresses the essence of a teamster's lot.

> Throughout the weeks he repeats his visits to the swamp and then the landing; . . . relieved by the companionship of his dumb but docile oxen, for whom he contracts an affection, and over whom he exercises the watchful vigilance of a faithful guardian, while he exacts their utmost service. He sees that each performs his duty . . . . He watches every hoof, the clatter of shoes, the step of each ox to detect any lameness.
>
> The jingling chains, as they trail along . . . discourse a constant chorus. With his goad-stick under his arm or as a staff, he leisurely walks along, musing as he goes, emitting from his mouth the curling smoke of his unfailing pipe, like a walking chimney or a locomotive; anon whistling, humming, or pouring forth with full-toned voice some favorite air or merry-making ditty. He varies the whole exercise by constant addresses to the oxen, individually and collectively: "Haw, Bright!" "Ge, Duke!" "Whoap! whoap!" "What ye 'bout there, you lazy ————." "If I come there, I'll tan your old hides for you!" "Pchip, pschip, go along there!" Knowing him not half in earnest . . . the oxen keep on the even tenor of their way, enjoying the only apparent comfort an ox can enjoy while away from his crib—chewing the cud.[17]

"It is by the use of an iron spade and pick-axe that miners dig for silver and gold; and it is also by the use of a plough, shod with iron, that the fields are ploughed and produce the corn and grain that feed mankind. Iron, then, is a greater blessing to man than silver or gold; and a blacksmith a more useful member of society than either a silversmith or a goldsmith."

Dr. John Trusler, 1791

Blacksmiths were as necessary to the live-oaking operation as they were to the shipyard, the town, and the country village. Of all the skilled craftsmen, the smith was the most respected, probably the most versatile, and usually the best spinner of yarns. Many children and adults would turn their errands into excuses to stop in at the smithy and hear a good story or pick up the latest news.

Around Marion, Massachusetts, they still chuckle about the town blacksmith, Rufus Briggs, and his tall tales. As a lad of seven or eight Howard Hiller frequented the smithy and for hours

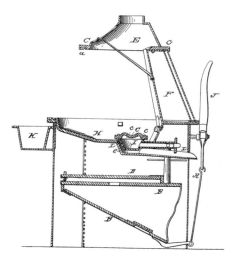

This *1848 patent drawing for Christopher V. Queen's portable blacksmith forge has a spout to carry off the rainwater.*

A *Cylindrical case (stand)*

B *Bellows*

C *Bracket for hood*

D *Tuyere (grate)*

E *Hood*

F *Wind screen*

H *Hearth*

I *Forge pan*

J *Bellows lever*

K *Trough for slack water*

L *Rain spout*

would listen to the stories while shooing away flies with an old horse tail tacked to the end of a stick. Rufus especially enjoyed reminiscing about the winter he went with a live-oak gang to Georgia where they found one "tre-men-dous" live-oak tree—so big it took three days to fell. From time to time while working on it they heard voices, occasional laughter, and wondered who it was. Then shortly before the tree was brought down, the gang walked around it and discovered that all along those voices were coming from live oakers chopping on the opposite side.[18]

The smith was acquainted with everyone in the community because he repaired or replaced a great many of the objects they used—barn-door latches and hinges; plowshares; firedogs and andirons; butchering tools; sled runners; wagon springs; boot scrapers; and the rivets, rings, bolts, hooks, and clips for harnesses. He shod farm animals; sharpened saws; made harpoon heads for whalemen and spikes for bridgebuilders; and fashioned tools for masons, carpenters, boatbuilders, fishermen, boilermakers, and farmers. It was his ability to fire-weld that made the smith unique, gaining him the reputation for being both practical and ingenious. He was the all-purpose repairman who fulfilled an extraordinary variety of functions for which we now must rely, less satisfactorily, on local hardware stores.

Not all smiths were content to stay put. Some spent years working on ships or traveling with marching armies, while others headed north to logging camps or south to the live-oak forests. A forge was a necessary part of their equipment, but hauling heavy bricks from place to place to build temporary forges on the spot was impractical, so portable iron forges were made that met the needs of traveling blacksmiths. Many were designed and sold; there were also less sophisticated temporary wooden forges (sometimes called "fire boxes"), lined with brick and sand, that were simple to build and could be mounted on wheels for portability.

Any smith who joined a live-oak gang was responsible for keeping the group's equipment in good working order. He made iron dogs for hewing; mended chains for snaking and hauling timber; and repaired the trace chains on ox harnesses, the pole rings

Blacksmith's patch on the iron tire of a timber cart at Jekyl Island, Georgia

and bow pins on ox yokes, and all the bolts, screws, washers, and pins that held the yokes and wheels together. Iron tires for cart wheels sometimes needed repairing, and at any time he could be called upon to replace bales for kettles, hooks for cooking cranes, iron bands for wooden buckets, and other utensils in the cook house.

Iron tires for small wheels could be made by smiths in camp, and lifted from forge to anvil by a man on either side; but tires for the huge timber-cart wheels were another matter. A ten-foot iron tire (six inches wide) made with half-inch stock weighed nearly 350 pounds, and moving it from forge to anvil for welding the joint would have required a crane. Buying a new set of wheels with tires or a new set of iron tires when needed was the only practical solution in a live-oak camp.[19]

In the hometown smithy there was a formidable array of tools; in camp, fewer tools were required because the smith's functions were less varied. Besides anvil, forge, vise, and bellows, he had hammers and sledges of different weights; round stock for making chain links, ox rings, and rivets; and bar stock for repairing tires and making axles. His equipment also included general-purpose flat-lipped tongs, bolt tongs, link tongs for chains, and pick-up tongs; drills and punches for making holes; set hammers to form sharp angles; and a cone mandrel for shaping ox rings, hardy tools, and fullers. There were a variety of cutters, including half-round ones for prying, and others for hot stock and cold stock; files for grinding down and cutting; flatters for smoothing surfaces; nail and bolt headers; and tools for removing tire bolts and ox-shoe nails.

Since there were too few draft animals in a live-oak camp to warrant hiring farriers (specialists who shoe animals), the smith took on that task as well. Southern oxen were rarely shod, but New England cattle needed protection from rocky ground and the clutter of shipyards; therefore, they were accustomed to it. But there was usually no necessity for replacing all eight shoes at one time, since they wore unevenly. On the other hand, shoeing an ox was more complicated than shoeing a horse, because the animal's cloven hoof required a pair of shoes for each foot, and since the

To prevent axes and other steel tools from losing their temper due to over-heating, a trough of water was set under the grindstone to cool it. Water also prevented the stone from being clogged with particles of dust and steel.

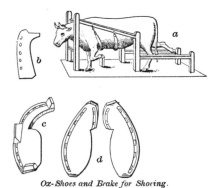

Ox-Shoes and Brake for Shoeing.

Transporting an ox-shoeing frame from New England to the South would have been impractical. An ox-brake, similar to the one shown above, could be put together quite easily at the live-oak camp. Three types of ox shoes are shown above, two of which have a projection that is bent into the cleft of the hoof and flattened to help keep the shoe in place.

animals were unable to stand on only three of their rather small feet, their tremendous weight had to be supported in a sling. Some oxen would face the prospect with equanimity; others would balk.

It is impressive to watch three strong men pushing and cajoling, pulling and goading an obstinate ox into position while staying clear of his great horns as he lunges suddenly and tries to turn or back away. Once the ox is inside the frame, his head is placed in a stanchion, then tied to supports on either side with a rope. A canvas sling fitted under his belly and raised by means of a winch supports, rather than suspends, his weight. Kicking is prevented by securing each leg to the frame with a rope, and the tail is anchored. One at a time, each foot requiring a shoe is pulled back with a hook or rope and tied down to a small wooden shelf for the smith's convenience.

Despite all these precautions some oxen still manage to thrash about. They strain to jump clear of the sling, and loud moaning and bellowing attests to great fear, although the shoeing itself is not painful. An experienced smith or farrier knows the oxen will be nervous, and anticipates explosive discharges; he is prepared with a good supply of wood shavings or straw to scatter about to make it easier to clean up the evidence.

121

The job of a live-oaking blacksmith offered variety, but it required the same physical strength and endurance as his work in the smithy at home. Although he was the most versatile man in camp, each member of the gang was depended upon for a particular role—hewer, axeman, teamster, cook. Cooperation among them was essential for accomplishing the job; it also helped morale and made a hard life easier to bear.

Chapter 7

Live-Oak Camp

The food that was placed before you then,
Would make your pulses thump . . . .

Orrington Brown

The tenor of life in a live-oak camp and morale of the men were contingent upon the extent of their daily labor; the weather; the rules and regulations; the competence and fairness of their superintendent; and, most of all, their food. From the time of embarkation until discharge, employers were usually obliged to feed the gang; however, the contrast is dramatic between our notions of good food and what they called "wholesome provisions." By our standards, theirs was a monotonous diet, a simple fare developed in this country by ordinary people of the seventeenth and eighteenth centuries. During their first hundred and fifty years in New England, inhabitants of shipbuilding towns on Cape Ann in Massachusetts were sustained by "pea and bean porridge, or broth, made of the liquor of boiled salt meat and pork mixed with meal, and sometimes hasty pudding and milk, both morning and evening."[1]

Writing on this topic, Henry Adams gave a lucid explanation of just why the nineteenth-century diet developed its particular character.

> Indian corn was the national crop, and Indian corn was eaten three times a day in another form as salt pork. The rich alone could afford fresh meat. Ice-chests were hardly known. In the country fresh meat could not be regularly got, except in the shape of poultry or

Food was preserved by salting, drying, pickling, and smoking, then shipped in barrels, casks, or kegs. It was expected that most of it would survive conditions fluctuating from cool and dry to warm and humid.

Announcing dinner

game; but the hog cost nothing to keep, and very little to kill and preserve. Thus the ordinary rural American was brought up on salt pork and Indian corn, or rye; and the effect of this diet showed itself in dyspepsia.[2]

Foreign visitors found the early nineteenth-century American diet an appalling combination of nearly insoluble salt meat; vegetables swimming in fat; and half-baked, greasy pastry. One perturbed critic observed their "whole day passes in heaping indigestions on one another; and to give tone to the poor, relaxed and wearied stomach, they drink Madeira; rum, French brandy, gin, or malt spirits, which completes the ruin of the nervous system."[3]

Dried salt fish, pork and beef; dried beans and corn; flour; cornmeal; salt; pepper; tea; coffee; and molasses were the provisions best suited to survive a journey to the live-oak camps. Hardtack or sea biscuit—that nearly indestructible, unleavened, dehydrated mixture of flour and water—was a staple familiar to all. Except for potatoes, the list omitted all vegetables and fruits as perishable. Purveyors were local businessmen trusted to sell reasonably good quality provisions and these were shipped on schooners with the gang. Discontent was less likely if familiar food appeared when the dinner horn sounded, and in early days ships returning to load timber during the winter could replenish dwindling supplies. By the time live-oak camps were well established in the 1850s, however, merchants in large coastal cities of the South were sufficiently well stocked to provide most necessities.

Every gang had its own cook, and bad meals provoked such grumbling that many considered him to be the camp's most important asset. Up long before sunrise, he was responsible for rousing the men. In Maine logging camps, some cooks announced reveille with the dinner horn, known as the "gaberel," while others emitted a long wail: "It's daaaylight in th' swaaamp!" Or, "Get up, get up, get up— . . . ain't you goin' to git up!"[4] Variations, well-laced with profanity, were probably also heard in palmetto country.

Throughout his day the cook needed assistance, and the young boys who were hired with the group could carry water, col-

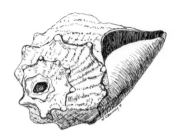

Some claimed the New England tin dinner horns could be heard for three miles around. In both the North and South, many used old ox horns or large conch shells brought home by seamen from warm waters off Florida reefs and the West Indies. The mouthpiece is a hole drilled in the apex. The tone of this primitive instrument sounds similar to a mellow French horn; with practice some people can play tunes. The above sketch was drawn from an antebellum conchshell horn in possession of Dr. and Mrs. Edwin F. Taylor.

lect kindling, chop wood, and maintain fires. Well banked, a fire would keep all night; if it went out, a new one would have to be started by striking sparks with flint and steel on tinder. This process was often tedious, lasting half an hour; safety matches as we know them were not invented until 1855.

Cast-iron equipment was used to cook meals for those cast-iron stomachs. Huge kettles were suspended over the open fire with chunks of salt meat or fish simmering for hours in their own broth. Dried beans were pit-baked in kettles we call "Dutch ovens." These were set in a heated "bean hole" dug in the ground, then covered with hot coals and dirt until the contents were done. Although bread could be baked in this same manner, johnny cake, often the favorite, was fried in lard. This stiff mixture of cornmeal, salt, and water was versatile; when mixed with additional water, it became cornmeal mush, better known as "hasty pudding." Doughnuts, those irregular, deep-fried lumps dubbed the cook's own langrage-shot,[5] became the familiar "pellets of indigestion."

It took a great deal of food to stoke the large gangs who worked for the Swifts in Louisiana, and they relied on a New Orleans firm of commission merchants to furnish provisions. For a two-month period during the 1857–58 season, a single order from H. F. Vredenburg included 70 barrels of "extra mess" beef, 35 barrels of Prime pork, 500 barrels of "superfine flour," 10 barrels of "good white beans," 500 pounds of corn, "Western butter" in lots of 300–400 pounds, and nearly 1,000 pounds of "Rio" coffee.[6] This suggests quantity cooking on a very grand scale indeed.

Meals were informal, and the men sat around on logs or simple split-log benches, the latter known in New England as "deacon seats." In the early days, pieces of salt pork were "tried out" in three-legged frying pans or "spiders" set directly over the coals. These in turn became common platters; each man took turns sopping up the melted hog lard with his bread, salt fish, or meat. This, it was claimed, served to lubricate the joints; molasses gave tenacity to the muscles. Later on, individual tin plates and cups were considered necessities; in 1816 Ebenezer Coffin bought the paraphernalia of civilization—knives, spoons, and

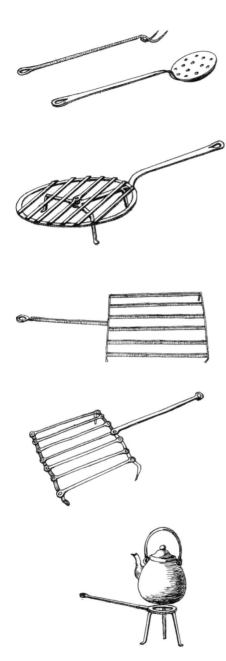

forks—for the small gang of shipwrights he employed from New York. It is tempting to assume that they fared relatively well, since Coffin purchased such luxuries as rice, turnips, veal, butter, and sugar in nearby Beaufort and added them to the usual fare. The utensils of their cook Marianne and her helper Dick, evidently Coffin's slaves, included even a waffle iron. The quality of their food and drink is unrecorded, but the quantity of spirits purchased was sufficient to allow each man almost a gallon of whiskey a week.[7]

Occasional surprises necessitated altering the predictable daily menu. A newly opened barrel of pork was found spoiled and unfit to eat, the hardtack got wet or became infested with maggots that "wouldn't budge," or they discovered the meal and flour alive with weevils. These small insects were no cause for alarm, but bread made with musty, moldy flour was unpopular. In a pinch there was always the reliable old shipboard special called "scouse" or "lobscouse"—a combination of finely pounded hardtack, bits of salt beef, and potatoes boiled together in water and presumably made palatable with salt and pepper.

The sweet served up was usually "duff," the dough pudding well known ashore and rated such a luxury among American seamen. Richard Henry Dana claimed that although duff was "heavy, dark and clammy," when eaten with molasses it formed "an agreeable variety with salt beef and pork" aboard ship.[8] Herman Melville once described a memorable duff he concocted aboard an American frigate in the 1840s. Combining the usual ingredients of flour, water, raisins, and beef fat (called "slush"), he tied the mixture in a canvas bag and boiled it in water for several hours. The big moment finally arrived. Attended by his mess mates, who watched in silent anticipation, he carefully removed the pudding from its cloth. "Bim! it fell like a man shot down in a riot . . . . It was harder than a sinner's heart; yea, tough as the cock that crowed on the morn that Peter told a lie."[9]

Whatever "vicious substances" were served in the early days, tea "strong enough to float an axe" concluded every meal to aid digestion. One method for brewing it combined three gallons of water, a pint of tea, and a pint and a half of molasses; this was

TABLE 4   A Sampling of Items Charged Against Individual
Accounts of Live Oakers in 1856–59

broad axe	$ 3.00	double gun	15.00
narrow axe	1.25	powder	.12
ox lash, .31; pair	.50	shot powder	1.12
straw hat	.37	bottle pain killer	1.00
wool jacket	3.25	compass	1.25
cotton drilling, 1 yd	.17	25 stamped envelopes	.80
striped shirt	1.25	½ bunch envelopes	.06
blue flannel shirt	1.75	6 pens	.06
undershirt	.87	trunk lock	.17
pair socks	.50	chest hinges	.20
felt hat	1.37	hand bag	1.50
2 pair overalls	1.24	pocket knife	.62
freight on chest	1.00	hank thread	.04
viol strings	.50	bar soap	.10
shoes	1.62	comb	.15
pr. pants	3.15	12 pipes	.12
buck shot	.12	sandfly netting, 7 yd	.70
tobacco	.40	shot pouch	1.12

SOURCE: J. & E. Swift Account Book, 1856–59. In possession of Oliver S. Chute.

boiled, then stirred with a stick "so as to give each man his fair share of sweetening and tea leaves."[10]

Some live oakers ate better than others. Impressed with a breakfast he once enjoyed in Florida, Audubon reported: "Our repast was an excellent one, and vied with a Kentucky breakfast; beef, fish, potatoes, and other vegetables, were served up, with coffee in tin cups, and plenty of biscuit. Every man seemed hungry and happy, and the conversation assumed the most humorous character." Later on, dinner would include a turkey shot by one of the men on his way to the hummock.[11]

After meals, clean-up was a matter of scouring pots, kettles, ladles, tin plates, and other utensils with whatever lay at hand; a wad of Spanish moss and sand often sufficed. Everything got a

Hardtack

A box of hardtack

rinsing in the nearby creek. The method was arduous, but it cut the grease and it was cheap; soap was reserved for an occasional bath and for washing clothes, as each man had to pay for his own.

In the evening a good many of the men pulled out their tobacco pouches, scraped and knocked out their pipes, and filled and lit them with red coals from the fire. Did they have the energy to sing, reread the letters from home, play cribbage, retell worn-out stories? Knowing that dawn would come apace to bring yet another exhausting day of axe work, more often they probably turned in early. Given the close proximity of fifty to a hundred bone-weary slumbering men, their nocturnal chorus must have been glorious.

Considering the hard labor, poor food, and casual standards of hygiene, it is not surprising that illness was common among the live oakers. From their account ledgers, journals, and letters comes evidence that daily sick lists were clearly a fact of camp life. First-hand information about their remedies is scarce, however. As the following rules and regulations suggest, moderate sanitation was recognized as desirable, if only to discourage swarms of flies and cockroaches, but no intermittent airing of bedding could eliminate lice, bedbugs, ticks, and fleas.

> 1st.   It is expected the Men in this Department will in all respects conform with the Articles they have signed.
> 2nd. For the Preservation of health all Clam Shells Oyster Shells and other nuisance will be emptied over the Bank into the River.
> 3rdly. To Prevent accident no Gun or other Fire arms to be discharged on any pretence whatever within 300 yds of the Buildings.
> 4th.   And lastly it is earnestly recommended to the Men to have their Beds & Beding aired as often as Convenient.
> Blackbeard Island
> Jany, 16th. 1818[12]

The early period of our republic was an unhealthy time. Henry Adams commented that "consumption, typhoid, scarlet fever, diphtheria, and rheumatic fevers were common, habits of drinking were still a scourge in every family, and dyspepsia

destroyed more victims than were consumed by drink."[13] Except for the smallpox inoculation (introduced in 1760), there was little notion of preventative medicine. Communicable diseases spread with particular rapidity among ships' crews and the populations of large seaport towns.

Medicine was primitive. Many sick recovered only if they "by the grace of God had a strong constitution." Taken ill aboard the schooner *Twins* bound from Philadelphia to Georgia in 1817, James Smith was treated with the customary "Emetic in the morning, a dose of Caster Oil at noon, & 40 Drops of Laudenum at night."[14] Improvement the following day indicated that at least his problem was not appendicitis.

Until research by Pasteur and Koch resulted in the acceptance of bacteriology as a science during the late nineteenth century, physicians widely accepted a theory that diseases were most often caused by an "excess excitability of the blood vessels." The result was a prolonged era of "heroic medicine"—rigorous treatments of blood-letting supplemented with sweating, blistering, purging the system, and inducing sleep. Treatments for physical injuries could be just as "heroic." A seaman unfortunate enough to develop a hernia was ordered to hang "by his heels until the prolapsus is reduced."[15]

The routine complaints in live-oak camps were stomach ailments, bowel disorders, colds, and the all-too-frequent agues that seemed to "arrive on horseback and leave on foot." Everyone had his favorite cure for the chills and fever of malarial attacks, which could be prolonged and violent. In 1800 Joshua Humphreys passed on to his son Samuel the advice of a friend: "drink no other drink than Porter and a little good Madeira wine" while in Georgia.[16]

Yellow fever also took its toll. Captain Albert C. Skiff of New Bedford, who danced and reminisced at his ninetieth birthday party in 1924, told of a live-oak gang he knew that stayed too long in the dangerous Southern climate. Struck suddenly with yellow fever, forty-seven of them died.[17] Some early medical authorities attributed attacks of fever to poor diet, fatigue, grief, and anxiety, "lying upon damp ground during evening dews, the suppression of accustomed evacuation," and the "miasmata arising from putrid stagnant water" in warm climates.[18] This last was actually close to the mark, since deadwater swamps were ideal breeding places for mosquitoes; however, proof that certain species transmitted both malaria and the much-dreaded yellow fever would have to wait until the early twentieth century.

By the 1820s Usher Parsons, an outstanding Boston physician with experience at sea, was advocating maintaining good health with pure, uncontaminated water, fresh fruits and vegetables, freshly baked bread, adequate rest, dry clothing and bedding, well-aired quarters, and the avoidance of intoxication and "violent exercise under a scorching sun."[19] Reports of the conditions under which the live oakers and seamen actually lived and worked would lead to the conclusion that Parsons' advice could have been received only with amusement by any live oaker, sailor, or sea captain.

Each season in camp a certain percentage of the men suffered severe gashes from sharp axes or sustained injuries from falling branches. The superintendent had no alternative but to bind or sew up the wounds as best he could. Sterilization of surgical instruments was unknown and the germ theory was a concept yet to be tested, but it was widely accepted that pouring on brandy or turpentine acted to prevent, as well as heal, infections. A man with a toothache would have to rely on an application of mustard or oil of peppermint, if such was available. The alternative was to have the offending tooth removed, but extraction procedures were crude, sometimes performed by blacksmiths. "It's simple," claimed one, "just pull the tooth as if you were pulling out a nail from a horse's shoe."[20] Those were the days when "Ya' pulled the wrong one!" became a perennial joke.

Whether the problem was an accident, illness, or minor complaint, men in camp depended on their superintendent to tend them, just as the crews of American merchant ships had to rely on their captain; neither group had a resident doctor. In either case, knowledge of pharmacy was limited to what could be gleaned from experience. When there seemed no prospect that a man's health would improve, he was removed. After a two-month ill-

A well-designed medicine chest, ca. 1800. What appear to be drawers are boxes with sliding tops containing dried preparations. In the right foreground is a pair of hand-held brass scales. A door at the back opens onto a double row of bottles.

ness on Blackbeard Island in 1818, Nathaniel Walker was given
half a month's pay and put in the care of Navy Agent Archibald S.
Bullock at Savannah, who was to send him back to Philadelphia
when he was able to travel.[21]

In serious cases they could sometimes seek help from the
surgeon of a large naval vessel or the doctor in a nearby community, but immediate attention was always out of the question,
since neither communication nor travel was rapid. A suffering
few, on land or sea, had to undergo treatment at the hands of their
companions:

> Symptoms don't count in our simple practice. We open our attack
> with a dose of Glauber or horse salts, which takes such a strong
> hold on the patient that he is bound to confess we are doing some-
> thing for him. It may happen that the patient grows worse, and a
> dose of castor oil to work off the salts is our next resource. He takes
> hope in the moving evidence of the medicine; and the more he
> endures the more he hopes. Should oil fail us, the ulterior of our
> modern healing art is to administer a rousing dose of calomel, with
> the intention that this shall work off salts, oils and itself. In severe
> cases, we repeat the entire course, and either kill or cure.[22]

Because disease and death were so prevalent among seamen
during the seventeenth and eighteenth centuries, our first American Congress passed an act in 1790 specifying that all vessels of
150 tons or more, having a minimum navigation crew of ten and
traveling to foreign ports, were to carry a medicine chest as standard equipment.[23] Apothecaries of "known reputation" were to
assemble these, reexamine the medicines once a year, and include
directions for administering them. In shipbuilding and seaport
towns these apothecaries did a brisk business, outfitting the
chests with assorted liquids and powders in numbered bottles and
boxes. Many they included are still familiar today—quinine, par-
egoric, castor oil, mercurial ointment, ipecac, and spirits of
ammonia.

Using their pamphlets of directions was simple. After deciding on the symptom and locating a description in the booklet that
seemed to fit it, the captain or superintendent could administer

treatment according to the numbers. These "symptoms books," not to mention the medicines themselves, left much to be desired, but they did contain certain proven remedies that offered more than some of the earlier treatments, and were an improvement over nothing at all. It was fortunate indeed when an employer sent a complete medicine chest along with his live oakers.

As an alternative to the heroism demanded for undergoing a cure at the hands of the medical profession, multitudes welcomed the nineteenth-century patent medicines, enticed by promises of easy cures. Far too many had already learned that a physician's cures could be worse than the patient's symptoms; such sentiments are reflected in the final verse of a Hutchinson family song.

> And when I must resign by breath,
> Pray let me die a natural death,
> And bid the world a long farewell,
> Without one dose of Calomel.[24]

In contrast to the often foul-tasting mixtures concocted by doctors, most of the nostrums had a pleasant taste that masked an alcoholic content of sometimes over 70 percent. These and opium solutions, which were freely administered, eased pain temporarily, but in the long run intensified the suffering of those who became victims of addiction.

In the days when health inspectors and federal drug laws were unknown, business flourished for the self-proclaimed "druggists" and "physicians." The claims they advertised for their pills and secret elixirs were as bogus as most of their products, but live oakers were no exception to those who eagerly sought panaceas that promised to ease a variety of complaints. Many an axeman may have refused the grog ration because of religious scruples, but discovered that a few swigs from his bitters bottle gave real comfort at the end of a long day in the swamp.

The enthusiasm for live oaking diminished as monotony settled in, and little distinguished one week from another. All

MEDICINE CHESTS

WITH
APPROVED DIRECTIONS,

COMPLETELY FITTED FOR

SHIPS,

BY

JACOB STONE, JR.

AT THE

NEWBURYPORT DISPENSARY,

Corner of ESSEX and STATE STREETS.

LIST OF UTENSILS CONTAINED IN THE CHEST.

LANCET, for bleeding, &c. SCISSORS.
LINT, for dressing sores. SYRINGE.
PALLET KNIFE, for spread- LEATHER and TOW.
  ing plasters, &c. CLYSTER PIPE and BAG.

CATALOGUE OF THE MEDICINES.

Basilicon Ointment,	*No.* 11	Mild Mercurial Ointment,	*No.* 14
Balsam Copaiva,	26	Opodeldoc,	30
Blistering Plaster,	15	Peruvian Bark,	4
Blue Stone,	29	Purging Pills,	16
Cream of Tartar,	3	Red Lavender,	35
Castor Oil,	20	Rhubarb Powders,	8
Diachylon Plaster,	13	Red Precipitate,	31
Elixir Salutis,	19	Salts,	1
Elixir Paregoric,	27	Sulphur,	2
Elixir Vitriol,	33	Sweet Spirits of Nitre,	22
Elixir, Stoughton's,	17	Spirits of Turpentine,	38
Essence of Peppermint,	25	Stomachic Spice Bitters,	34
Goulard's Extract,	37	Spanish Flies Pulv'd,	36
Huxham's Tincture of Bark,	18	Turner's Cerate,	12
Injection Powders,	9	Tincture of Camphor,	21
Jalap and Calomel Powders,	7	Turlington's Balsam,	28
Laudanum,	23	Vomits of Tartar Emetic,	5
Magnesia,	32	Vomits of Ipecac,	6
Mercurial Pills,	10	Volatile Spirits,	24

PRINTED BY W. & J. GILMAN, 9, STATE-STREET,
NEWBURYPORT.

1828.

MEDICINES.

No. 1. *Salts.*

A COOLING and useful purge in inflammatory cases. Dose, two large spoonfuls dissolved in a tumbler of water. It is good for cooling the stomach after excessive drinking.

No. 2. *Sulphur.*

Useful as a purge in eruptions of the skin; good also for coughs and asthmas, and for carrying off the bad effects of mercury. Dose, three tea-spoonfuls mixed with molasses. Equal parts of this and hog's lard make an ointment infallible in the cure of the itch.

No. 3. *Cream of Tartar.*

This is a cooling powder. A solution of a table spoonful in a quart of water, forms an excellent beverage to quench thirst in fevers, and the patient may drink freely of it. Equal parts of this and sulphur, mixed with molasses, is a remedy for the piles.

No. 4. *Peruvian Bark.*

This is good in intermittent fever, or fever and ague, having taken a vomit. The dose is a tea-spoon or two, to be taken every four or six hours, between the fits, in red wine, or chamomile tea: increase or diminish the dose as the fits become more or less frequent. If it should purge, you may add five drops of No. 23, to each dose; if, on the contrary, it should render the bowels costive, give a dose of No. 8, when requisite. It is also recommended in all cases of debility; in cases of venereal ulceration; in erysipelas; scrofula, &c. Dose, one to three tea-spoonfuls in wine, spirit, or water, twice a day.

No. 5. *Tartar Emetic Vomits.*

These are necessary in the commencement of fevers, ague, flux, and foul stomach attended with sickness, indigestion, loss of appetite, pain and dizziness in the head, &c. Dissolve the contents of one paper in 6 large spoonfuls of water; take two spoonfuls every half hour until it produces vomiting. Drink freely of chamomile tea or warm water, after each operation. If a discharge from the bowels does not follow the operation of an emetic, a dose of salts the next day is necessary. After the operation, if pains in the stomach ensue, take a dose of No. 23.

The earliest "symptoms books" identified medicinal preparations by number rather than by name, probably to encourage owners of medicine chests to purchase refills from the same apothecary. This gave rise to a well-known yarn of the ship's captain who was treating an ill crew member when he discovered the prescribed dose in bottle No. 15 was empty. Presumably in good faith, he gave a teaspoon of medicine from bottle No. 6 and a teaspoon from bottle No. 9, the sum of these being 15. The patient did or did not recover, depending on who told the tale.

that kept many from quitting was the contemplation of lost wages, but a few made off anyway. In March 1820 Edmund Pratt, Benjamin E. Smith, and James Mahuren, all employees of Green & Emerson of Bath, Maine, were apprehended and fined $29.75 each for "sheriffs fees, jail fees and other expenses of running away."[25] They were soon back on the job.

The Sabbath and Christmas Day were free; other days off were mostly forced upon them by heavy rains or by the high winds that blew up sandstorms and prevented working near the beaches. Long periods of idleness bred a dangerous discontent.

On Sundays the men relaxed by sleeping late, writing letters home, washing and mending clothes, repairing tools, and (when the need arose) replacing worn-out mattress straw with the Spanish moss so conveniently at hand. Bible reading was rare; probably reading was limited to family letters and hometown newspapers. All recreation was of their own making, and given half a chance a predictable few would drink themselves into a stupor. Others would gamble their wages in games of chance.

The sea islands abounded with deer, bear, cougar, wildcat, wild boar called "tuskers," and opossum. Wild turkeys, geese, and ducks were the plentiful game birds; salt-water fish were available with the incoming tides; and rivers and marsh creeks yielded oysters, crab, and shrimp. Some of the men collected sea shells and observed the antics of porpoises and unfamiliar shore birds; others found a more curious population along the marshes at low tide.

In the tidal waters on the landward side of the islands nested the alligators, those amphibious monsters that vented such terrifying roars in springtime. There was actually little to fear unless the alligators were frightened by attack; then they could run with remarkable speed, their tails becoming lethal weapons against any adversary. Among the reptile population, though, the men were more concerned with poisonous snakes, which despite hibernation would move out of their nests on warm winter days. In late December 1817 one group killed a large rattlesnake with twelve rattles and "on opening it found it had swallowed a full

Sunday clean-up

grown Rabit."[26] By the change of season in mid-March, the snake population began to manifest itself on Blackbeard Island.

> The weather these two days past has the appearance of Spring the singing of the feathered tribe in Boughs of the trees is delightful to the ear whilst the Serpentine race watching like a Fiend of Darkness for his Prey; strikes the mind with horror—a mixture of pleasure & Pain . . . . This day the Men killed 19 Mocasons . . . John Ratcliff brought one to the house alive.[27]

Today coastal residents still warn outsiders against venturing into the swamps and woods because of rattlesnakes they claim to be "six feet long and big around as a man's arm."

The age-old method of discouraging wildlife at campsites is to eliminate natural refuges by clearing underbrush, dead branches, tree limbs, and fallen logs; and to secure all edible stores against invasion, especially by raccoons, skunks, and other nocturnal foragers. But there is no defense against flying insects. Unless a cold snap eliminates the mosquitoes, they remain a problem into late autumn, while warm winter rains bring the misery of villainous sand flies that attack without mercy.

The woods yielded unlimited firewood, and the men soon discovered that dried-out knots of resinous pitch pine, called "fat-pine" or "ligh'ood," made excellent kindling. Open fires were their only defense against the dank chill of gray winter fog, when Georgia temperatures crouched a few degrees above freezing and the rain and blustery northwest winds seemed never-ending. Salvaging mildewed clothing and bedding was possible only when a break in the weather brought clear days and warm sunshine.

What little illumination they had at night, other than firelight, was supplied with candles. Early lanterns, which were made of sheet iron or tin pierced with a nail, cast attractive patterns, but little light. Tin candle lanterns of a later vintage had glass globes; those most useful in camp were made with frames of tin with four to six glass sides protected with wire bands. These could be hung from a nail or peg by the convenient carrying hoop. Kerosene, patented in 1854 and usually known as "coal oil," was considered unsafe for years because its volatility posed a great danger in the woods.

Actually, any open flame was a potential hazard. Within a week of arriving at camp, James Keen wrote, "At one O'clock this morning, Awoke up with the Cry of Turnout, Turnout, we are all on Fire, the wind blowing at this time a gale from the West. The fire Caught from the Chimney of the Cook house which was soon extinguished." Within two weeks they were alerted to flames in the house chimney.[28] Vigilance was essential.

If anyone hoped for an uneventful season it was the superintendent. Again from James Keen's journal comes a good sampling of the daily problems that confronted the man in charge. Among his fifty-nine live oakers, a good quarter were troublemakers. He contended with disobedience everywhere, quarreling in the carpenter's department, fighting in the cook house, and disputes with a Navy employee over who had authority to make decisions about camp regulations. Once he was indignant to learn that slaves detailed to cut roads several miles north of headquarters were in fact building a fence to enclose a private cotton field, "whilst in the pay of the Government & eating the provisions of the same." On another occasion one of the slaves was sent to draw a molasses ration in place of whiskey for three sick black men, causing a great hullabaloo because it threatened to "create a jealousy among the White Men who were not allowed whiskey when on the sick list nor anything in lieu of it."[29]

Most of Keen's troubles, in fact, stemmed from "old demon rum"; he frequently contended with Sunday fighters who became Monday malcontents.

> This Morning Rider, Hartford & Loyd refused to go to work unless they got their Whiskey, they having been drunk all night disturbing by [their] noise the Sober men. I refused to let them have any & they refused to go into the woods to work. At 10 O'Clock . . . Glenn Cut Tee's leg very badly they were both Drunk yesterday.[30]

Overindulgence and fighting were sporadic; those who made them a habit risked being discharged, but withholding the rum ration altogether would have violated both agreement and custom.

Green and Emerson's live oakers from Bath seem to have supplied their own daily grog, for they bought quantities of rum from
the company. In 1820 Isaac Thomas obtained three gallons prior
to sailing from Maine to Georgia. At twenty-five cents a quart, it
cost him five cents less than a bar of soap. Through the winter he
purchased clothing, some tobacco, and as much as half a gallon of
rum a day. The following March notice of his demise was entered
simply as one more item against his account: "Funeral Expenses,
$2.00."[31]

Some did not drink, either out of preference or because they
were Quakers or of another religious sect barring alcohol. The
temperance movement and prohibition laws that ultimately eliminated the grog ration in shipyards were also having an effect in
the live-oak forests. There was ample and irrefutable evidence to
prove grog's detrimental effect. The combination of alcohol, rainy
days, and idle hands triggered altercations, reduced useful work,
and sometimes resulted in serious injury.

Wandering along the St. Johns River in 1832, John J. Audubon
met a few live oakers and their families who lived in Florida year-
round. They remained, even though suffering poor health from
the climate, living in simple dwellings with little furniture and
sleeping on bear skins. Several miles away in the hummocks
where they worked, the men put up shanties where a cook prepared their meals. On a particularly stormy night the naturalist
was invited to join one of these hospitable families. The cheerful
housewife prepared a bountiful supper for the group and they visited late into the evening. Audubon recorded this nearly disas-
trous incident the husband told of his experience in the woods
some four years previously.

Walking to the hummock where live oaks were felled, he lost
his way in the tall grasses; an early morning fog prevented him
from seeing beyond thirty or forty yards in any direction. Every
tree resembled every other tree, and the ill-defined, intersecting
trails increased his confusion. As the heavy fog lifted, he saw the
noon sun, but not a single familiar object. Without a gun to shoot

game, becoming frantic and famished, he allayed his hunger with grasses and weeds at sundown, then spent the night in "the greatest agony and terror." For several days he resumed his quest for food and water with no recollection of what had happened. Finally, running "wildly through those dreadful pine barrens I met with a tortoise . . . although I knew that, were I to follow it undisturbed, it would lead me to some water, my hunger and thirst would not allow me to refrain from satisfying both by eating its flesh and drinking its blood. With one stroke of my axe the beast was cut in two; in a few moments I despatched all but the shell . . . . how much I thanked God, whose kindness had put the tortoise in my way." Forty days elapsed before he at last reached the riverbank, his "clothes in tatters, his once bright axe dimmed with rust, his face begrimed with beard, his hair matted, and his feeble frame little better than a skeleton covered with parchment, there he laid himself down to die." The faint sound of oars seemed only a dream; it died away, then again woke him from his lethargy and he saw a boat. On his knees he gave one feeble cry, then another with shrill voice, and was rescued almost immediately.

As it turned out, the hummock and cabin were scarcely eight miles apart; the axeman's place of rescue on the St. Johns was some thirty-eight miles distant. They calculated the live oaker had probably covered four hundred miles, rambling around in circles for about ten miles a day. Audubon concluded that "nothing but the great strength of his constitution and the merciful aid of his Maker could have supported him for so long a time."[32]

As spring advanced and available timber was cleared, employers began closing down their operations. In camps where live oakers numbered a hundred or more men, dismissal took place gradually over a period of weeks. Each man packed his belongings, checked over his account in the ledger, signed it before a witness, was paid off (minus what he owed his employer), and returned North. The superintendents and teamsters were the last to leave.

Most of the men returned home as they had arrived, by ship. It was the least expensive way, and they had to pay their own passage; besides, railroad facilities were poor. Even so, in the mid-nineteenth century a ship passage from Louisiana to Massachu-

setts cost about $50, over half the total wages for some. There-
fore, the expense of transportation home made live oaking no
more profitable than whaling to an ordinary seaman.

After a season in camp there was nothing ambiguous about
the meaning of *toil*, and many bid the job goodbye forever. Each
gang's experience was unique; together they endured common
dangers and hardships, together they shared camaraderie and
humor. Whether a man returned to camp or not, he took home
memories enough to last a lifetime.

Home again

Contrary to a misconception based on a nineteenth-century
statement, live oak *was* used in shipbuilding well before 1740.[33]
The early American colonists were too dependent on sailing vessels to survive without building their own, and they were quick
to appreciate the excellent timber at hand for construction. Although southern live oak was extremely difficult to work, they
used it anyway; they proclaimed its value in descriptions of the
New World's resources, and even named their ships for it.

Prior to the Revolutionary War, shipbuilders at least as far
north as Philadelphia found live oak worth the expense of freighting to their yards. During the war, it was an important component
of frigates as well as other ships. Following the Revolution,
domestic needs for the timber were limited to merchant vessels;
efforts of southern planters to export it for naval use in Britain
and France met with little success, although it was much favored
in commercial shipyards abroad.

A major change occurred in 1794, when the United States
was forced into building a navy to protect her commercial inter-
ests from the devastation of Barbary corsairs; Georgia live oak
was required by the War Department as a prime component in the
first six frigates. The government's recruitment of skilled shipwrights from Massachusetts, Connecticut, and along the Delaware River to go south and live in camps of their own making,
to fell and hew the timber to mould, ushered in a practice resulting in large-scale operations that continued for nearly a hundred
years.

Demands for naval and commercial ships' timber increased for decades after the War of 1812, both here and in Europe. Such demand precipitated the federal government's attempt to protect its needs by designating more than a quarter million acres of land as public domain exclusively for naval timber. The problem of protecting so vast a semitropical wilderness from illegal cutting, however, was never satisfactorily solved; neither legislative action nor limited patrols of the area could effectively stop indiscriminate pillage. Although decimation of the forests was deplored in some quarters, the one innovative attempt at conservation—cultivating live oak in a government-sponsored nursery—soon ended because of bitter animosity between political factions and the nation's tenaciously held myth of inexhaustible resources. Meanwhile, the finest whaleships, clippers, and packets were those whose builders and owners could boast were "live-oak built."[34]

In recent years, there has been a sharp reminder that live oak was considered both important and valuable during the nineteenth century. The ceding of Florida by Spain to the United States opened the way for increasing numbers of settlers, traders, surveyors, and timber cutters. This intensified difficulties with the Indians, at times causing a temporary halt to government timber surveys and curtailment of live-oaking activities. When the major Florida Wars ended in 1843, approximately 3,800 Seminoles were forcibly removed to Indian Territory in Oklahoma as part of the Five Civilized Tribes, leaving behind several hundred defiant survivors secluded in the Everglades. In 1950 and 1951, under the Act of 13 August 1946, Seminole Indians of the State of Florida and the Seminole Nation of Oklahoma brought suit against the United States Government for Seminole aboriginal lands in Florida relinquished under the treaties of 1823 and 1832. Valuable stands of live oak and red cedar were figured among their losses and, in accordance with a compromise settlement agreement, the Indian Claims Commission awarded the plaintiffs $16,000,000 compensation in 1976.[35]

Throughout most of the nineteenth century along the Atlantic and Gulf coasts from Maine to Louisiana, the terms *live oak-*

ing and *live oaker* were in common use from high government official to shipyard worker. As Congress authorized construction of naval vessels and the Navy Department advertised for live oak in quantities of thousands of cubic feet "cut to mould," bids were eagerly submitted by northern shipbuilders who could hire the skilled labor necessary to supply it. Their undertaking—locating available timber and obtaining cutting rights; recruiting, organizing, and transporting large groups of men and equipment, oxen, timber carts, and provisions for five- to six-month periods; overseeing the operation; and chartering and scheduling vessels to ship the timber north—seems formidable. Setting up camps; overcoming the physical hazards in cutting roads for hauling through a veritable jungle; felling immense trees; hewing and hauling the timber to landings; loading it onto scows; then reloading onto schooners for twelve, fourteen, or more hours a day while living under primitive conditions is a testimony to remarkable endurance and skill. Untold thousands of men were involved in the work, until it tapered off as the age of sail gave way to transport by steel ships and railway trains powered by steam engines. Live oaking then became a thing of the past; it has faded from memory and is now all but forgotten.

This is understandable. The live oakers lived in a time when most people earned a living by hard physical labor, working six days out of seven from dawn until after dusk; such arduous schedules left them little energy or leisure for other pursuits. Had they been given the time to record details of their daily routine, surely most of them would have questioned the sense of it, for "everybody knew" what they did. Their parents and grandparents had accomplished the same jobs in the same way; methods seemed to change not a whit from one generation to another.

It was partly for these reasons that until recently historians have generally ignored the pursuits of early working-class men and women. The observations and recollections of the high-born and well-educated tend to monopolize historical literature. As Frederick Law Olmstead remarked, it better suited the vanity of literary men to study the activities and fortunes of their peers or superiors; ordinary people, because they left few records and were viewed as accounting for few grand events, tend to disappear from history.

By now, time and technology have separated us so completely from common folk of the nineteenth century that learning about their daily lives and their methods of working depends entirely on gleanings from the little evidence they left behind in their surviving tools and equipment, letters, diaries, financial accounts, and pictures. We can never reconstruct the era of the live oakers, but these fragments give us some hint of its flavor and evoke a special appreciation for ordinary Americans whose combined efforts made many of the world's finest wooden sailing ships a reality.

Appendix

The following sample letters reflect live oakers' lives at camp and their concerns about matters at home.

Oliver C. Swift to his father, Elijah Swift, in Falmouth, Massachusetts, 23 October 1825

Port Royal Harber [South Carolina] Octr 23ᵈ. 1825.

Honᵈ Father

It's with pleasure I now inform you of our arrval here after a passige of 6 days all well, we came in over Port Royal Bar this day 2 O. C. and are now at anchor off Station Creek—have been onshore and engaged a pilot to take us to Chaplins Bluff where we expect to proceed tomorrow.

There was a smart frost here on the Night's of the 19th and 20th Inst. The Cotton Crops are nearly distroyed throu-aught the Sea Islands by the Catipiller, not more than one fifth of a crop will be made.

We have had a brisk Notherly wind during our passage except a few hours, on the Night of the 19th it blew a gale came too under a ballonn mainsail for the night oxen laboured very hard, but have trav'd it like hiroes, except the white famous he appears yet sick will not eat—

Our men have been quite contented and happy throughout the passage our Boats came safe and in fact we have not lost a straw—

Yours
Oliver C. Swift

Oliver C. Swift to his father, Elijah
Swift, in Falmouth, Massachusetts,
8 November 1825

Beaufort Nov 8ᵗʰ 1825

Honᵈ Father

I have been here for two days a wating the arrival of Capt Hatch, he last night arriv'd all well, the vessel has gone down this mornings ebb to proceed up St Hellinas Creek to [Dr.] Fullars landing, near which our house is to be located. I shall take from Mr Stutson Mr Leach & 8 men, from Mr Jenkins 10 more and establish a seperate gang on Chaplins Island in a palmeter Camp   Mr Jenkins had amt about 2000 feet when I last estimat the quantity for timber on Chaplins at 10000 feet or upwards the timber on St Helina is very scattering.

Yours in haste
O. C. Swift

PS have about 50 sticks halled

Oliver C. Swift to his father, Elijah
Swift, in Falmouth, Massachusetts,
22 November 1825

Charleston [South Carolina] Nov 22d 1825

Honrd Father Sir

I left Chaplins Isle on th 19 inst after having establishd a detachd gang from Mr Jenkins on the south end of Chaplins Isle; intent for Beaufort thinking to make some arrangement about oxen as three of our Nothern oxen had sickened and died, but was then informed that Mr Newall had arriv'd in persute of timber, thinking any delay dangerous I left immediately in persute of timber and arrivd here yesterday have a prospect of purchasing a fine lot on Chisolums Isle. which I saw on my route and of our as to smaller lots, can not hear any thing of Mr Newall here, if he has actually arrivd in quest of timber I fear it will be a serious consequence to us althoug I have some prospect of getting the timber on Bulls, was you here now to attend to ingaging timber it would be of great importance to us, as the ishew of the business seems to depend intirely on the purchase of timber. The timber on St Helina is of not much importance as it is something rotten   Our Chartered vessels have not yet arrived.

I shall draw on you for 1,000 Dollars in a few Days. I shall assertain tomorrow on my return to home respecting the prospect of timber to the South of Bulls Island and write you immediately, if I should not succeed wile I may want your assistance as I shall want to go to St. Johns E. Florida—

I have been trying to sell a bill on you to day at 10 days sight at the Branch Bank and at the brokers they regain ½ per cent and two indorsers belonging in the City I offerd at the Bank Mr Black and Mr Young a ship Chandler who was rejected, I at last found a Gentleman of Mr Blacks acquaintance who offered to buy a Draft of 1000 in the course of 10 days you will conceive the difficulty of selling drafts and doubtless be appraised of the necessity of appropriating funds here at my disposeal, as the payments for the timber will have to be punctually paid on shipment and in some cases advances required before the timber is cut

Yours
Oliver C Swift

PS   Uncle Thomas Lawrence wished me to see he is in town. Well, our Falmouth People are all well I am now about leaving for Beaufort Island in my Boat shall write you at Beaufort hope you will be in ready to come this way in case I have to go to Florida—

O C Swift

Oliver C. Swift to his father, Elijah Swift, in Falmouth, Massachusetts, 25 December 1825

Beaufort [South Carolina] Decm 25th 1825

Honrd Father Sir

I have just now receivd a letter from Capt Myrick dated the 18th Inst he has again arrivd in port a wreck he left Charleston in company with me in my schr Hope to follow me in to port Royal, got blown off & sprung a leak in Bow and his vessel is now again repairing   I think I shall not venture to give him a cargo at any rate I shant for Boston, the Captain and vessel are about alike—

We have now 14 or 15 tho [thousand] feet timber hewn and mostly in the woods with the exception of these cargos at the landing, halling and shipping will require my utmost exertion I cannot get a vessel in Charleston or Savannah. You had better Charter 2 vessels if possible as vessels will be in dimand in the Spring. I hope you have made some arrangement to invest funds in Charleston as it is so difficult to dispose of Drafts there owing to the late falures there the merchants have lost all confidence in each other which makes business extremely dull.

I am now moving Mr Stutson from St Helina to Port Royal Mr Leach I have had to put down on account of his drinking I have established Mr. Winkly with a small gang near Chaplins Isle.

Should you charter a vessel you will please send her to Beaufort for orders and ship me 3 Buls [barrels] Beans 4 quintles Codfish as we are about out and they can not be obtained here

Yours
O. C. Swift

26th P.S.   I have this day drawn on E. Swift & Sons for favour of Charles Bourn for Five hundred Dollars at 10 day sight am now bound to Chaplins Island this morning—

O C Swift

John Jenkins to his brother-in-law, Oliver C. Swift, in Falmouth, Massachusetts, 11 March 1841

Charleston [South Carolina], 11th March 1841

Dear Brother,

I wrote to you two days ago, informing I should leave the next morning for the Island, but the desire of obtaining a vessel to ship the pine timber and the constant rain, have detained me here—and I am happy to inform you that I have today chartered the schr. Temperance *of Salem 137 tons low deck, copper fastened, to proceed from this port to Wilmington in ten days, and there load with fine lumber & timber for Woods Hole at $8. pr Ht [hundred feet?] for all the sawed stuff and $10. pr. Ht for the ranging timber. She will take I think 85 or 90 Ht I have ordered 15 Ht of Heading besides all the sawed stuff for the ship, and shall have her after taking all the sawed stuff & Bowsprit & topmast to fill up with timber from 12 to 16 inches Square—and I hope she will reach you in time.*

I have also chartered the Sloop West Falmouth *Capt Nye, to proceed to Stono the first wind and take the balance of the ships frame which will be left by the* Isaac Jackson, *and shall fill her up with promiscuous timber. I was induced to do this on ascertaining yesterday that the M——— [undecipherable] had not arrived at St. Augustine on the 7th and as we had heavy westerly gales after she sailed I am apprehensive she was blown off the coast, and that she will not return here in time to enable her to deliver the balance of the ships frame at Woods Hole by the time you will need it. Have also ordered 10 Bbls. thin tar to by [be] shipped from Wilmington by the* Temperance. *Mr. Morris has just informed me that he shall return to Wilmington tomorrow, and will commence immediately sawing our lumber, and that there shall be no delay in loading the schr. as soon as she shall arrive there.*

Truly Yours
John Jenkins

It has rained constantly the last two days and is now raining in torrents. We averaged about 2 days work in a week
The water is 2 ft. above the railroad where it crosses Edisto River. Passengers are detained from travelling, and it is almost impossible to get about. The country is completely inundated. If I had the two Steamers B. Hooks I think I should discharge the gang immediately.
Annexed is copy of Charter party with Capt. Legee—Frt. [freight] of tar to be the N. York rates of frt.

Charter Agreement Between Oliver C. Swift & Co. and Captain Jacob Legee, Jr.

This Charter Party made this 11th day of March AD 1841 by O. C. Swift & Co. of Falmouth, Mass. of the one part, and Jacob Legee Jr. Master of Sch. Temperance *of Salem Mass. of the other part witnesseth, That for the consideration hereinafter mentioned the said Jacob Legee Jr. hereby agrees with the said Swift & Co. that at the expiration of ten working days from the date of this charter party, he will proceed from this port with said sch.* Temperance *without any delay, excepting contrary winds & weather, to the port of Wilmington N.C. and there take on board and load said schooner with a full cargo of boards, plank & ranging timber to be furnished by the Agent of said Swift Co. and from thence he, the said Legee will proceed with all possible despatch to Woods Hole, Falmouth, Mass. and there deliver the said cargo to the order of said Swift & Co. And the said Legee further agrees that said Schl. Temperance shall be tight, staunch & strong and sufficiently manned, tackled & apparreled with all things necessary for such a vessel & voyage, and that he the said Legee will defray all the expenses of manning & victualling said vessel and pay all pilotage & port charges which may accrue during said voyage.*

And the said O. C. Swift & Co. on their part hereby agree that after fifteen days from the date of this Charter party, their Agent at Wilmington shall have the lumber ready to load said sch. Temperance as fast as her crew can take it on board; and for all delay of loading, occasioned by the lumber not being furnished as before expressed, they, the said Swift & Co. will pay to said Jacob Legee a demurrage of fifteen dollars pr. day for every day the said Sch. may be so detained by their Agents neglecting or refusing to furnish the cargo. And upon the fulfilment of this charter party in all it stipulations by the said Legee, the said O. C. Swift & Co. hereby agree to pay to said Legee, on delivery of the cargo aforesaid at Woods Hole in full for freight of the same, Eight Dollars per thousand for all the sawed stuff, and Ten Dollars pr. —— for the ranging timber.

To the faithful performance of the foregoing agreements, the parties aforesaid, hereby bind themselves each one to the other in the penal sum of Five Hundred Dollars.

In testimony of which the parties aforesaid have hereunto affixed their signatures at the port of Charleston, this Eleventh day of March AD 1841.

[signed] Jacob Legee Jr.
[signed] O. C. Swift & Co.

Signed in presence of C. Gibbs

Thomas L. Swift to his brother, Oliver C. Swift, in Falmouth, Massachusetts, 18 January 1842

Charleston [South Carolina] Jany 18/42

Dear Brother

My letter of 13th inst informed you I should write in 5 days. Here it is. In the first place I give the list of wants on the frame To wit

1 Stern post
1 do Knee, have one, may answer, if we cannot get another
1 Main Transom have a tree that will make it think it sound
1 Upper Apron   do   do   do   do   [ditto]
2 Breast Hooks out of 5
2 Counters
21 Floors, have got 14 and 2 more in progress
36 1st Futtocks
38 2d   do [ditto]
36 3d   do [ditto]
11 tops

Have got about 330 ps. [pieces] and want about 150 ps on same   If you can sell the frame in Washington do so you see what I have got and I think I can get the balance. I am willing to risk it any how—but mind ye, on top of my opinean comes Mr Caways to this effect—that thus far it is the finest frame ever got out in this country and you must get a good price for it if you sell it in Washington, not less than 1.75 pr ft if you can avoid it   On Mr Dwight we shall cut rising 5000 ft Mr C's measure. Our promiscuous timber sides 9 p, 10 p, 11 p, 12, 14, 16, 18, 20, 22, never less than 12 ft in length, except 2 or 3 sticks which were but little work to side out, at 10 ft. It is rather a short growth of timber, but the sidings up to 14 ft are long enough, and the others do very well, not many sticks of the 2 highest sidings, of 12, 14, 16, 18, quite a smart chance, Mr Cowing says no better timber ever grew or was got out, very sound, but tremendous hard. I hope you will be able to go to Washington soon for I am anxious to know what to do with the timber soon as possible, as I can now ship any where at very low rates. Soon as you can leave and make arrangements about it, write me. Stick them hard for a price. I shall soon hear from Mr Legare and will write you, if you wish me to ship that I will do so, and if the flat is then worth moving shall have her towed to Bulls—Capt Silas Mowane wishes you to inform his family that he is well and not any prospect of a freight You wish to know how much timber I can cut, above you have the amount we have cut, but we shall now get out timber faster than before, for these reasons, we have an easier lot of timber and less mould timber to get

I have partly agreed with a man by name Malloon, I think you know him, a first rate fellow away from grog. I can manage that and shall ship one more good fellow if I can find him. I shall discharge 2 or 3 men very early. Make such a contract with the commissioners as you think proper, of course you want crowd too hard upon me in quantity for I do not wish to cut much after the middle of April

I have cut no promiscuous timber low as 9 inch, if you wish me to do so, advise me. Make your contract extend 2 years if you can, and get all to Norfolk, and as little to Philadelphia as possible. By the Bye if you wish to take a trip this way when you get in Washington I should be very happy to see you. I think the prospect for the season looks well, and will not require your attention here particularly—at the same time I should be happy to see you and profit by your advice in the way of business you can come in 2 days and thus far few interuptions have taken place on the line. With much respect I remain your afet Brother

Thomas L Swift

Duplicate sent to Washington directed

William Ellis to his father, Stephen Ellis, in Sippican, Rochester, Massachusetts, 19 December 1852

St Marks [Florida] Dec 19 1852

Dear father

I suppose you feel some what anxious to know how we are getting along here and what the prospect is for making money Business has been dull enough up to the present time but I am in hopes it will soon change for the better There has been so much

rain that we could do but very little and after the rains abated
we might have done something I was taken sick and unable to
do a thing yesterday was the first time I worked for several days
I had a disorder of the head and the fever and ague and was
pretty sick part of the time Charles is a little complaining to day
but will probably feel a better tomorrow he has got the bowel
complaint I herd from New Port to day where Thomas Oglesbey
has been confined for some time and it is not expected he will
live the day out Poor fellow that he is Most gone there is no
doubt his complaint is of the lungs The doctor says they are
nearly all consumed

I never was so sick of any place in my life as I am of this
and have wished myself to home many a time since I got here
and if I had money enough to get home with I would leave Florida
forever I dont think we will make much this winter—and I
guess you will se us to home pretty early without we get along
more prosperously

The prospect is much more favorable for the coming part of
the season if the weather is dry and we have our health It is
warm here and has been through the winter so far nights frosty
so as to keep it generally healthy The J Vail is ready for sea and
is a waiting for a time to go down the bay heard from Harper
yesterday he is well and the vessel is a bout loaded Sam Spencer
is going to leave Florriday in a few days to engage in business in
some other state A wise plan Tell Sarah and Ellen they must be
good children and I will bring them something when I come
home Give my respects to the folks

William Ellis

Ben to Jonathan Hiller in
Mattapoisett, Massachusetts,
11 March 1858

Attakapas [Louisiana] Sunday March 11th. [18] 58

*Brother Jonathan   i have just recieved your letter and it was as
good as a feast To get a few words from poisett once in a while
This is what i call a hard old country and most eny thing new
goes well after being shut up in The woods for four months   it is
now twelve oclock and The horn is blowing for dinner so i will
go and see what They have got so nice*

*well i have got my dinner down. They had what They call duff a
passel of flour boiled up in a rag one pound of it is as heavy as
Two pounds of lead   Taking our group on an everage i Think wee
have lived very well for a Live oak gang wee have had plenty of
sweet potatoes and dough nuts evry night wee have Two Cooks
They cook a flour barrel full of Them evry day   Thair is Thirty
seven men all told in our gang Twenty hewers wee have now
Twenty five thousand feet of Timber and one hundred and
Twenty five sticks rowled up for morning The other two gangs i
suppose have about The same wee begin to have the weather
pretty warm now   The Trees are leafed out The black bury vines
have been in bloom about a month and begin To fall of i suppose will be ripe The last of next month   i rather Think wee shall
get away for home by The 2nd of April   i dont Think our Timber
will hold out eny longer Then That   wee will not moove agane at
eny rate wee have had it very muddy The most of The Time but
it is now getting quite dry wee havnt had eny rain of eny account
for a month The snakes and Aligators begin to crawl out quite
smart one of our boys killed a morgason yesterday mesureing six
feet and eight inches and another fellow a rattle snake with nign
rattles   i have not got the paper you sent me yet i suppose likely
some one will read it before i get it   it generaly Takes a paper one
week longer To come Then it does a letter i expect you Fellows
will make your whack on building That ship   Tell Dan not to
work To hard on Them plank i wish i was Thair To help him
Tell him That i Think he missed it awfully by not comeing out
hear for the privalidge of leaving hear for home will be worth a
few hundred   Tell him not to curse old Deacon quite so bad   Tell
Bill darkey it pears like its going to rain   Tell Studly to keep that
steam box hot for i calculate to be Thair To put Them bottom
plank on The boys plague Burbank all most to death he sez ile be*

*damed if i would go live oaking agane if They would give mee all
of Louiseanna for thair is nothing goes but a pack of god damed
hogs he sayed when wee first get hear if eny one got to fighting
they should be discharged so evry once in a while after dark
about a dozen of Them will mat in and pretend to be fighting
untill They get The old fellow to rairing They keep him in a fret
about all the Time They dont like him atal and i rather Think
when They get payed of he will get knocked if he dont keep
scarse give my how de do to all hands and tell them i hope to bee
among them soon*

Ben

*Nathaniel P. Hiller was nineteen years
old when he wrote to his father from
Georgia in 1851; eight years later he
was spending another winter live oaking on the east coast of Florida.*

Nathaniel P. Hiller to his father,
Nathaniel Hiller in Rochester,
Massachusetts, 26 January 1851

Jan the 26 1851

*Dear Father   having a few spare moments I thought that I
would write to you to let you know that i am well hopeing to
that these few lines will find you enjoying the same blessing. we
are all well at present and we could enjoy our selfs well if it was
not for the sand flys they are very plenty we have had some rain
within this last three weeks which is fild the swamps up which
is made it bad wheeling i recieved Anns letter the twenty first
of January and i was very glad to here from home. we are a gitting timber quite fast now but should git it faster if it was not so
much rotton we are a going over to Black Hammock to morrow
a plantation about three miles from hear we have to go over in a
boat. the plase that we are now in is Camden County [Georgia]
and the post office that at Brunswick is about ten miles by water
and fifty by land we have a house about twenty feet square we
live down below and sleep up stares there here is thirteen in the
gang now with us that belongs out here we should live well if we
had a good cook he is an old man from Nantucket the name of
our fore man is Mr Charles Fish of Falmouth he is a very cleaver
man the place wher our house now stands is on the Pine barren
Sorounded on all sides by Saw palmettos with hear and there an
old fat pine log the place wher we land our timber is cald Honey*

154

creek. we come over St. Simons bar to git here I expect that we shal move frome here in about a month eather four to the west or ten miles to the north i write this letter in a hurry as you will see for Mr Cummings is going to care [carry] them we carry the letters down to a plantation about two miles off. i send my love and respects to. we have changed post office direct the letters now Langsburg Po Camden county Ga in the care of John H Parker.

Nathaniel P H

Nathaniel P. Hiller to his father,
Nathaniel Hiller in Rochester,
Massachusetts, 20 February 1859

New Smyrna [Florida] Feb 20 1859

Dear Father, haveing a chance to Send a note In Williams Laetter I thought I would write you a few lines. Father Dexter Sems anchious about that business with Isaac Corbin and wants to know If It is Setled or If there has bin anything done about it, I would be glad to have a letter from you but If you do not wish to write a letter Send a note In Melvin thos letter, pleas to write the perticulars for he wants to know all about It. We are all well and git along very well, the weather Is very pleasent we have not lost more then a coupple days on account stormy weathear since we have bin at work, we are not much troubled with watter under foot but have a plenty to drink and very good to for this Country ther Is some very good Brookes which runs over the land we work on, the Timber In some Placeses proves very unsound but fore an eaverage, there Is 12 hewers of us, last week we hewd out 2573 ft cub[ic]

Give my respects to Mother and to all the neighbours, tell Isaac I should like to have a letter from him and like to have him bring along Some Sweet Potatoes for we do not have any, my paper Is gitting small I will quit hopeing these few lines may [find] you all well,

Nathaniel P Hiller

Notes

INTRODUCTION

1. William D. Weekes, "The Awesome Live Oak," *American Forests* 85 (February 1979): 20.

CHAPTER 1

1. Eugenio Ruidíaz y Caravia, ed., *La Florida Su Conquista y Colonización por Pedro Menéndez de Avilés* (Madrid: Hijos de J. A. Garcia, 1893), 2:99; *Barcia's Chronological History of the Continent of Florida . . . from the Year 1512, in which Juan Ponce de Leon discovered Florida, until the year 1722,* trans. Anthony Kerrigan (Gainesville: University of Florida Press, 1951), pp. 20, 112.

2. *A True Declaration of the Estates of the Colonie in Virginia . . .* (London: Printed for William Barret, 1610), p. 54.

3. See: William A. Baker, *Colonial Vessels: Some Seventeenth-Century Craft* (Barre, Mass.: Barre Publishing Co., 1962).

4. [Thomas Ash?] *Carolina: or A description of the present state of that country, and the natural excellencies thereof; . . .* (London: Printed for W. C., and to be sold by Mrs. Grover, 1682), p. 10.

5. *South-Carolina Gazette,* 7–14 December 1747, 9 July 1748.

6. "Ship Registers in the South Carolina Archives 1734–1780," introduction by R. Nicholas Olsberg, *South Carolina Historical Magazine* 74 (1973):242; Lilla Mills Hawes, ed., *The Letter Book of Thomas Rasberry, 1758–1761,* Collections of The Georgia Historical Society

(Savannah, Ga., 1959), 13:30; *Georgia Gazette*, 2 June 1763, 16 July, 8 October 1766.

7. *South-Carolina and American General Gazette*, 8 August 1771.

8. P. Fatio, "Considerations on the Importance of the Province of East Florida to the British Empire (on the supposition that it will be deprived of its Southern Colonies) By the Situation, its produce in Naval Stores, Ship Lumber, & the Asylum it may afford to the *Wretched & Distressed* Loyalists," 14 December 1782, CO 5/560:913.

9. Chas. Inglis to Rear Admiral of the Blue John Montagu, Esqr., 11 July 1772. ADM. I/484, PRO.

10. Ibid.

11. Bernard Pool, *Navy Board Contracts 1660–1832. Contract Administration under the Navy Board* (Hamden, Conn.: Archon Books, 1966), pp. 62–63, 83–84. Perhaps it never occurred to the British that American colonists would often hastily construct ships of green timber for sale, while reserving the best quality timber for themselves. See: Samuel Trask Dana, *Forest and Range Policy, Its Development in the United States* (New York, Toronto, London: McGraw-Hill, 1956), p. 15.

12. Robert Greenhalgh Albion, *Forests and Sea Power: The Timber Problem of the Royal Navy 1652–1862* (Cambridge: Harvard University Press, 1926), pp. 23–25.

13. *Georgia Gazette*, 23 February 1774.

14. *Georgia Gazette*, 28 December 1774, 11 October 1775.

15. P. Lee Phillips, *Notes on the Life and Works of Bernard Romans* (Deland: Florida State Historical Society, 1924), p. 20.

16. Bernard Romans, *A Concise Natural History of East and West Florida* (New York: Printed for the author, 1775), p. 124.

17. Leclerc Milfort [Louis Le Clerc Milfort], "Memoir or Short Sketch of my different voyages and my stay in the Creek Nation (1775–1795)," trans. with explanatory notes Oliver G. Ricketson, Jr. [ca. 1945–1950], in possession of Mary Ricketson Bullard, copy at the Georgia Historical Society.

18. *American Husbandry; Containing an Account of the Soil, Climate, Production and Agriculture of the British Colonies in North America . . .*, 2 vols. (London: J. Bew, 1775), 1:377, 2:75.

19. Wharton and Humphreys Ship Yard Accounts, 1773–1795. Joshua Humphreys Papers, Historical Society of Pennsylvania; *Naval Documents of the American Revolution*, ed. William Bell Clark (vols. 1–4), William James Morgan (vols. 5–8) (Washington, D.C.: U.S. Government Printing Office, 1968), 3:1039–40, 5:1046.

20. Charles Oscar Paullin, ed., *Out-Letters of the Continental Marine Committee and Board of Admiralty. August, 1776–September, 1780* (New York: Naval History Society, 1914), pp. 275–76; *Naval Docu-*

ments Related to the United States Wars with the Barbary Powers . . . (Washington, D.C.: U.S. Government Printing Office, 1939), 1:72; Allen D. Candler, *The Revolutionary Records of the State of Georgia* (Atlanta: The Franklin-Turner Company, 1908), 2:105–06.

21. *Naval Documents of the American Revolution*, ed. William James Morgan (Washington, D.C.: U.S. Government Printing Office, 1976), 6:60, 111–12, 1465, 1471: 7:468, 637, 1306.

22. Ibid., 7:839, 915, 946.

23. Ibid., 7:946.

24. Wm. Butterworth [Henry Schroeder], *Three Years Adventures of a Minor, In England Africa the West Indies South-Carolina and Georgia* (Leeds: Edwd. Baines, [1831]), pp. 342–43.

25. Gilbert Chinard, "André and François-André Michaux and their Predecessors. An Essay on Early Botanical Exchanges between America and France," *Proceedings of the American Philosophical Society* 101 (1957):344–50; Gilbert Chinard, "Recently Acquired Botanical Documents," *Proceedings of the American Philosophical Society* 101 (1957):508–22.

26. Nathanael Greene to John Houstoun, [12 September 1784] Nathanael Greene Papers, William R. Perkins Library, Duke University.

27. Houstoun to Greene, 12 November 1784, Nathanael Greene Papers, William R. Perkins Library.

28. Joseph Byrne Lockey, *East Florida: 1783–1785: A File of Documents Assembled and Many of Them Translated* (Berkeley and Los Angeles: University of California, 1949), p. 491.

29. John McQueen to Nathanael Greene [23 May 1785], Nathanael Greene Papers, William R. Perkins Library.

30. B^{3}788 (Marine) fols, 367–69. Archives de la Marine, Paris. See also: Paul Walden Bamford, *Forests and French Sea Power 1660–1789* (Toronto: University of Toronto Press, 1956), p. 190.

31. Nathanael Greene to Le Marquis Charles de Castries, December 1785, Nathanael Greene Papers, Clements Library, University of Michigan.

32. John Baker Holroyd Sheffield, *Observations on the Commerce of the American States, by John Lord Sheffield; A New Edition, Much Enlarged . . .* (London: Printed for J. Debrett, Opposite Burlington House, Piccadilly, 1784), p. 84. The first edition of this work, published in 1783, was written in opposition to a proposal of William Pitt's concerning altering the navigation acts to favor the United States.

33. Marquise de Lafayette to Nathanael Greene, 29 December 1785, Nathanael Greene Papers, Clements Library.

34. James Penman to N. Greene, 9 February 1786, Nathanael Greene Papers, William R. Perkins Library.

35. Ibid.

36. "Precis de Memoires envoyes par M. Rolland . . . 1786." B⁷ 460 (Marine), Archives de la Marine. See also: Bamford, *Forests and French Sea Power* . . ., p. 190.

37. Chinard, "André and François-André Michaux . . .," *Proceedings of the American Philosophical Society* 101 (1957):351–52. See also: "Journal of André Michaux 1787–1796, with introduction by C. S. Sargent, *Proceedings of the American Philosophical Society* 26 (1888): 1–145.

38. Chinard, "André and François-André Michaux . . .," p. 352.

39. Arthur Preston Whitaker, *Documents Relating to the Commercial Policy of Spain in the Floridas with Incidental Reference to Louisiana* (Deland: Florida State Historical Society, 1931), p. 127.

40. Peter P. Hill, " 'A Masked Acquisition'—French Designs on Cumberland Island, 1794–95," *Georgia Historical Quarterly* 64 (Fall, 1980):309.

41. Ibid., 313.

CHAPTER 2

1. *Naval Documents Related to . . . Wars with the Barbary Powers,* 1:1–6. (See also the index).

2. Ibid., 1:54–56.

3. Act of 27 March 1794, ch. 12, 1 Stat., 350.

4. *American State Papers, Naval Affairs* (Washington: Gales and Seaton, 1834), 1:6.

5. Ibid., 1:8.

6. Tench Coxe to John T. Morgan, 12 June 1794. Letters of Tench Coxe, Commissioner of the Revenue, Relating to the Procurement of Military, Naval, and Indian Supplies, 1794–1796, RG75, Microcopy M-74; Naval Records Collection of the Office of Naval Records and Library. Correspondence on Naval Affairs when Navy was under the War Department 1790–1798, RG45, Entry 374, National Archives.

7. Coxe to Jedediah Huntington, 15 June 1794, Letters of Tench Coxe, RG75, Microcopy M-74.

8. Ibid.; *American State Papers, Naval Affairs,* 1:9.

9. Coxe to Huntington, 18 June 1794. Letters of Tench Coxe, RG75, Microcopy M-74.

10. Coxe to Isaac Holmes, Daniel Stevens, John Habersham, Joseph Clay, 17 June 1794. Letters of Tench Coxe, RG75, Microcopy M-74.

11. John T. Morgan to Joshua Humphreys, 30 August 1794. Joshua Humphreys Letter Book, 1793–1797. Historical Society of Pennsylvania.

12. Ibid.

13. Coxe to John Barry, 3 October 1794, RG75, Microcopy M-74.

14. John Barry to Tench Coxe, 10 November 1794, as quoted in Margaret Davis Cate, *Our Todays and Yesterdays. A Story of Brunswick and the Coastal Islands*, 2nd rev. ed. (Brunswick, Ga.: Glover Bros., Inc., 1930), pp. 87–88.

15. Morgan to Humphreys, 21 October 1794. Joshua Humphreys Letter Book, 1793–1797.

16. Barry to Coxe, 10 November 1794, in Cate, *Our Todays and Yesterdays*, p. 88. Much of the timber cut on St. Simons and Hawkins islands belonged to Richard Leake; the slaves that Morgan rented belonged to Thomas Spalding, Leake's son-in-law, and John Cooper [Couper?], all of whom were prominent coastal planters.

17. Coxe to Habersham, Clay, and Morgan, 18 October 1794, RG75, Microcopy M-74.

18. Coxe to Morgan, 23 October 1794, RG75, Microcopy M-74.

19. Report on progress in building the frigates, 20 December 1794. Joshua Humphreys Letter Book, 1793–1797. See also: *American State Papers, Naval Affairs*, 1:17–20.

20. Morgan to Barry, 29 December 1794. John Barry Papers, New York Historical Society. See also: *Naval Documents Related to the United States Wars with the Barbary Powers* (Washington, D.C.: U.S. Government Printing Office, 1939), 1:122.

21. RG45, Entry 374, National Archives. See also: *Naval Documents . . . Barbary Powers*, 1:80.

22. War Department to Coxe, 25 October 1794, RG45, Entry 374; Coxe to Secretary of War, 25 October 1794, RG75, Microcopy M-74; War Department to Morgan, 30 July 1795, RG45, Entry 374, National Archives.

23. War Department to James Hackett, 4 November 1795, RG45, Entry 374.

24. Humphreys to Morgan, 29 December 1795. Joshua Humphreys Letter Book, 1793–1797.

25. *Naval Documents . . . Barbary Powers*, 1:103.

26. Ibid., 1:154.

27. Act of 20 April 1796, ch. 14, 1 Stat., 453. See also: *Naval Documents . . . Barbary Powers*, 1:139.

28. Thomas Truxtun to Josiah Fox, 24 March 1796. Josiah Fox Papers, item 74, Peabody Museum of Salem. See also: *Naval Documents . . . Barbary Powers*, 1:122–25.

29. Samuel Nicholson to Josiah Fox, 25 August, 22 December 1796. Josiah Fox Papers, items 101, 115.

30. Josiah Fox to Tench Francis, 7 June 1797. Josiah Fox Papers, item 103.

31. In Portsmouth, New Hampshire, the 36-gun *Congress* was launched 15 August 1799 and served during the War of 1812; in 1834 she was found unfit for repair and broken up at the Norfolk Navy Yard. The 36-gun *Chesapeake* was launched 2 December 1799 at the Gosport Yard in Virginia, and the 44-gun *President* was launched 10 April 1800 in New York. Both of these frigates were captured by British ships during the War of 1812 and taken into the Royal Navy; *President* was broken up in 1817 and *Chesapeake* in 1820.

Of the original three frigates, only USS *Constitution* is still in service; tied up at her berth in Boston harbor she is the oldest commissioned warship in the world. *Constellation* is best remembered for the famous battle off Nevis in the West Indies where she captured the 40-gun frigate *L'Insurgente* in February 1799. In 1853–54 she was modified and rebuilt as a corvette; in 1955 she was stricken from the Navy list and transferred to Baltimore for restoration by a group of patriotic citizens. Annually, thousands of visitors go aboard the vessel at her berth in Baltimore's Inner Harbor. The 44-gun *United States* was destroyed after the Civil War when she was ordered broken up in late 1865. The fact that all of these ships survived for more than a decade underscored the value of using excellent quality timber.

32. Act of 30 April 1798, ch. 35, 1 Stat., 553; Act of 4 May 1798, ch. 39, 2 Stat., 556; Act of 22 June 1798, ch. 55, 2 Stat., 569; Act of 30 June 1798, ch. 64, 2 Stat., 575.

33. *American State Papers, Naval Affairs*, 1:27, 65–66.

34. Camden Co., Ga., Deed Book D, Folios 228–29, affidavit of George Gibbs, 1 June 1799.

35. Act of 25 February 1799, ch. 13, 3 Stat., 621. See *Naval Documents Related to the Quasi-War with France* (Washington, D.C.: U.S. Government Printing Office, 1935–1938), 2:131–32, 3:382, 5:131–32; *American State Papers, Naval Affairs*, 1:65–66.

36. Camden Co., Ga., Deed Book E, Folios 58–65; McIntosh Co., Ga., Deed Book A, Folios 6–10, copy in Title Papers, 1838–1943, Records of the Public Buildings Service, RG121, Entry 80, National Archives; H. Doc. 114, 19th Cong., 2d sess.

37. RG45, File AC, Box 10, National Archives.

38. Ebenezer Jackson to Sec. of the Navy Benjamin Stoddert, 17 March 1801. Ebenezer Jackson Letter Book, 1801–1820, William R. Perkins Library, Duke University.

39. Phineas Miller to Thomas Shubrick, 21 June 1800, RG45, File AC, Box 10, National Archives.

40. Ibid.

41. Miller to Sec. of the Navy Benjamin Stoddert, 1 July 1800, RG45, File AC, Box 10, National Archives.

42. Jackson to Sec. of the Navy Benjamin Stoddert, 7 April 1801. Ebenezer Jackson Letter Book, 1801–1820.

43. RG45, File AC, Box 10, National Archives.

44. Jackson to Sec. of the Navy Benjamin Stoddert, 8 March 1801; Jackson to Thomas Turner, 12 March 1801; Jackson to William Crofts, 17 March 1801. Ebenezer Jackson Letter Book, 1801–1820.

45. Jackson to Samuel Humphreys, 30 March 1801. Ebenezer Jackson Letter Book, 1801–1820.

46. Joshua Humphreys to Samuel Humphreys, 4 May 1801. Joshua Humphreys Letter Book, 1800–1835.

47. Jackson to Sec. of the Navy, pro. tem, 13 May 1801. Ebenezer Jackson Letter Book, 1801–1820.

48. Act of 3 March 1801, ch. 20, 2 Stat., 110.

49. James Hackett to Timothy Pickering, 29 May 1795, quoted in Joshua Humphreys Correspondence, 1775–1831.

50. Thomas Shubrick to Sec. of the Navy Benjamin Stoddert, 4 Feb. 1800, RG45, File AC, Box 10, National Archives.

51. See: *Naval Documents . . . Barbary Powers*, vols. 1–7.

52. Dunbar Rowland, ed., *Official Letter Books of W. C. C. Claiborne, 1801–1816* (Jackson, Miss.: State Department of Archives and History, 1917), 5:285–86.

53. [Christopher Claxton], *The Naval Monitor . . .* (London: Printed by A. J. Valpy, 1815), pp. 86–87.

54. Act of 29 April 1813, ch. 138, 3 Stat., 321; *American State Papers, Naval Affairs*, 1:306.

55. For reports on the burning of Washington, see: *American State Papers, Military Affairs*, 1:575–80; *American State Papers, Naval Affairs*, 4:220. Records of Sec. of the Navy Levi Woodward indicated that 15,000 cubic feet of live-oak timber was burned at the Washington Navy Yard in 1814. An additional 44,500 cubic feet of live oak was lost during the War of 1812 when three vessels were burned: the 36-gun frigate *New York*, the 44-gun frigate *Columbia*, and the 16-gun sloop *Argus*. See: *American State Papers, Naval Affairs*, 4:218, 220.

56. Great Britain–United States Claims Under the Treaty of Ghent, 24 December 1814, RG76, Entry 185, Claim 75, National Archives.

CHAPTER 3

1. *American State Papers, Naval Affairs*, 1:321; Act of 3 March 1815, ch. 82, 3 Stat., 226.

2. Summary of Information Respecting Live Oak Timber of the Carolinas and Georgia, October 1815–November 1817. RG45, Entry 239, National Archives.

3. Ibid.

4. Act of 29 April 1816, ch. 138, 3 Stat., 321.

5. Act of 1 March 1817, ch. 22, 3 Stat., 347.

6. Records of the Bureau of Land Management, RG49, National Archives. Journal and Report of James L. Cathcart and James Hutton, Agents Appointed by the Secretary of the Navy to Survey Timber Resources Between the Mermentau and Mobile Rivers, 1818–19. Microfilm Publication M8; Journal of John Landreth on an Expedition to the Gulf Coast, Nov. 15, 1818–May 19, 1819. Microfilm Publication T12. See also: Walter Prichard, Fred B. Kniffen, and Clair A. Brown, "Southern Louisiana and Southern Alabama in 1819: The Journal of James Leander Cathcart," *Louisiana Historical Quarterly* 28 (January, 1945): 735–921.

7. Journal and Report of James L. Cathcart . . . , 23 January 1819. For a comment on the unfulfilled live-oak contract of Edward Livingston, see: Prichard, et al., "Southern Louisiana and Southern Alabama in 1819 . . . ," *Louisiana Historical Quarterly* 28:770.

8. Ibid., 7 February 1819.

9. Journal of John Landreth . . . , 21 January 1819.

10. Journal and Report of James L. Cathcart . . . , 13, 21 January 1819.

11. *American State Papers, Naval Affairs*, 3:48; See also: Franklin B. Hough, *Report Upon Forestry* (Washington, D.C.: U.S. Government Printing Office, 1878), p. 10; Bess Glenn, "Cathcart's Journal and the Search for Naval Timbers," *The American Neptune* 3 (1943):239–49; Jenks Cameron, *The Development of Governmental Forest Control in the United States*, Institute for Government Research, Studies in Administration (Baltimore: Johns Hopkins Press, 1928), pp. 32–33.

12. Hough, *Report Upon Forestry*, p. 11, indicated 244,452 acres; however, this does not include the islands of Blackbeard and Grover or the Santa Rosa tract. H. Ex. Doc. 161, 40th Cong., 2d sess. (1868) indicates 264,449.77 acres, which included Santa Rosa but not Blackbeard and Grover.

13. Clarence Edwin Carter, comp. and ed., *The Territorial Papers of the United States. The Territory of Florida, 1821–1824* (Washington, D.C.: U.S. Government Printing Office, 1956), 22:370, 375–76, 430–31, 693, 701, 791–92.

14. Act of 23 February 1822, ch. 9, 3 Stat., 651.

15. *American State Papers, Naval Affairs*, 3:47–48; H. Doc. 114, 19th Cong., 2d sess.

16. Act of 3 March 1827, ch. 94, 4 Stat., 242. See also: *American State Papers, Naval Affairs*, 3:917–58.

17. *American State Papers, Naval Affairs*, 3:945–49; See also: William R. Adams, "Florida Live Oak Farm of John Quincy Adams," *Florida Historical Quarterly* 51 (1972), 132; William F. Keller, *The Nation's Advocate. Henry Marie Brackenridge and Young America* (Pittsburgh: University of Pittsburgh Press, 1956), pp. 331–48.

18. *American State Papers, Naval Affairs*, 3:922–25.

19. Ibid., 3:922.

20. Ibid.

21. Ibid.

22. Ibid., 3:923, 924.

23. Ibid.

24. Charles Francis Adams, ed., *Memoirs of John Quincy Adams: Comprising Portions of His Diary from 1795–1848* (Philadelphia: J. B. Lippincott & Co., 1874–77), 7:323–24 (see also: 8:51).

25. *American State Papers, Naval Affairs*, 3:926; 4:939.

26. Adams, *Memoirs . . .*, 8:322–23. See also: Adams, *Florida Historical Quarterly* 51 (1972), 138–41; Keller, *The Nation's Advocate . . .* (1956), pp. 338–47; Cameron, *Development of Governmental Forest Control . . .* (1928), pp. 52–65.

27. Ibid. Keller, *The Nation's Advocate*, p. 348.

28. Act of 1 March 1817, ch. 22, 3 Stat., 347; Act of 23 Feb. 1822, ch. 9, 3 Stat., 651; Act of 2 March 1831, ch. 66, 4 Stat., 472. See also: Carter, *Territorial Papers of Florida*, 22:375; 26:695, 772; S. Doc. 38, 27th Cong., 1st sess.

29. "Historical Statement of the use of Live Oak Timber for the Construction of vessels of the Navy, and Vessels Built with it;—the Quantity on Lands Reserved from Sale by the United States and on Private Land, and the Necessity for its Preservation for Future Use," *American State Papers, Naval Affairs*, 4:191–223. See also: Ibid., 4:116; H. Ex. Doc. 23, 22d Cong., 2d sess.

30. Ibid., 4:201. For a list of live-oak naval vessels built during the period 1797–1831, see: *American State Papers, Naval Affairs*, 4:218.

31. Ibid., 4:488.

32. Records of the General Land Office. Live Oak Correspondence, RG49, National Archives.

33. George S. Kephart, "Live Oak, the Tree with a Past," *American Forests* 78 (1972):58. See also: S. Doc. 97, 27th Cong., 3d sess.

34. *American State Papers, Naval Affairs*, 4:81.

35. Logbook of U.S. Schooner *Spark*, RG24, National Archives.

36. David M. Ludlum, *Early American Hurricanes 1492–1870* (Boston: American Meteorological Society, 1963), pp. 140–42.

37. *American State Papers, Naval Affairs*, 4:159, 161; H. Ex. Doc. 23, 22d Cong., 2d sess.

38. Cameron, p. 94.

39. William Acken, 5 April 1839, fragment of a letter, formerly in possession of Elizabeth F. Smith.

40. *American State Papers, Naval Affairs*, 3:957.

41. See: Cameron, p. 80; *Congressional Globe*, 10 Jan. 1843, p. 119.

42. S. Doc. 97, 27th Cong., 3d sess.

43. Ibid.

44. Ibid.

45. Ibid.

46. Cameron, p. 82; S. Doc. 97, 27th Cong., 3d sess.

47. St. Augustine *News*, 10 June 1843; Washington, D.C. *Daily National Intelligencer*, 17 June 1843; Carter, *Territorial Papers of Florida*, 26:425–26, 573–75, 639–41.

48. Ibid., 26:639–41, 663–64, 666–68, 673–74.

49. Live Oak Letters and Letters from Timber Agents, June 1828–February 1836, June 1839–December 1859, RG45, Entry 259, National Archives. See also: Abandoned Military Reservations File—Live Oak Reserves, Florida, correspondence of 2 October 1859, RG49, National Archives.

50. Joshua Humphreys Notebook, 1719–1842, p. 347, Historical Society of Philadelphia.

51. [Maria Audubon, ed.], *The Life of John James Audubon, the Naturalist* (New York: G. P. Putnam & Son, 1869), p. 218.

52. *Report of the Commissioner of Agriculture for the Year 1866* (Washington, D.C.: U.S. Government Printing Office, 1867), p. 491.

53. Ibid., p. 489.

54. Ibid., p. 488.

55. Act of 5 August 1882, ch. 391, 22 Stat., 291; Act of 3 March 1883, ch. 97, 22 Stat., 477.

56. Charles C. Stebbins, personal interview, Darien, Ga., June 1975.

57. United States Naval Shipyard, Portsmouth (New Hampshire), Memorandum. Subject: Oak, the U.S.F. *Constitution*, and related facts and fallacies, 24 May 1962. Copy in possession of author.

58. Today, the unavailability of sufficient stands of live oak precludes its use in repair work aboard U.S.S. *Constitution*. During her 1973–76 overhaul, all knees and breasthooks in need of replacement were made successfully with laminated white oak. Her future timber needs are ensured by a Navy-owned forest of white oaks on a 25,000-acre tract near Crane, Indiana. It was dedicated on 8 May 1976, and appropriately named "Constitution Grove."

CHAPTER 4

1. Notation of 25 February 1797 in Joshua Humphreys Letter Book, 1793–1797.

2. New Bedford *Mercury*, 17 February 1832.

3. Nantucket *Inquirer*, 19 November 1831.

4. Carl C. Cutler, *Greyhounds of the Sea. The Story of the American Clipper Ship* (New York and London: G. P. Putnam's Sons, 1930), pp. 145–46, 168; New York *Commercial Advertiser*, 6 August 1849.

5. Cutler, *Greyhounds of the Sea*, p. 150.

6. John M. Bullard, *The Rotches* (New Bedford: Privately printed, 1947), pp. 259–60.

7. Ibid., pp. 260–61.

8. Ibid., p. 263.

9. New Bedford *Mercury*, 21 July 1832, 21 June 1833, 28 March 1834; Elizabeth A. Little, "Live Oak Whaleships," *Historic Nantucket* 19 (1971):30–33.

10. J. H. Easterby, "Shipbuilding on St. Helena Island in 1816," *South Carolina Historical and Genealogical Magazine* 47 (1946):117–20.

11. Henry F. Willink to Jonathan Handy, 18 January 1841, in possession of Marion L. Channing.

12. Account Book of Jonathan Handy, 1834–1853, in possession of Marion L. Channing.

13. Theodate Geoffrey [Dorothy Wayman], *Suckanesset; Wherein May Be Read a History of Falmouth, Massachusetts* (Falmouth: Privately printed, 1930), p. 85.

14. Contracts of the War Department and Navy Department, June 1794–December 1842, RG45, Entry 235, National Archives.

15. Geoffrey, *Suckanesset*, p. 89.

16. Swift family correspondence in possession of Oliver S. Chute, Milton, Massachusetts.

17. New Bedford *Mercury*, 3 October 1828, 28 September, 26 October 1832; Nantucket *Inquirer*, 13 November 1830. H. Doc. 308, 22d Cong., 1 sess., v.1.

18. Swift family correspondence in possession of Oliver S. Chute, Milton, Massachusetts.

19. Act of 30 June 1834, ch. 143, 4 Stat., 721.

20. Ianthe Bond Hebel, "Live Oak Barons. A Romantic Bit of Lumber History," *Southern Lumber Journal* 54 (1950):48–50, 52, 54, 74. See also: Volusia County Historical Commission, *Centennial History of Volusia County, Florida, 1854–1954*, ed. Ianthe B. Hebel (Daytona Beach: College Publishing Company, 1955), pp. 3–4.

21. Hebel, "Live Oak Barons," pp. 50, 52, 54.

22. Ibid., p. 54.

23. Hugh D. Langdale, personal interview, Newport, Florida, 3 June 1975.

24. Franklyn Howland, *A History of the Town of Acushnet, Bristol County . . . , Massachusetts* (New Bedford, Mass.: Published by the author, 1907), pp. 352–55; *Niles National Register*, 23, 30 June 1838.

25. Act of 3 March 1843, ch. 83, 5 Stat., 617.

26. H. Doc. 195, 28th Cong., 2d sess.

27. Ibid.

28. *Congressional Globe*, 28, 31 January 1845.

29. H. Doc. 195, 28th Cong., 2d sess.

30. Ibid.

31. New Bedford *Evening Standard*, 11 May 1892; San Francisco *Daily Examiner*, 11 July 1883; San Francisco *Chronicle*, 12, 13 July 1883.

32. The House Committee on Expenditures of the Navy Department published "Aledged Abuses" in June 1860 citing W. C. N. Swift's 1858 contract as a "violation of law . . . improper, and injurious to the public good." President James Buchanan, Secretary of the Navy Isaac Toucey, and William Plitt of Philadelphia were implicated in the report. H. Rept. 621, 36 Cong., 1st sess.

33. Grace Williamson Edes, *Annals of the Harvard Class of 1852* (Cambridge: Privately printed, 1922), pp. 174–76, 367, 384–85.

34. H. Rept. 632, 36th Cong., 1st sess.

35. New Bedford *Daily Evening Standard*, 19 August 1857.

36. Boston *Herald*, 14 October 1857.

37. Virginia Steele Wood, ed., "Elijah Swift's Travel Journal from Massachusetts to Florida, 1857," *Florida Historical Quarterly* 55 (1976): 183.

38. *Official Records of the Union and Confederate Navies in the War of the Rebellion*, 1st ser. (Washington, D.C.: U.S. Government Printing Office, 1901), 12:655–56.

39. S. L. Thorndike to Paul Joseph Revere, 14 August 1862, Paul Joseph Revere Papers, Massachusetts Historical Society; *Massachusetts Soldiers, Sailors, and Marines in the Civil War* (Norwood, Mass: Published by the Adjutant General, 1932), 4:3.

40. New Bedford *Evening Standard*, 5 April 1901.

41. New Bedford *Daily Mercury*, 4 October 1872.

42. An elderly gentleman dictated this song to Mrs. Lillian M. Young of Cambridge, Maine, about 1896 and part of the fifth verse is missing. Other variations are entitled "Mauling Live Oak." Fannie Hardy

Eckstorm and Mary Winslow Smyth, *Minstrelsy of Maine. Folk-Songs and Ballads of the Woods and the Coast* (Boston and New York: Houghton Mifflin Company, 1927), pp. 65–67.

CHAPTER 5

1. John W. Griffiths, *A Treatise on Marine and Naval Architecture or Theory and Practice Blended in Ship Building* (London: George Philip & Son, [1856?]), pp. 47, 91.

2. "The Building of the Ship," *Harper's New Monthly Magazine* 24 (1862): 610.

3. Walter E. Channing, personal interview, Marion, Mass., October 1975.

4. "The Building of the Ship," p. 610. See also: Dorothy O'Keefe, "Lofting and Mold Making," *Salt* 5 (June, 1980):51–58.

5. *Mattapoisett and Old Rochester Massachusetts*, Prepared under the Direction of a Committee of the Town of Mattapoisett (New York: The Grafton Press, 1907), pp. 280–81.

6. Marion Nicholl Rawson, *Of the Earth Earthly. How Our Fathers Dwelt Upon and Wooed the Earth* (New York: E. P. Dutton and Co., Inc., 1937), p. 273.

7. Dana Story, *The Building of a Wooden Ship* (Barre, Mass.: Barre Publishers, 1971), n.p.

8. Samuel H. Barnes, personal interview, Norwood, Mass., November 1974.

9. Rawson, *Of the Earth Earthly*, p. 277.

10. Story, *The Building of a Wooden Ship*, n.p.

11. Richard C. McKay, *South Street: A Maritime History of New York* (New York: G. P. Putnam's Sons, 1934), pp. 160–61.

12. See: John Allen Krout, *The Origins of Prohibition* (New York: Alfred A. Knopf, 1925); Richard W. Howland and Joe W. Howland, "200 Years of Drinking in the United States: Evolution of the Disease Concept," in *Drinking. Alcohol in American Society—Issues and Current Research*, ed. John A. Ewing and Beatrice A. Rouse (Chicago: Nelson-Hall, 1980), pp. 39–60.

13. William Hutchinson Rowe, *The Maritime History of Maine. Three Centuries of Shipbuilding and Seafaring* (New York: W. W. Norton & Co., 1948), p. 127.

14. Henry William Blair, *The Temperance Movement; Or, the Conflict Between Man and Alcohol* (Boston: William E. Smythe Company, 1888), p. 425.

15. By 1860 the per capita consumption of beer dropped to 4.79 gallons, and distilled spirits to 4.70 gallons; in 1978 the per capita consumption of beer was 29.78 gallons and distilled spirits was 2.60 gallons. Statistical data from: Table 3, "Apparent Consumption of Alcoholic Beverages and Absolute Alcohol in each Class of Beverage, in U.S. Gallons per Capita of the Drinking-Age Population, U.S.A. 1790–1978," in Merton M. Hyman et al., *Drinkers, Drinking and Alcohol-Related Mortality and Hospitalizations. A Statistical Compendium* (New Brunswick, N.J.: Center of Alcohol Studies, Rutgers University, 1980), p. 3.

16. Lyman Beecher, *Lectures on Political Atheism and Kindred Subjects; Together with Six Lectures on Intemperance* (Boston: John P. Jewett & Company; Cleveland: Jewett, Proctor & Worthington, 1852), p. 352.

17. *National Philanthropist*, 4 March 1826, name changed to *Genius of Temperance, Philanthropist and People's Advocate*.

18. The text of several pledges appears in Deets Pickett, ed., *The Cyclopedia of Temperance Prohibition and Public Morals* (New York and Cincinnati: The Methodist Book Concern, 1917), pp. 202–03. The favorite juvenile pledge of temperance leader Frances E. Willard is found in her *Glimpses of Fifty Years; Autobiography of an American Woman* (Chicago: Woman's Temperance Publication Association, [1889]), p. 331.

19. *Maine Inquirer*, 10 December 1830; William Avery Baker, *A Maritime History of Bath, Maine and the Kennebec River Region* (Bath, Maine: Marine Research Society of Bath, 1973), 1:344–45, 361.

20. Act of 14 July 1862, ch. 164, 2 Stat., 565.

21. Swift Brothers, New Bedford, and Bertram Cunningham, Jefferson County, Maine, live oaking contract, 10 October 1872. In possession of Mrs. Charles A. Davis.

22. Swift Brothers of New Bedford, collection of live oaking contracts and permissions of minors, 1855 and 1857. In possession of Obed N. Swift.

23. Ibid.

24. Ibid.

25. Holograph contract between Ezra Burbank and Swift Brothers of New Bedford, 7 September 1857. In possession of Obed N. Swift.

26. "Live-Oaking in Southern Forests. Jacob W. Chase, One of the Few Surviving Woodmen Who Worked for Swift Brothers in 1855," New Bedford, *Sunday Standard*, 13 February 1910.

27. See: Basil Greenhill and Ann Giffard, *Travelling by Sea in the Nineteenth Century* (New York: Hastings House Publishers, 1974), p. 14.

28. "Live-Oaking in Southern Forests. . . ."

29. Ibid.
30. Ibid.

CHAPTER 6

1. "Live Oaking in Southern Forests. . . ."
2. Warren (Maine) Historical Society, *From Warren to the Sea 1837–1852. Letters of the Counce and McCallum Families* (Middletown, N.Y.: Whitlock Press, 1970), pp. 19–20.
3. Ibid., p. 20.
4. "Live Oaking in Southern Forests. . . ."
5. [Maria Audubon, ed.], *The Life of John James Audubon*, p. 216.
6. Ibid., p. 217.
7. Ibid., pp. 217–18.
8. Samuel H. Barnes, personal interview, Norwood, Mass., November 1974.
9. "Log Carts, with Enormous Wheels, Carried 100-Foot Pines to Sawmill," Tampa *Tribune*, 13 January 1957; "'Frog' Smith discusses the Old Log Cart—Team of Mules and No Brakes," Tampa *Tribune*, 27 January 1957; J. Brewer Owens, personal interviews, Brunswick, Ga., 18 March 1973 and June 1975.
10. J. Brewer Owens, personal interview, Brunswick, Ga., 18 March 1973.
11. Tampa *Tribune*, 27 November 1957.
12. J. Brewer Owens, personal interviews, Brunswick, Ga., 18 March 1973 and June 1975.
13. Joseph B. Felt, *History of Ipswich, Essex, and Hamilton* (Cambridge: Charles Folsom, 1834), p. 45.
14. Dawes Markwell, "Handy Oxen," *The Chronicle of the Early American Industries Association, Inc.* 35 (June 1972):18; See also: Lewis F. Allen, *American Cattle: Their History, Breeding and Management* (New York: Taintor Brothers & Co., 1868), pp. 293–96.
15. Isaac Stephenson, *Recollections of a Long Life 1829–1915* (Chicago: Privately printed, 1915), p. 50.
16. *Ludowici News* (Ludowici, Georgia), 1 November 1973 (reprinted from an unidentified newspaper of Macon, Georgia, ca. 1920.)
17. John S. Springer, *Forest Life and Forest Trees . . .* (New York: Harper & Brothers, 1856), pp. 108–09.
18. Howard Hiller, personal interview, Rochester, Mass., 17 April 1975.
19. William M. Wasson, personal interview, Freeport, Maine, 8 May 1977.

CHAPTER 7

1. Felt, *History of Ipswich*, p. 30.

2. Henry Adams, *History of the United States of America During the First Administration of Thomas Jefferson, 1801–1805* (New York: Charles Scribner's Sons, 1889), 1:45.

3. Adams, *History of the United States*, 1:44–45.

4. Stewart H. Holbrook, *Holy Old Mackinaw. A Natural History of the American Lumberjack* (New York: Macmillan Company, 1938), p. 46.

5. The *Oxford English Dictionary* cites *langrage* (also *langridge*) as a nautical and military term of unknown origin. It means "case-shot loaded with pieces of iron of irregular shape, formerly used in naval warfare to damage the rigging and sails of the enemy."

6. Swift Brothers Account Book, 1858–1859, Whaling Museum, Old Dartmouth Historical Society.

7. Easterby, "Shipbuilding on St. Helena," pp. 218–19.

8. Richard Henry Dana, *Two Years Before the Mast. A Personal Narrative of Life at Sea* (New York: Harper & Brothers, 1840), p. 25.

9. Herman Melville, *White-jacket; or The World in a man-of-war* (New York: Harper & Brothers, 1850), pp. 74–76.

10. Richard Henry Dana, *Two years Before the Mast . . .* , p. 387.

11. [Audubon], *The Life of John James Audubon*, pp. 219–20.

12. Virginia Steele Wood, ed., "James Keen's Journal of a Passage from Philadelphia to Blackbeard Island, Georgia, for Live Oak Timber, 1817–1818," *The American Neptune* 35 (1975):245.

13. Adams, *History of the United States*, 1:19–20.

14. Wood, "James Keen's Journal," p. 233.

15. *The Ship's Medicine Chest and First Aid at Sea*, compiled by U.S. Public Health Service and U.S. War Shipping Administration (Washington, D.C.: U.S. Government Printing Office, 1947), p. 2.

16. Joshua Humphreys to Samuel Humphreys, 8 April 1800. Joshua Humphreys Letter Book, 1797–1800. Historical Society of Pennsylvania.

17. New Bedford *Standard Times*, 23 December 1924.

18. James Thacher, *American Modern Practice; Or, A Simple Method of Prevention and Cure of Diseases* (Boston: Ezra Read, 1817), pp. 289–90.

19. Usher Parsons, *Sailor's Physician, Containing Medical Advice, for Seamen and other Persons at Sea, on the Treatment of Diseases, and on the Preservation of Health in Sickly Climates* (Providence: Barnum Field & Co., 1824), p. 167.

20. Mildred McClary Tymeson, "The Family Dentist," *New*

England Galaxy 7 (1966):7. See also: Josiah Flagg, *The Family Dentist* (Boston: Joseph W. Ingram, 1822).

21. Wood, "James Keen's Journal," p. 241.

22. Karl Vogel, "Medicine at Sea in the Days of Sail," in *Milestones in Medicine* (New York: Appleton-Century Co., Inc., 1938), p. 361.

23. Act of 20 July 1790, ch. 29, 2 Stat., 134; See also: Act of 2 March 1805, ch. 28, 2 Stat., 330.

24. *Book of Words of the Hutchinson Family Songs* (Boston: J. S. Potter & Co., 1855), p. 42.

25. Green and Emerson Account Ledger, 1819–1821, Maine Maritime Museum.

26. Wood, "James Keen's Journal," p. 234.

27. Ibid., pp. 242–43.

28. Ibid., p. 234, 235–36.

29. Ibid., p. 243.

30. Ibid., p. 244.

31. Green and Emerson Account Ledger, 1819–1821, Maine Maritime Museum.

32. [Audubon], *Life of John James Audubon*, p. 225–27.

33. J. Leander Bishop, *A History of American Manufactures from 1608 to 1860 . . .* (Philadelphia: Edward Young & Co., 1868), 1:85.

34. The type of wood used in construction of particular merchant ships was sometimes mentioned in newspaper notices of launchings. Other published sources for this information include *American Lloyd's Registry of American and Foreign Shipping* (New York: R. C. Root, Anthony & Co., 1857), superseded by the American Bureau of Shipping, *Record of American and Foreign Shipping* (New York, 1869–1932; issued 1869–1908 under an earlier name for the bureau, the American Shipmasters' Association).

35. 60 Stat. 1049, 25 USC 70; 87 Stat. 466, 12 USC 1401; The Seminole Indians of the State of Florida, and The Seminole Nation of Oklahoma, Plaintiffs, v. The United States of America, Defendant.

Bibliography

MANUSCRIPTS

Ann Arbor, Mich. Clements Library, University of Michigan. Nathanael Greene Papers.

Barnstable, Mass. Barnstable County Register of Probate. Estates of the Swift family.

Bath, Maine. Maine Maritime Museum. Green & Emerson Account Ledger, 1819–1821; John A. Lord Papers.

Boston, Mass. Massachusetts Historical Society. Paul Joseph Revere Papers; Samuel Brown Papers.

———. U.S.S. *Constitution* Museum Foundation, Inc. U.S. Navy Memorandum No. IX21/L9-3 (M). Subject: U.S. Frigate *Constitution*; Research Memorandum, 27 November 1931, concerning restoration and repairs.

Crawfordville, Fla. Fragment of a letter signed William Acken, 5 April 1839, formerly in possession of Elizabeth F. Smith.

Durham, N. C. William R. Perkins Library, Duke University. Nathanael Greene Papers; Ebenezer Jackson Papers.

East Falmouth, Mass. Mrs. Charles A. Davis. Swift Brothers, New Bedford, Mass. and Bertram Cunningham, Jefferson Co., Maine, live-oaking contract, 10 October 1872.

Kew, Surry. British Public Record Office. Colonial Records. Chas. Inglis to Rear Admiral of the Blue John Montagu, 11 July 1772, ADM. I/484, PRO; P. Fatio, Considerations on the Importance of the Province of East Florida to the British Empire . . . ." 14 December 1782, CO 5/560:913.

Marion, Mass. Marion L. Channing. Jonathan Handy Account Books, 1822–1826, 1834–1853; Henry Yonge to Jonathan Handy, 26 December 1838; Henry F. Willink to Jonathan Handy, 18 January 1841.

———. Sippican Historical Society. Barnabas Hiller Account Book, 1843–1864, on loan from Ellen H. Michaud, Bedford, Mass.

———. Charles A. Ellis, Jabez Delano to William Ellis, 9 August 1841; William Ellis to Stephen Ellis, 19 December 1852.

Milton, Mass. Oliver S. Chute, J. & E. Swift Account Book, 1856–1859; Oliver C. Swift to Elijah Swift, 23 October, 8, 22 November, 25 December 1825; John Jenkins to O. C. Swift, 11 March 1841; Thomas L. Swift to Oliver C. Swift, 18 January 1842.

New Bedford, Mass. Swift Brothers of New Bedford. Collection of live-oaking contracts, 1855 and 1857, in possession of Obed N. Swift.

———. Whaling Museum, Old Dartmouth Historical Society. Swift Brothers Account Book and Letter Book, 1858–1859.

New York, N. Y. New York Historical Society. Pendleton Papers, John Barry Collection.

Paris. Archives de la Marine. Series B, including correspondence, B^3 788 (Marine) fols. 367–69; B^7 460 (Marine) and D^3 16 "Précis des memoires envoyes par M. Rolland . . . sur les bois que produit la Nouvelle Angleterre. . . ."

Philadelphia, Pa. Historical Society of Pennsylvania. Joshua Humphreys Papers.

Portsmouth, N. H. United States Naval Shipyard. Memorandum. Subject: Oak, the U.S.F. *Constitution*, and related facts and fallacies, 24 May 1962.

Rochester, Mass. Mrs. Howard Hiller, East-Over Farm. Barnabas Hiller to Nathaniel Hiller, 26 December 1841; Nathaniel P. H. [Hiller?] to his father [unnamed], 26 January 1851; Ben [surname not given] to Jonathan Hiller, 11 March 1858; Nathaniel P. Hiller to his father, 20 February 1859.

Salem, Mass. Peabody Museum of Salem. Josiah Fox Papers.

South Dartmouth, Mass. Mary Ricketson Bullard, "The Cumberland Islands: Their Division Between the Heirs of Lynch and the Estate of General Greene," unpublished Ms, June 1977. Le Clerc Milfort, "Memoir or Short Sketch of my different voyages and my stay in the Creek Nation (1775–1795)." Trans. from the French with explanatory notes by Oliver G. Ricketson, Jr., unpublished Ms, ca. 1945–1950.

Tallahassee, Fla. Robert Manning Strozier Library, Florida State University. Daniel Ladd Account Book, 1859–1860.

———. Florida State Library. Florida Tax Rolls for Jefferson County, 1856, 1857, 1858.

Taunton, Mass. Bristol Country Register of Probate. Probate records of the Swift family.

Washington, D.C. National Archives. Record Group 24: Records of the Bureau of Naval Personnel; Record Group 45: Naval Records Collection of the Office of Naval Records and Library; Record Group 49: Records of the Bureau of Land Management; Record Group 75: Records of the Bureau of Indian Affairs; Record Group 76: Records of Boundary and Claims Commissioners and Arbitrations; Record Group 121: Records of the Public Buildings Service.

―――. U.S. Navy Memorial Museum, Washington Navy Yard. William Doughty file.

PERSONAL INTERVIEWS

Barnes, Samuel H., Norwood, Mass., November 1974 and 25 September 1975.

Channing, Walter E., Marion, Mass., October 1975.

Hiller, Howard B., Rochester, Mass., 17 April 1975.

Langdale, Hugh D., Newport, Fla., 3 June 1975.

Owens, J. Brewer., Brunswick, Ga., 18 March 1973 and June 1975.

Stebbins, Charles C., Darien, Ga., June 1975.

Wasson, William M., Freeport, Me., 8 May 1977.

PUBLISHED GOVERNMENT DOCUMENTS

American State Papers. Naval Affairs . . . , 1789–1836. 7 vols. Washington: Gales & Seaton, 1834–1861.

Bates, William W. "Ship Timber in the United States." In *Report of the Commissioner of Agriculture for the Year 1866.* Washington: U.S. Government Printing Office, 1867.

Carter, Clarence Edwin, ed. *The Territorial Papers of the United States. The Territory of Florida, 1821–1845.* 5 vols. Washington: The National Archives, 1958–1962.

Congressional Globe, 28, 31 January 1845.

Dictionary of American Naval Fighting Ships. 8 vols. Washington: Department of the Navy, Office of the Chief of Naval Operations, Navy History Division, 1959–1981.

Fowells, H. A., comp. *Silvics of Forest Trees of the United States.* Agriculture Handbook No. 271. Washington: Division of Timber Management Research Forest Service, U.S. Department of Agriculture, 1965.

Hough, Franklin B. *Report upon Forestry*. Washington: U.S. Government Printing Office, 1878.

Naval Documents of the American Revolution. 8 vols. Edited by William Bell Clark (vols. 1–4), William James Morgan (vols. 5–8). Washington: Department of the Navy, Naval History Division, 1964–1980.

Naval Documents Related to the Quasi-War Between the United States and France, 1798–1801. 7 vols. Washington: U.S. Government Printing Office, 1935–1938.

Naval Documents Related to the United States Wars with the Barbary Powers, 1785–1807. 7 vols. Washington: U.S. Government Printing Office, 1939–1945.

Official Records of the Union and Confederate Navies in the War of the Rebellion. 30 vols. Washington: U.S. Government Printing Office, 1894–1922.

Report of the Commissioner of Agriculture for the Year 1866. Washington: U.S. Government Printing Office, 1867.

The Ship's Medicine Chest and First Aid at Sea. Miscellaneous Publication No. 9. U.S. Public Health Service and the War Shipping Administration. Washington: U.S. Government Printing Office, 1947.

Torres, Louis. *Historic Resource Study. Cumberland Island National Seashore, Georgia, and Historic Report Historical Data Section of the Dungeness Area*. Denver: Denver Service Center, Historic Preservation Division, National Park Service, November 1977.

Wood Handbook: Wood as an Engineering Material. U.S. Department of Agriculture Handbook No. 72. Washington: USDA Forest Products Laboratory, Forest Service, Rev. 1974.

PUBLISHED BOOKS

Abell, Sir Wescott. *The Shipwright's Trade*. Cambridge: The University Press, 1948.

Adams, Charles Francis, ed. *Memoirs of John Quincy Adams: Comprising Portions of His Diary from 1795–1848*. 12 vols. Philadelphia: J. B. Lippincott & Co., 1874–1877.

Adams, Henry. *History of the United States of America During the First Administration of Thomas Jefferson, 1801–1805*. New York: Charles Scribner's Sons, 1889.

Albion, Robert Greenhalgh. *Forests and Sea Power: The Timber Problem of the Royal Navy, 1652–1862*. Cambridge: Harvard University Press, 1926.

Albion, Robert Greenhalgh and Pope, Jennie Barnes. *The Rise of New York Port [1815–1816]*. New York: Charles Scribner's Sons, 1939.

Allen, Lewis F. *American Cattle: Their History, Breeding and Management*. New York: Taintor Brothers & Co., 1868.

American Husbandry; Containing an Account of the Soil, Climate, Production and Agriculture of the British Colonies in North America . . . . 2 vols. London: J. Bew, 1775.

[Ash, Thomas?] *Carolina; or A description of the present state of that country, and the natural excellencies thereof; . . . .* London: Printed for W. C., and to be sold by Mrs. Grover, 1682.

[Audubon, Maria, ed.] *The Life of John James Audubon, the Naturalist*. New York: G. P. Putnam & Son, 1869.

Bailey, L. H., ed. *Cyclopedia of American Agriculture*. 4 vols. New York: The Macmillan Co., 1907–1909.

Baker, William A. *Colonial Vessels: Some Seventeenth-Century Craft*. Barre, Mass.: Barre Publishing Co., 1962.

———. *A Maritime History of Bath, Maine and the Kennebec River Region*. 2 vols. Bath, Me.: Marine Research Society of Bath, 1973.

Bamford, Paul Walden. *Forests and French Sea Power, 1660–1789*. Toronto: University of Toronto Press, 1956.

Barcia Carballido Y Zuniga, Andres Gonzalez de. *Chronological History of the Continent of Florida . . . from the year 1512, in which Juan Ponce de Leon discovered Florida, until the year 1722*. Translated by Anthony Kerrigan. Gainesville: University of Florida Press, 1951.

Bartram, John. (See: Stork, William.)

Bartram, William. *Travels Through North & South Carolina, Georgia, East & West Florida*. Philadelphia: James & Johnson, 1791.

Bealer, Alex W. *Old Ways of Working Wood*. Barre, Mass.: Barre Publishers, 1972.

Beecher, Lyman. *Lectures on Political Atheism and Kindred Subjects; Together with Six Lectures on Intemperance*. Boston: John P. Jewett & Company; Cleveland, Ohio: Jewett, Proctor & Worthington, 1852.

Belmore, Bruce W. *Early Princeton, Maine*. Princeton, Me.: Southworth-Anthoensen, 1945.

Bishop, J. Leander. *A History of American Manufactures from 1608 to 1860 . . . .* 3 vols. Philadelphia: Edward Young & Co., 1868.

Blair, Henry William. *The Temperance Movement; Or, the Conflict Between Man and Alcohol*. Boston: William E. Smythe Co., Philadelphia: E. R. Baxter and Company, 1888.

Book of Words of the Hutchinson Family Songs. Boston: J. S. Potter & Co., 1855.

Bryant, Ralph Clement. *Logging. The Principles and General Methods of Operation in the United States.* New York: John Wiley & Sons, Inc., 1914.

Bullard, John M. *The Rotches.* New Bedford: Privately printed, 1947.

Butterworth, Wm. [Henry Schroeder]. *Three Years Adventures of a Minor, In England, Africa, the West Indies, South-Carolina, and Georgia.* Leeds: Edwd. Baines, [1831].

Cameron, Jenks. *The Development of Governmental Forest Control in the United States.* Baltimore: Johns Hopkins Press, 1928.

Candler, Allen D. *The Revolutionary Records of the State of Georgia.* 3 vols. Atlanta: The Franklin-Turner Company, 1908.

Catalogue of Fruit and Ornamental Trees and Plants . . . Cultivated at the Linnaean Botanic Garden, William Prince, Proprietor, Flushing Long-Island, near New-York. New York: T. and J. Swords, 1822.

Cate, Margaret Davis. *Our Todays and Yesterdays. A Story of Brunswick and the Coastal Islands.* 2d rev. ed. Brunswick, Ga.; Glover Bros., Inc., 1930.

Catesby, Mark. *The Natural History of Carolina, Florida, and the Bahama Islands. . . .* 2 vols. London: published by author, 1731–1743.

Channing, Marion L. *Laura Russell Remembers.* Marion, Mass.: Channing Books, 1970.

Chapelle, Howard I. *The History of American Sailing Ships.* New York: Bonanza Books, 1935.

––––––. *The History of the American Sailing Navy. The Ships and Their Development.* New York: W. W. Norton & Co., Inc., 1949.

Cutler, Carl C. *Greyhounds of the Sea. The Story of the American Clipper Ship.* New York and London: G. P. Putnam's Sons, 1930.

Dana, Richard Henry. *Two Years Before the Mast . . . .* New York: Harper & Brothers, 1840.

Dana, Samuel Trask. *Forest and Range Policy, Its Development in the United States.* New York, Toronto, London: McGraw-Hill Book Company, Inc., 1956.

Eckstorm, Fannie Hardy, and Smyth, Mary Winslow. *Minstrelsy of Maine. Folk-Songs and Ballads of the Woods and the Coast.* Boston and New York: Houghton Mifflin Company, 1927.

Edes, Grace Williamson. *Annals of the Harvard Class of 1852.* Cambridge: Privately printed, 1922.

Felt, Joseph B. *History of Ipswich, Essex, and Hamilton.* Cambridge: Charles Folsom, 1834.

Fitch, Samuel Sheldon. *A System of Dental Surgery.* 2nd ed. Philadelphia: Carey, Lea, & Blanchard, 1835.

Flagg, Josiah. *The Family Dentist.* Boston: Joseph W. Ingram, 1822.

Geoffrey, Theodate [Dorothy Wayman]. *Suckanesset: Wherein May Be Read a History of Falmouth, Massachusetts.* Falmouth: Privately printed, 1930.

Greenhill, Basil, and Giffard, Ann. *Travelling by Sea in the Nineteenth Century.* New York: Hastings House Publishers, 1974.

Griffiths, John W. *A Treatise on Marine and Naval Architecture or Theory and Practice Blended in Ship Building.* London: George Philip & Son, [1856?].

Hawes, Lilla Mills, ed. *The Letter Book of Thomas Rasberry, 1758–1761.* Collections of The Georgia Historical Society, vol. 13. Savannah: The Georgia Historical Society, 1959.

Hegarty, Reginald. *Birth of a Whaleship.* New Bedford, Mass.: New Bedford Free Library, 1964.

Holbrook, Stewart H. *Holy Old Mackinaw: A Natural History of the American Lumberjack.* New York: The Macmillan Company, 1938.

Howland, Franklyn. *A History of the Town of Acushnet, Bristol County . . . , Massachusetts.* New Bedford, Mass.: Published by author, 1907.

Howland, Richard W. and Joe W. "200 Years of Drinking in the United States: Evolution of the Disease Concept." In *Drinking. Alcohol in American Society—Issues and Current Research*, edited by John A. Ewing and Beatrice A. Rouse, pp. 39–60. Chicago: Nelson-Hall, 1980.

Hutchins, John G. B. *The American Maritime Industries and Public Policy, 1789–1914. An Economic History.* Harvard Economic Studies, vol. 73. Cambridge: Harvard University Press, 1941.

Hyman, Merton M., et al. *Drinkers, Drinking and Alcohol-Related Mortality and Hospitalizations. A Statistical Compendium.* New Brunswick, N.J.: Center of Alcohol Studies, Rutgers University, 1980.

Ise, John. *The United States Forest Policy.* New Haven: Yale University Press, 1920.

Kauffman, Henry J. *American Axes. A Survey of Their Development and Their Makers.* Brattleboro, Vermont: The Stephen Greene Press, 1972.

Keller, William F. *The Nation's Advocate. Henry Marie Brackenridge and Young America.* Pittsburgh: University of Pittsburgh Press, 1956.

Krout, John Allen. *The Origins of Prohibition.* New York: Alfred A. Knopf, 1925.

Lawson, John. *A New Voyage to Carolina: Containing the Exact Description and Natural History of That Country . . . .* London: J. Knapton, 1708–1710.

Lockey, Joseph Byrne. *East Florida: 1783–1785. A File of Documents Assembled and Many of Them Translated.* Berkeley & Los Angeles: University of California Press, 1949.

Loudon, J. C. *Arboretum et Fruticetum Britannicum; Or, The Trees and Shrubs of Britain . . . .* 8 vols. London: Printed for the author; and sold by Longman, Orme, Brown, Green, and Longmans, 1838.

Ludlum, David M. *Early American Hurricanes, 1492–1870.* Boston: American Meteorological Society, 1963.

Martin, Tyrone G. *A Most Fortunate Ship, A Narrative History of "Old Ironsides."* Chester, Conn.: The Globe Pequot Press, 1980.

Massachusetts Soldiers, Sailors, and Marines in the Civil War. 8 vols. Norwood, Mass.: Published by the Adjutant General, 1932.

Mattapoisett and Old Rochester Massachusetts. Prepared under the Direction of a Committee of the Town of Mattapoisett. New York: The Grafton Press, 1907.

McKay, Richard C. *South Street: A Maritime History of New York.* New York: G. P. Putnam's Sons, 1934.

Medicine Chests Carefully Prepared for All Climates, with Directions for Using the Medicines, and Treatment of Diseases Incident to Seamen. Gregg & Hollis, No. 30, Union Street . . . Boston. Boston: Moore and Prowse, 1826.

Melville, Herman. *White-jacket; or The World in a man-of-war.* New York: Harper & Brothers, 1850.

Mercer, Henry C. *Ancient Carpenter's Tools.* Doylestown, Pa.: The Bucks County Historical Society, 1929.

Michaux, André. *Historie Des Chênes De L'Amérique.* Paris: 1801.

Michaux, F. Andrew. *The North American Sylva.* 3 vols. Philadelphia: J. Dobson, 1841.

Packard, Francis R. *History of Medicine in the United States.* 2 vols. New York: P. B. Hoeber, Inc., 1931.

Parsons, Usher. *Sailor's Physician, Containing Medical Advice, for Seamen . . . at Sea, on the Treatment of Diseases, and on the Preservation of Health in Sickly Climates.* 2nd ed. Providence: Barnum Field & Co., 1824.

Partridge, Bellamy, and Bettmann, Otto. *As We Were. Family Life in America, 1850–1900. In Pictures and Text.* New York: Whittlesey House, McGraw-Hill Book Company, Inc., 1946.

Paullin, Charles Oscar. *Paullin's History of Naval Administration, 1775–1911.* Annapolis: U.S. Naval Institute, 1968.

Paullin, Charles Oscar, ed. *Out-Letters of the Continental Marine Committee and Board of Admiralty. August, 1776–September, 1780.* 2 vols. New York: Naval History Society, 1914.

Phillips, P. Lee. *Notes on the Life and Works of Bernard Romans*. De-land, Fla.: Florida State Historical Society, 1924.

Pickett, Deets, ed. *The Cyclopedia of Temperance Prohibition and Public Morals*. New York and Cincinnati: The Methodist Book Concern, 1917.

Pool, Bernard. *Navy Board Contracts, 1660–1832. Contract Administration under the Navy Board*. Hamden, Conn.: Archon Books, 1966.

Quarterman, Luther H. *Reminiscences of a Country Boy*. Savannah, Ga.: Privately printed [1961].

Ramsay, David. *The History of South-Carolina from Its First Settlement in 1670, to the Year 1808*. 2 vols. Charleston: Published by David Longworth, for the Author, 1809.

Rawson, Marion Nicholl. *Candle Days. The Story of Early American Arts and Implements*. New York and London: The Century Co., 1927.

——. *Of the Earth Earthly. How Our Fathers Dwelt Upon and Wooed the Earth*. New York: E. P. Dutton & Co., Inc., 1937.

Reed, Parker McCobb. *History of Bath and Environs. Sagadahoc County, Maine, 1607–1894*. Portland, Me.: Lakeside Press, 1894.

Rees, Abraham. *The Cyclopaedia; or Universal Dictionary of Arts, Sciences, and Literature*. First American edition adapted to this country. 43 vols. text, 4 vols. plates. Philadelphia: Samuel F. Bradford and Murray Fairman and Co., [ca. 1807].

Robins, Frederick W. *The Smith. The Traditions and Lore of an Ancient Craft*. London: Rider and Company, 1953.

Romans, Bernard. *A Concise Natural History of East and West Florida*. New York: Printed for the author, 1775.

Rowe, William Hutchinson. *The Maritime History of Maine. Three Centuries of Shipbuilding and Seafaring*. New York: W. W. Norton & Co., 1948.

Rowland, Dunbar, ed. *Official Letter Books of W. C. C. Claiborne, 1801–1816*. 5 vols. Jackson, Miss.: State Department of Archives and History, 1917.

Ruidíaz y Caravia, Eugenio, ed. *La Florida Su Conquista y Colonización por Pedro Manéndez de Avilés*. 2 vols. Madrid: Hijos de J. A. Garcia, 1893.

Ryder, Alice Austin. *Lands of Sippican on Buzzards Bay*. New Bedford, Mass.: Reynolds Printing, 1938.

Sargent, Charles Sprague. *Silva of North America*. 8 vols. Boston and New York: Houghton Mifflin and Company, 1895.

Sloane, Eric. *A Museum of Early American Tools*. New York: Funk & Wagnalls, 1964.

Springer, John S. *Forest Life and Forest Trees* . . . . New York: Harper & Brothers, 1856.

Stephenson, Isaac. *Recollections of a Long Life, 1829–1915.* Chicago: Privately printed, 1915.

Stork, William. *A Description of East-Florida, With a Journal, Kept by John Bartram of Philadelphia, Botanist to His Majesty for the Floridas: Upon a Journey from St. Augustine up the River St. John, as far as the lakes.* London: Sold by W. Nicoll and G. Woodfall, [1766].

Story, Dana A. *The Building of a Wooden Ship "Sawn Frames and Trunnel Fastened."* Barre, Mass.: Barre Publishers, 1971.

———. *Frame-Up! The Story of Essex, Its Shipyards and Its People.* Barre, Mass.: Barre Publishers, 1964.

Sturt, George. *The Wheelwright's Shop.* Cambridge, England: The University Press, 1923.

Tannahill, Reay. *Food in History.* New York: Stein and Day, 1973.

Teal, Mildred and John. *Portrait of an Island.* New York: Atheneum, 1964.

Thacher, James. *American Modern Practice; Or, A Simple Method of Prevention and Cure of Diseases.* Boston: Ezra Read, 1817.

A True Declaration of the Estates of the Colonie in Virginia . . . . London: Printed for William Barret, 1610.

Van Wagenen, Jared, Jr. *The Golden Age of Homespun.* Ithaca: Cornell University Press, 1953.

Vogel, Karl. "Medicine at Sea in the Days of Sail." In *Milestones in Medicine.* New York: Appleton-Century Co., Inc., 1938.

Volusia County Historical Commission. *Centennial History of Volusia County, Florida, 1854–1954.* Edited by Ianthe B. Hebel. Daytona Beach: College Publishing Company, 1955.

Warren [Maine] Historical Society. *From Warren to the Sea, 1827–1852. Letters of the Counce and McCallum Families.* Middletown, New York: Whitlock Press, 1970.

Watson, Aldren A. *The Village Blacksmith.* New York: Thomas Y. Crowell Company, 1968.

Whitaker, Arthur Preston. *Documents Relating to the Commercial Policy of Spain in the Floridas with Incidental Reference to Louisiana.* Deland: Florida State Historical Society, 1931.

Williams, John Lee. *The Territory of Florida: Or Sketches of the Topography, Civil and Natural History from the First Discovery to the Present Time.* New York: A. T. Goodrich, 1837.

Winthrop, Theodore. *Life in the Open Air and Other Papers.* Boston: Ticknor and Fields, 1863.

Wood, Virginia Steele, ed. *St. Simons Island, Georgia, Brunswick and Vicinity. A Description and History Written by William W. Hazzard, 1825.* Belmont, Mass.: Oak Hill Press, 1974.

Wymer, Norman. *English Country Crafts. A Survey of Their Development from Early Times to Present Day.* London: B. T. Batsford Ltd., 1946.

Young, James Harvey. *The Toadstool Millionaires. A Social History of Patent Medicines in America Before Federal Regulation.* Princeton: Princeton University Press, 1961.

PERIODICAL ARTICLES

Adams, William R. "Florida Live Oak Farm of John Quincy Adams." *Florida Historical Quarterly* 51 (1972): 129–42.

Bourdeau, Philippe F., and Oosting, Henry J. "The Maritime Live Oak Forest in North Carolina." *Ecology* 40 (1959):148–52.

"The Building of the Ship." *Harper's New Monthly Magazine* 24 (1862):608–20.

Chinard, Gilbert. "André and François-André Michaux and their Predecessors. An Essay on Early Botanical Exchanges between America and France." *Proceedings of the American Philosophical Society* 101 (1957):344–50.

———. "Recently Acquired Botanical Documents." *Proceedings of the American Philosophical Society* 101 (1957):508–22.

Easterby, J. H. "Shipbuilding on St. Helena Island in 1816. A Diary of Ebenezer Coffin." *South Carolina Historical and Genealogical Magazine* 47 (1946):117–20.

Hebel, Ianthe Bond. "Live Oak Barons. A Romantic Bit of Lumber History." *Southern Lumber Journal* 54 (1950):48, 50, 52, 54, 74.

Hill, Peter P. "'A Masked Acquisition'; French Designs on Cumberland Island, 1794–95." *Georgia Historical Quarterly* 64 (Fall, 1980): 306–16.

Kephart, George S. "Live Oak, the Tree with a Past." *American Forests* 78 (1972):37–39, 58–61.

[Kimber, Edward.] "Itinerant Observations in America." *London Magazine* (November 1745):395, 549–52.

Lipman, Arthur G., and Osborne, George E. "Medicine and Pharmacy Aboard New England Whaleships." *Pharmacy in History* 11 (1969):119–31.

Little, Elizabeth A. "Live Oak Whaleships." *Historic Nantucket* 19 (1971):24–38.

"Live Oak Plantations." *Country Gentleman: A Journal for the Farm the Garden and Fireside . . .* 11 (1858):93.

Markwell, Dawes. "Handy Oxen." *The Chronicle of the Early American Industries Association, Inc.* 35 (1972):17–21.

Miller, Genevieve. "Directions for the Use of an Early American Marine Medicine Chest." *Bulletin, History of Medicine* Supplement No. 3 (1944):217–22.

O'Keefe, Dorothy. "Lofting and Mold Making." *Salt* 5 (1980):51–58.

Prichard, Walter; Kniffen, Fred B.; and Brown, Clair A. "Southern Louisiana and Southern Alabama in 1819: The Journal of James Leander Cathcart." *Louisiana Historical Quarterly* 28 (1945):735–921.

Sargent, Charles S. "The Live Oak." *Garden and Forest: A Journal of Horticulture, Landscape Art and Forestry* 1 (1888):476–77.

Sargent, C. S., ed. "Portions of the Journal of André Michaux, Botanist, written during his Travels in the United States and Canada, 1785 to 1796." *Proceedings of the American Philosophical Society* 26 (1888): 1–145.

"Ship Registers in the South Carolina Archives, 1734–1780." Introduction by R. Nicholas Olsberg. *South Carolina Historical Magazine* 74 (1973):189–279.

Smith, Joseph Coburn. "The Tools of the Maine Woodsmen [in 1926]." *Chronicle of the Early American Industries Association, Inc.* 25 (1972):49–54.

Stephens, Edwin L. "Annals of the Live Oak Society." *Louisiana Conservation Review* 6 (1936):15–20, 30–31.

———. "'I Saw in Louisiana a Live Oak Growing.'" *Lousiana Conservation Review* 4 (1934):17–22.

———. "The Live Oak Society." *Louisiana Conservation Review* 5 (1935):25–32.

Tymeson, Mildred McClary. "The Family Dentist." *New England Galaxy* 7 (1966):3–11.

Weekes, William D. "The Awesome Live Oak." *American Forests* 85 (February 1979):20–23, 56–58.

Wood, Virginia Steele, ed. "James Keen's Journal of a Passage from Philadelphia to Blackbeard Island, Georgia, for Live Oak Timber, 1817–1818." *The American Neptune* 35 (1975):227–47.

———. "Elijah Swift's Travel Journal from Massachusetts to Florida, 1857." *Florida Historical Quarterly* 55 (1976):181–88.

Newspapers

Barnstable, Mass. *Patriot*, 27 January 1852; 27 January 1874.

Bath, Me. *Daily Times*, 9 May 1882.

Boston *Daily Journal*, 14 October 1857.

Boston *Herald*, 14 October 1857.

Columbian Museum & Savannah Advertiser, 7 July 1798.

Daytona *News-Journal*, 22 April 1963.

Falmouth, Mass. *Enterprise*, 20 May 1966.

Georgia Gazette, 2 June 1763; 16 July, 8 October 1766; 23 February, 28 December 1774; 11 October 1775.

Honesdale, Pa. *Wayne County Herald*, 7 November 1889.

Ludowici, Ga. *News*, 1 November 1973.

Maine Inquirer, 10 December 1830.

Maryland Journal and Baltimore Advertiser, 1 January 1777.

Nantucket *Inquirer*, 23 October, 13 November 1830; 19 November 1831; 26 April 1834; 2 November 1836.

National Philanthropist, 4 March 1826.

New Bedford *Daily Mercury*, 4 October 1872.

New Bedford *Evening Standard*, 19 August 1857; 11 May 1892; 5 April 1901.

New Bedford *Mercury*, 3 October 1828; 17 February, 21, 27 July, 11, 28 September, 26 October 1832; 21 June 1833; 28 March 1834.

New Bedford *Standard Times*, 23 December 1924.

New Bedford *Sunday Standard*, 13 February 1910.

New York *Commercial Advertiser*, 6 August 1849.

New York *Maritime Register*, 5, 12 February 1908.

Niles National Register, 23, 30 June 1838.

St. Augustine *News*, 10 June 1843.

San Francisco *Chronicle*, 12, 13 July 1883.

San Francisco *Daily Examiner*, 11 July 1883.

South-Carolina and American General Gazette, 8 August 1771.

South-Carolina Gazette, 7–14 December 1747; 9 July 1748; 2 April 1750.

Tampa *Tribune*, 13, 27 January 1957; 27 November 1957.

Washington, D.C. *Daily National Intelligencer*, 17 June 1843.

Credits

FRONTISPIECE

ii. From William Cullen Bryant, *Picturesque America* . . . (New York: D. Appleton, 1872), n.p.

INTRODUCTION

4. From André Michaux, *Historie des Chênes de l'Amérique* (Paris, 1801), p. 10. Photograph courtesy of Arnold Arboretum Library, Harvard University.

5. Map courtesy of the U.S. Department of Agriculture.

6. Photograph by Charles J. Williams, courtesy of Patrick M. Williams and The American Forestry Association.

CHAPTER 1

9. Drawing by Walter E. Channing, from *St. Simons Island, Georgia; Brunswick and Vicinity, Description and History*, ed. Virginia Steele Wood (Belmont, Mass.: Oak Hill Press, 1974), p. 22.

11. Photograph by Gordon Brown, courtesy of the Institute of Archeology and Anthropology, University of South Carolina.

12. From Daniel Lescallier, *Planches du Dictionnaire de Marine* (Paris, 1797), plate 103. Courtesy of Houghton Library, Harvard.

13. Map by Walter E. Channing.

13. Map by Walter E. Channing.

14. From W. H. Pyne, *Microcosm* (London, 1806). By permission of the Houghton Library, Harvard University.

CHAPTER 2

27. From the *Connecticut Gazette*, 26 June 1794. Courtesy of the New London County Historical Society.

27. From the *Connecticut Gazette*, 25 September 1794. Courtesy of the New London County Historical Society.

27. From the *Connecticut Gazette*, 18 June 1795. Courtesy of the New London County Historical Society.

29. From W. H. Pyne, *Microcosm* (London, 1808), vol. 2, p. 262. Courtesy of the Hugh M. Morris Library, University of Delaware.

33. Drawing by Walter E. Channing.

33. Drawing by Walter E. Channing.

35. From the Newburyport *Herald*, 8 October 1799. Courtesy of Widener Library, Harvard University.

36. From the *Columbian Museum & Savannah Advertiser*, 4 April 1800. Courtesy of the Georgia Historical Society.

38. From the Charleston, South Carolina *City-Gazette and Daily Advertiser*, 2 April 1801. Courtesy of Widener Library, Harvard University.

40. Courtesy of the Library of Congress.

42. From H. M. Brackenridge, *History of the Late War* . . . (Philadelphia: Kay, 1839), pp. 47, 223.

CHAPTER 3

45. Drawing by Joshua Shaw, ca. 1810–25. Photograph courtesy of the Museum of Science and Industry, Chicago.

47. From William Cullen Bryant, *Picturesque America* . . . (New York: D. Appleton, 1872), vol. 1, p. 27.

48. From A. J. Coolidge and J. B. Mansfield, *A History and Description of New England, General and Local* (Boston: Coolidge, 1859), vol. 1, n.p.

54. From the *Georgian*, 18 October 1832. Courtesy of the Georgia Historical Society.

57. From William Cullen Bryant, *Picturesque America . . .* (New York: D. Appleton, 1872), vol. 1, p. 29.

58. From the Providence, Rhode Island *Republican Herald*, 28 July 1832. Courtesy of the Rhode Island Historical Society.

59. From William Cullen Bryant, *Picturesque America . . .* (New York: D. Appleton, 1872), vol. 1, p. 28.

61. Drawing by Walter E. Channing.

63. From *Gleason's Pictorial Drawing-Room Companion*, 17 May 1851, p. 1. Courtesy of Widener Library, Harvard University.

65. Photograph courtesy of the Maine Maritime Museum.

66. Photograph by Howell Baldwin, courtesy of the U.S. Navy.

66. Photograph by Howell Baldwin, courtesy of the U.S. Navy.

67. Photograph by Howell Baldwin, courtesy of the U.S. Navy.

67. Photograph by Howell Baldwin, courtesy of the U.S. Navy.

67. Photograph by Howell Baldwin, courtesy of the U.S. Navy.

68. Etching by Christopher Murphy. Used with the permission of Margaret A. Murphy.

68. Photograph by Howell Baldwin, courtesy of the U.S. Navy.

68. Photograph courtesy of the Library of Congress.

CHAPTER 4

70. From Fredrik Henrik af Chapman, *Architectura Navalis Mercatoria* (Holmise, 1768), plate 36. Courtesy of the Library of Congress.

71. Photograph by M. W. Sexton, courtesy of the Peabody Museum of Salem.

75. Photograph courtesy of Oliver S. Chute and the Falmouth Historical Society.

75. From Frederick Freeman, *The History of Cape Cod* . . . (Boston, 1862), vol. 2, n.p.

76. Photograph courtesy of Oliver S. Chute.

77. Photograph courtesy of Oliver S. Chute.

79. Map by Walter E. Channing.

81. From Franklyn Howland, *A History of the Town of Acushnet* . . . (New Bedford, 1907), p. 352.

81. From Franklyn Howland, *A History of the Town of Acushnet* . . . (New Bedford, 1907), p. 353.

84. Photograph courtesy of the Harvard University Archives.

86. Photograph courtesy of the Whaling Museum, Old Dartmouth Historical Society, New Bedford, Mass.

CHAPTER 5

89. Drawing by Samuel F. Manning and used with his permission.

89. From Henry Wadsworth Longfellow, *The Building of the Ship* (Boston: Fields, Osgood, 1870), n.p. Photograph courtesy of the National Archives.

90. From *Register of Officer Personnel, U.S. Navy and Marine Corps, and Ships' Data 1801–1807* (Washington: U.S. Government Printing Office, 1945).

91. Drawing by Walter E. Channing.

92. From *Harper's New Monthly Magazine*, April 1862, p. 609. Courtesy of Widener Library, Harvard University.

93. From *Ballou's Pictorial*, 19 May 1855, p. 1. Courtesy of Widener Library, Harvard University.

94. From Henry Moses, *Sketches of Shipping Drawn and Etched by Henry Moses* (London: Ackerman, 1837), n.p. Photograph courtesy of Pennsylvania State University Press.

95. From *The Glass; or, The Trials of Helen More . . .* , ed. Maria Lamas (Philadelphia: Martine Harmstead, 1849), frontispiece. Courtesy of Widener Library, Harvard University.

96. From the *New-Bedford Mercury*, 29 October 1841. Courtesy of Widener Library, Harvard University.

96. From Charles Carleton Coffin, *Building the Nation* (New York: Harper & Brothers, 1883), p. 273.

97. Courtesy of Stephen M. Swift.

98. Courtesy of Stephen M. Swift.

101. Map by Walter E. Channing.

102. Map by Walter E. Channing.

105. Photograph courtesy of Mr. and Mrs. Howard Hiller.

CHAPTER 6

107. From James A. Henshall, *Camping and Cruising in Florida* (Cincinnati: Clarke, 1884), p. 39.

107. From Thomas Jeffrey, *A General Topography of North America and the West Indies* (London: Sayer, [1768]). By permission of the Houghton Library, Harvard University.

108. Drawing by Walter E. Channing.

109. Drawing by Walter E. Channing.

109. Drawing by Walter E. Channing.

109. From Edward H. Knight, *Knight's American Mechanical Dictionary* (New York: Hurd and Houghton, 1876), vol. 3, p. 1850.

110. Drawing by Walter E. Channing. From George S. Kephart, *Campfires Rekindled; A Forester Recalls Life in the Maine Woods of the Twenties* (Marion, Mass.: Channing Books, 1977), p. 42.

111. From Peter Guillet, *Timber Merchant's Guide* (Baltimore, 1823), p. 15. Courtesy of Kress Library of Business and Economics, Baker Library, Harvard Business School.

112. Drawing by Walter E. Channing.

112. Drawing by Walter E. Channing.

112. Drawing by Walter E. Channing.

113. From W. H. Pyne, *Microcosm* (London, 1806). By permission of the Houghton Library, Harvard University.

113. Drawing by Walter E. Channing.

114. Drawing by Walter E. Channing.

114. Drawing by Walter E. Channing.

115. Drawing by Walter E. Channing.

116. Photograph courtesy of the U.S. Department of Agriculture.

118. From Edward Hazen, *Panorama of Professions and Trades; or Every Man's Book* (Philadelphia: Uriah Hunt, 1837), p. 283. Courtesy of Kress Library of Business and Economics, Baker Library, Harvard Business School.

119. Photograph courtesy of the National Archives.

120. Photograph by Virginia S. Wood.

121. From W. H. Pyne, *Microcosm* (London: 1806). By permission of the Houghton Library, Harvard University.

121. From Edward H. Knight, *Knight's American Mechanical Dictionary* (New York: J. B. Ford, 1875), vol. 2, p. 1586.

CHAPTER 7

124. From *The Youth's Picture Book of Trades* (Cooperstown, N.Y.: Phinney, 1842), n.p. Courtesy of Kress Library of Business and Economics, Baker Library, Harvard Business School.

124. From Harriet Beecher Stowe, *Palmetto-Leaves* (Boston: Osgood, 1873), p. 321.

125. Drawing by Walter E. Channing.

125. Drawing by Walter E. Channing.

125. Drawing by Walter E. Channing.

126. Drawing by Walter E. Channing.

126. Drawing by Walter E. Channing.

126. Drawing by Walter E. Channing.

126. Drawing by Walter E. Channing.

127. Drawing by Walter E. Channing.

128. From John D. Billings, *Hardtack and Coffee or The Unwritten Story of Army Life* (Boston: George M. Smith, 1887), p. 114.

129. Drawing by Walter E. Channing.

129. Photograph by David Gunner. Courtesy of the Francis A. Countway Library of Medicine, Boston.

132. From Jacob Stone, Jr., *Medicine Chests with Approved Directions . . .* (Newburyport, Mass.: Gilman, 1828), n.p. Photograph by David Gunner, courtesy of the Francis A. Countway Library of Medicine, Boston.

134. From John D. Billings, *Hardtack and Coffee or The Unwritten Story of Army Life* (Boston: George M. Smith, 1887), p. 84.

139. From Henry Wadsworth Longfellow, *The Building of the Ship* (Boston: Fields, Osgood, 1870), p. 43.

Acknowledgments

People who care about wooden ships are exceptionally helpful and generous. They include the late Walter E. Channing, who not only agreed to draw maps and other illustrations for the book, but who willingly shared his knowledge of ship construction with me and spent many hours explaining theories and concepts of which I had no prior knowledge. I deeply regret that he did not live to see the completed work. Marion L. Channing's enthusiasm for the project and her many practical questions and suggestions have led me to a fascinating variety of places. A special acknowledgment is due both of them for unfailing moral support and encouragement.

For an early critical reading of the manuscript, I am indebted to the late William A. Baker, Curator of the Francis Russell Hart Nautical Museum, Massachusetts Institute of Technology; and to Commander Tyrone G. Martin, USN (Ret.), former Commanding Officer of the U.S.S. *Constitution*. Both responded with patience and alacrity to numerous questions. Commander Martin provided opportunities for me to make thorough examinations of *Constitution* from spardeck to bilge, and generously shared source material from his research files.

Mary Ricketson Bullard of South Dartmouth, Massachusetts, and Cumberland Island, Georgia, and Dr. R. Hardy Meade of the

New England Medical Center, read parts of the manuscript. Dr. William S. Dudley, Naval Historical Center, read the final draft. All of them made suggestions of great value.

Without the enthusiastic interest of several people, a good portion of the original source material would never have been located. Those who gave free access to manuscripts in their possession include Marion L. Channing, Dorothy C. Hiller, Oliver S. Chute, Obed N. Swift, Mary Ricketson Bullard, Mrs. Robert Michaud, and Charles A. Ellis.

I am especially grateful to Preston W. Lane, former Refuge Manager, Savannah National Wildlife Refuge, for a trip to Blackbeard Island; and to Dr. and Mrs. Robert Christian for a visit to neighboring Sapelo Island, Georgia. Others who shared their first-hand knowledge of the sea islands—and of ship building, timber hauling, oxen, blacksmith work, etc.—include the late Samuel H. Barnes; J. Brewer Owens; William W. Wasson; the late Howard B. Hiller; Russell McDonald; the late Dr. Mode Stone; George S. Kephart; William M. Wasson; Hugh D. Langdale; the late Dr. John Lyman; Dr. Nesta Ewan; Dr. and Mrs. Edwin F. Taylor; Colonel Sidney Britt, USA (Ret.); Les Bardon; Ralph V. Wood, Jr.; William E. Covil, Jr.; the late Elizabeth F. Smith; the late Charles C. Stebbins; Mary Lyman Cammann; and Donal McLaughlin.

To several friends in the South I owe a special debt for driving miles through the countryside to help me locate places related to live oaking. Such friends include Mrs. A. O. Townsend, Mrs. B. H. Scarborough, Dr. Linda M. Malone, Mrs. Eugene A. Stanley, Beth B. Engel, Alfred W. Hartridge, Floreda Duke Varick, Mr. and Mrs. Roy Huntsman, and Mrs. Kenneth Berrie.

Much of value was contributed by the late Walter Muir Whitehill; Richard K. Showman; Mary Mac Showman; Dr. Dorothy Dodd; Ruth S. Baker; Captain W. J. L. Parker, USCG (Ret.); Malcolm Bell, Jr.; John Gardner; Herbert Mason; Mary G. Mason; Alfred W. Jones; Mr. and Mrs. Robert G. Fuller; William and Ann M. Griever; Dr. Jean Bruneau; Lavinia Bruneau; Mr. and Mrs. Raymond Small; the late Admiral Samuel Eliot Morison, USN; and the late Marion V. Brewington.

Personnel at the former Boston Navy Yard who were involved with the 1973–1976 restoration of U.S.S. *Constitution* are due special thanks for their assistance. They include Captain Earl deR. Barondes, USN (Ret.); Captain William J. Norris; USN (Ret.); John F. Langan, former Chief Planner and Estimator; Warren Hawkes; Robert Deery; and Donald Turner.

Staff members at a number of institutions have made my research easier. I wish to convey my particular appreciation to Marte E. Shaw, formerly at Houghton Library, Harvard University; Lilla Mills Hawes, former Director, and Anthony R. Dees, Director, Georgia Historical Society; Philip C. F. Smith, Curator, Philadelphia Maritime Museum, and former managing editor of *The American Neptune*; Richard C. Kugler, Director of the Whaling Museum, Old Dartmouth Historical Society; Ralph L. Snow, former Director, and Marnee Lilly, Curator of Collections, Maine Maritime Museum; Melba Martin Bruno, National Agricultural Library; Bruce E. Barnes, formerly at the New Bedford Free Public Library and now at Southeastern Massachusetts University Library; Elizabeth K. Ehrbar, Florida State Division of Recreation and Parks; Joyce Y. LeBlanc, Louisiana Forestry Commission; and Dr. Edward D. Ives, University of Maine at Orono.

Other institutions whose staff members have been most helpful include the National Archives; Boston Athenaeum; Kress Collection, Baker Library, Harvard Business School; Widener Library, Francis A. Countway Library of Medicine, Gray Herbarium and Arnold Arboretum Library, Frances Loeb Library, all at Harvard University; Massachusetts Historical Society; Historical Society of Pennsylvania; Strozier Library, Florida State University; P. K. Yonge Library of Florida History, University of Florida; Florida State Archives; National Maritime Museum, London; Library of Congress; Georgia Surveyor-General Department; The Mariners Museum; Old Sturbridge Village; Mugar Memorial Library, Boston University; Maine State Library and Museum; Special Collections, University of Southwestern Louisiana; Archives de France; Navy Department Library, Naval Historical Center; Nantucket Atheneum; American Institute of the History of Pharmacy; United States Department of Agriculture, Forest Products Laboratory; South Carolina State Commission of Forestry; Special Collections, University of Georgia Libraries; American Forestry Association; and New York Historical Society.

Additionally, for their competence and cheerful support, I have the highest praise for the staff of Northeastern University Press. In particular, I wish to acknowledge the help of Robilee A. Smith, assistant director, and Katherine Talmadge, editor.

The Kittridge Educational Fund awarded me a generous grant for travel and for the illustrations.

Index

The **Naval Institute Press** is the book-publishing arm of the U.S. Naval Institute, a private, nonprofit society for sea service professionals and others who share an interest in naval and maritime affairs. Established in 1873 at the U.S. Naval Academy in Annapolis, Maryland, where its offices remain, today the Naval Institute has more than 100,000 members worldwide.

Members of the Naval Institute receive the influential monthly magazine *Proceedings* and discounts on fine nautical prints and on ship and aircraft photos. They also have access to the transcripts of the Institute's Oral History Program and get discounted admission to any of the Institute-sponsored seminars offered around the country.

The Naval Institute also publishes *Naval History* magazine. This colorful bimonthly is filled with entertaining and thought-provoking articles, first-person reminiscences, and dramatic art and photography. Members receive a discount on *Naval History* subscriptions.

The Naval Institute's book-publishing program, begun in 1898 with basic guides to naval practices, has broadened its scope in recent years to include books of more general interest. Now the Naval Institute Press publishes more than seventy titles each year, ranging from how-to books on boating and navigation to battle histories, biographies, ship and aircraft guides, and novels. Institute members receive discounts on the Press's nearly 400 books in print.

For a free catalog describing Naval Institute Press books currently available, and for further information about subscribing to *Naval History* magazine or about joining the U.S. Naval Institute, please write to:

Membership & Communications Department
U.S. Naval Institute
118 Maryland Avenue
Annapolis, Maryland 21402-5035

Or call, toll-free, (800) 233-USNI.